Trade Him!

TRADE

100 years of baseball's greatest deals

Edited by JIM ENRIGHT

FOLLETT PUBLISHING COMPANY
Chicago

Library of Congress Catalog Card Number: 75-14655
ISBN: 0-695-80623-8

First Printing

Above left and right, Charles A. Comiskey. The Old Roman was a builder of championship teams in both St. Louis and Chicago and built baseball's first palace—Comiskey Park—to house his beloved White Sox. *Right,* Willie Kamm—first of the $100,000 "Beauties" moving from minors to White Sox in 1922.

THE AMERICAN LEAGUE BASE BALL CLUB OF CHICAGO   No. A 465

CHAS. A. COMISKEY, PRES.

Chicago, June 6 1922

Pay to the order of John H. Farrell Secty Nat'l Ag $ 100,000.00

One hundred thousand Dollars ##   Dollars.

To FIRST NATIONAL BANK,   THE AMERICAN LEAGUE BASE BALL CLUB OF CHICAGO

2-1   CHICAGO, ILL.   Chas. A. Comiskey

St. Louis Cardinals   George Brace Photo   St. Louis Cardinals

Above center, Jimmy Ring, a so-so pitcher who went along for the ride in trade of superstars: Frankie Frisch, *left,* for Rogers Hornsby, *right. Below,* Casey Stengel, jack-of-all-trades, and master of one: the Yankees. He is shown at different stages of his career: as a Brave, as a Yankee and as a Met.

George Brace Photo   George Brace Photo   George Brace Photo

Above left, Cy Young (509 career victories, five 30-game winning seasons). What're the odds that one of the winners of his awards might sometime match his feats? *Above right,* Babe Ruth. He was so tremendous with the Yankees that most fans-buffs have forgotten he concluded his career with the Boston Braves. *Right,* Clark Griffith. The Ol' Fox's trades ranged from two son-in-laws to a live turkey.

Center, John McGraw. They didn't call him "Little Napoleon" for nothing: he was strong, stern, stimulating. *Top left,* Jimmie Dykes did more with a little than any other manager of his era. *Top right,* Lou Boudreau. Had Boudreau been blessed with always having Shortstop Boudreau during his entire managerial career, he'd now possess a record nobody would match. *Bottom left,* Roy Campanella. A crippling injury cut short a great career for an outstanding gentleman. *Bottom right,* Joe Cronin. His career was assured when Tom Yawkey decided not to buy Peewee Reese.

8

Top left, Tris Speaker: superstar, super gentleman. *Top right,* Ty Cobb. He went to his grave thinking he was the best player ever, and who can dispute it? *Bottom left,* Warren Spahn. Remember Boston Braves' favorite chant in 1948? "Spahn and Sain, and two days of rain." *Bottom right,* Hank Aaron. Few great players have been spurred to greater heights by hate mail: many bushel baskets full.

Chicago National League Ball Club (Inc.)

George Brace Photo

Above left, Riggs Stephenson and Hack Wilson—the Cubs' best one-two punch until Ernie Banks and Billy Williams arrived some 30 years later. Wilson's 56 HRs and 190 RBIs still stand as records and high-spot the shame he's not in the Hall of Fame. *Above right,* Mel Ott. Master Mel stepped in the bucket 511 times as a home-run hitter. *Below left,* Bill Veeck, Senior, was a baseball writer under the name of Bill Bailey. Later his astute deals as the Cubs' president blueprinted many of the team's glory days. *Below center,* Bill Veeck, Junior, has done more for the sale of sport shirts than Cecil B. DeMille did for the film industry. Veeck, Jr. can apply the fastest needle in pro sports. *Below right,* Leo Durocher. The game passed him by after his leadership failed the Cubs in 1969.

George Brace Photo

George Brace Photo

Houston Sports Association, Inc.

10

George Brace Photo   Cincinnati Reds, Inc.

Above left, Hank Greenberg. His scissors swing at the plate was an action picture most artists couldn't paint. *Above right,* Johnny Bench. Both offensively and defensively he's a combination of Bill Dickey and Mickey Cochrane. Johnny is an excellent managerial prospect. *Below left,* Randy Jones could be another Tom Seaver as a prize pitching discovery by an expansion club. *Below right,* Chuck Klein. The Cubs paid $65,000 to get him and shelled out $50,000 to unload him.

San Diego Padres Baseball Club   George Brace Photo

11

St. Louis Cardinals

Below left, Bob Feller. At the outset of his high school days in Van
Meter, Iowa, Bob was regarded as a better basketball than baseball
prospect. How opinions do change! *Below right, top,* Sparky Anderson is
short on playing ability, long on managerial finesse. *Below right, bottom,*
Willie Mays. The Say Hey Kid never enjoyed the same pleasure playing in
San Francisco that he did in New York.

George Brace Photo

Cincinnati Reds, Inc.

San Francisco Giants

12

Left, Fleet feet carry Cardinals' Lou Brock to one of record 118 stolen bases against the Cubs in 1974. *Below left,* Johnny Vander Meer. His successive no-hitters proved lightning can strike twice in the same place. *Below center, top,* Honus Wagner, a most unlikely looking shortstop ever to step on the field. Nevertheless, he was one of the superstandouts. *Below center, bottom,* Bill Madlock gets tremendously long mileage out of a short swing. *Below right, top,* Ernie Banks. No one player ever did a better job of "carrying" a team than Banks, and his successive MVP's were most deserving. *Below right, bottom,* Ernie Broglio—big loser in a big deal.

Pittsburgh Athletic Co., Inc.

Chicago National League Ball Club (Inc.)

Chicago National League Ball Club (Inc.)

Chicago National League Ball Club (Inc.)

Cincinnati Reds, Inc.

13

Top left, Rusty Staub, a swinger and a good player. *Top right,* Gil Hodges, a hep Hoosier. *Center left,* Dave Kingman—his "stats": 36 HRs and 153 strikeouts. *Center right,* Tom Seaver. The Mets drew his name out of a hat. *Bottom left,* Dodgers' Walter Alston signed 23 one-year contracts as manager.

Above left, Dennis McLain could make a bankroll disappear faster than Houdini, and a Jesse Crawford he wasn't at the organ. *Above right,* Carl Hubbell was another scouting blunder. The Tigers failed to protect him in minors, and he won 253 games for the Giants. *Below,* Twin Winners—St. Louis Cardinals of 1926 won both the pennant and the World Series under Rogers Hornsby *(circled).*

15

San Diego Padres Baseball Club

San Diego Padres Baseball Club

George Brace Photo

Philadelphia Phillies

Philadelphia Phillies

Chicago White Sox

Los Angeles Dodgers

Father & son combos: *Top left and center,* Buzzie Bavasi and Peter Bavasi—their astute direction and Ray Kroc's bankroll proved to be big help to the Padres. The Bavasis were smart enough not to deal Randy Jones. *Bottom left and center,* Bob and Ruly Carpenter. Until recent seasons the Phillies were engulfed in a country club atmosphere, offering new proof it's impossible to buy a pennant.

Above right, top, Ed Barrow never received the full credit he deserved building the Yankee dynasty. *Above right, bottom,* Frank Lane was blessed with bulldog determination. He never would accept no for an answer. Annually, especially when he was in his prime, Lane's telephone bills were bigger than a full year's salary for some men in baseball. His deal for Chico Carrasquel, with Lane as general manager of the White Sox, was one of his best fleece jobs ever. *Right,* Dazzy Vance won 50 games (28–22) in successive seasons with a ragamuffin Dodger team in 1924–1925.

16

Left, The Cubs have a happy note for this centennial season. They played and won their first game April 25, 1876, beating Louisville 4–0. The Cubs also won a pennant that first season. *Below left,* Branch Rickey lulled more of his counterparts (trade makers) with fancy sweet talk than anybody else in the game. He always made it a point to trade off a star before he reached his peak rather than wait until the star was over the hill. Rickey did it for two reasons: (1) it was a savings in the salary budget, and (2) it assured top dollar return in every trade. *Below right,* Jackie Robinson. There were two main men in his life. Branch Rickey off the field, Peewee Reese on the field.

17

Baseball, Office of the Commissioner

Above left to right, Ford Frick—
Happy Chandler—Bowie Kuhn. This
picture is a first: three commissioners
in attendance at the same social func-
tion. Frick was a baseball writer in
his youth. Chandler represented Kentucky both as governor and U.S. Senator. Kuhn is a lawyer, a ready com-
modity in present-day pro sports.
Chandler was regarded as a players'
commissioner, and this never sat well
with the owners, mainly Lou Perini
and Del Webb. *Right top,* Kenesaw
Mountain Landis—flock of firsts as
first commissioner. *Right bottom,*
General William D. Eckert—fourth
commissioner of baseball who faded
like an AWOL private.

George Brace Photo

Baseball, Office of the Commissioner

Contents

To Helen and Lenna for their inspiration,
and twenty-four Good Guys on the baseball beat for their
expertise . . .

Acknowledgments

Helpers in the production of *Trade Him!* could field a baseball team of their own without making a single trade. First the idea: it hadn't been done before! Then it was Operation Go with twenty-three of the nation's foremost baseball writers or sports columnists and a former catcher (and author and raconteur): Joe Garagiola.

After Follett staffers Vytautas Babusis and Allen Carr climbed aboard the bandwagon, the rest was easy. For this I say thanks to Frank Slocum, Pete and Delores Stoneham, all the individual club publicity directors in the American and National Leagues, Ken Smith and Cliff Kachline of the Hall of Fame staff, Lowell Reidenbaugh of *The Sporting News*, Joe Reichler, and Bob Wirz of the Commissioner's Office.

A special thank you goes to Chicagoan George Brace, a free-lance photographer with almost a million pictures to prove it.

Jim Enright

Foreword

To a ballplayer who has never been traded, the thought isn't really something scary. After all, being traded is something that happens only to other players.

The first time you're traded, it's a jolt. A ballplayer joins an organization thinking that he will stay with them for the length of his baseball career. When he's traded, he feels like he's been sold out by his own family.

While I don't think it would be honest to say that a player ever gets used to the idea of being traded, after it's happened to you a couple of times, it loses its shock. You start to adopt little ways to make it more pleasant for yourself. You tell yourself that you must be a pretty good player or your new club wouldn't have wanted you. That lasts until you report to the new club and immediately hear rumors that you'll soon be on your way in another trade.

I have seen guys cry when they were traded, and I've seen guys jump with joy. Me, I never cared too much either way. Home-run hitters might be influenced by the fences in the park they're leaving and the park they're going to. Pitchers might consider which club offered them the best opportunity to start regularly. But my feeling always was that one bullpen is pretty much like any other.

To me, being traded was like celebrating your one hundredth birthday. It might not be the happiest occasion in the world, but then you have to consider the alternatives. You ask a guy who has spent ten years with one club how he feels about being traded, and he makes it sound like they're sending him to Devil's Island. But ask a player who has been sent to the minor leagues, or one who has been given his unconditional release, and he'll tell you that being traded from one big league club to another is a pleasure.

To some players, being traded is the escape hatch. A guy isn't playing with his present club and feels that somewhere else he might get to play regularly. That's when he tells the press about his ultimatum to his bosses, "Play me or trade me." I always went more for a variation of that. When Phil Linz was with the Yankees, he was honest enough with himself to realize that he might not be quite the player he dreamed about being. Also, he knew that the Yankees had an excellent shot at the pennant and the World Series shares that went with it. So Linz issued an ultimatum that went, "Play me or keep me."

There are some myths about being traded, too. If you read the papers, you get the idea that when a new player comes over in a trade, everybody welcomes him with open arms and tells him what a big factor he's going to be. When I was traded by the Pirates to the Cubs, I joined the Cubs in New York. All the way to New York from Pittsburgh, I kept telling myself, "This is it, Joe. You have finally found a home. This club will give you the chance to be a regular and to stay in one place for a while."

When I got to the Commodore Hotel in New York, where the Cubs were staying, the first person I met was Wid Matthews, the man who had made the deal for me. You want to know what an ego-building greeting he gave me? He said, "Hiya, Joe. Wait until you see Chiti. He looks just great." Chiti was Harry Chiti, who belonged to the Cubs, but was then in the service. Even more to the point, Chiti, like me, was a catcher. I hadn't put on a Chicago uniform yet, and my job was in jeopardy.

Newspapers can be great for your confidence, too. Describing a trade I was involved in, one newspaper said, "This can really be described as an even trade. It should hurt both clubs."

In this book, you'll read the public side and the private side of trades involving every major league club. What you won't be reading as much about are the deals general managers tried to make, and couldn't. It is a baseball cliché that sometimes the best deals are the ones you don't make. But some general managers just can't resist the urge to make trades. In this book you'll come across the name Frank Lane a lot, because Lane was a general manager who not only was not afraid to make trades, but he was afraid not to. They used to say that the toughest job on any club Frank Lane was running belonged to the guy who had to take the team picture.

I guess if I had to describe the reaction of players to being traded, I would first have to qualify it by saying that I'm talking about fringe players like me, not superstars. For a fringe guy, the prospect of being traded is like waiting for the other shoe to drop. I found out early in my career that I could never discount the possibility of being traded. The late Mr. Branch Rickey was discussing our ball club with me one day, and said, "Joe, you figure in our plans." Three days later I was with the Cubs.

Before you turn to the stories of each club and its trades, *I want to thank Jim Enright for asking me to join the very impressive lineup of contributors he has put together for this book. It is one of the most impressive I've ever seen, and I'm sure you've got some entertaining reading ahead.*

JOE GARAGIOLA

BILL GLEASON
Sports Columnist, *Chicago Sun-Times*

Bill Gleason, of the *Chicago Sun-Times,* is regarded as the "new" Warren Brown among Chicago sports columnists. His touch on a typewriter ranges from the flick of a flyweight to the pulverizing punch of a heavyweight in typical Warren Brown manner. He has been newspapering since he was seventeen years old, starting with Hearst before joining the Field Enterprises. Bill has written three books. Many critics consider his *Daley of Chicago* to be the only definitive biography of the mayor. His other titles are *The Liquid Cross,* a novel about Chicago's Skid Row, and *Footsteps of a Giant,* the life story of the late Emlen Tunnell, National Football League Immortal.

Introduction

For the boy White Sox fan it was always winter. If he had had the power, summer would have been called off on account of rain. Summer was the time of disappointment; winter the time of hope. He could not know, as he picked up his newspapers for delivery, that only once, in all the years ahead, would the hope of winter be rewarded, that there would be one summer of fulfillment, the summer of 1959.

Had he known that, he would not have been discouraged. He was a White Sox fan as were his father and his Tipperary-County-born grandfather. Love of the White Sox was something that the male line inherited, as the sons of Russian princes inherited hemophilia.

Because the boy had been a White Sox fan forever, his expectations were small. He did not dream of great things. He withdrew, instead, into the time of his father and his grandfather, the time when the White Sox were champions. He wondered how that could have been. He knew, deep within the place where the nun at St. Columbanus said his soul was, that Buck Weaver had not thrown the World Series of 1919.

His newspaper was the *Chicago Daily Times*. The *Times* was the perfect paper for the South Side of that time, Number Five in circulation in a "league" of five. The *Times* was the only Chicago paper that really stuck up for President Roosevelt, and any paper that was for Roosevelt had to be for the White Sox. The boy's instinct told him that the Cubs were Republicans who had voted for Hoover.

The *Times*, like the South Side, was belligerent and so superior about its inferiority. Born just before the depression, the tabloid had been sold exclusively on newsstands during the first few years of its struggling existence. The boy was in the first group to have a *Times* home delivery route. On the first day he had had one address tag on his huge metal ring, had delivered one news-paper, and had gone home, sure of his place in newspaper history, to report to his mother, who had found "the job" for him. The boy was ten years old.

The boy had a sense of mission. The *Times* was his family's newspaper. His father would not allow the *Tribune* in the house. The *Tribune* was against Roosevelt.

The boy was a newspaper fan, too. Starting on the back page, he would read almost every word in the *Times* before he fell asleep each night. The *Times* had a contentious sports editor, whose name was Marvin McCarthy, and two baseball writers who made the games come alive—were they, he asks his memory now, John C. Hoffman and Herb Simons?

On the route, especially on Sunday mornings, there was time for reading on the back porch stairways of three-flats in Park Manor. And so it was that he found out Al Simmons, Mule Haas, and Jimmie Dykes belonged to the White Sox.

The boy was warmed by the hot stove of winter expectation. Santa Claus had come back into his life. This was not a trade. It was bigger than a trade. J. Louis Comiskey, the corpulent man who had truly and financially inherited the White Sox from his father, spent $150,000 to buy Simmons, Haas, and Dykes from the Phila-delphia Athletics. That would shut up the kids who were always saying, "The Comiskeys are too cheap to get any good players." The boy had heard that from some grown men who professed to be White Sox fans. He never had heard it from his father.

Al, Mule, and Jimmie. He said the words over and over, a litany of achievement. Al, Mule, and Jimmie. Only a season had passed since they had played in the World Series. Sure, they had lost to the Cardinals but, gee, just being in the World Series. . . . Al, Mule, and Jimmie. Sure, they were getting old, but the boy couldn't remember a White Sox team that had three famous players. . . .

Al, Mule, and Jimmie. With those three stars in the lineup, the White Sox weren't going to finish in no seventh place again, 56½ games out of first place. Now the White Sox were good enough to compete against the New York Yankees, a team the boy had begun to hate with a passion that would grow as he did.

The Deal that was better than a trade made winter a joyous one. School was interesting. Food tasted better. Joe Penner and Jack Benny were funnier. Myrt and Marge weren't quite as sad. The boy's ankles didn't wobble so much when he tried to ice-skate in Meyering Playground. He began to like his younger sisters.

Summer came as it always does for a White Sox fan. Al, Mule, and Jimmie. They played and the White Sox did not finish seventh, 56½ games out. They finished sixth, 31 games out. The boy was impressed. Soon the litany became a devotion. Jimmie! Virtually by forfeit James Dykes became manager of the White Sox. A doer of small miracles, Dykes made the wait for winter more bearable.

Jimmie improved the franchise without money. He traded for players other teams did not want—the sore-armed, the soul-scarred, the drinkers. Young as he was, the boy understood. Beer had come back in the year Jimmie came to the White Sox, and the saloons had come back disguised as taverns. The paper route took the boy up to 75th, the border street between the Irish and Swedes. Almost every Sunday morning he would see a representative or two of those combative races meandering along home, blood on shirt and suit, eyes blackened, nose bent, cheeks scratched.

Dykes and his consummate pitching coach, "Muddy" Ruel, took unto themselves discarded pitchers with romantic names like Thornton Lee, Bill ("Bullfrog") Dietrich, and Edgar Smith.

Edgar Smith. He was a left-hander who drank a lot and pitched a lot. It was Smith's duty to pitch against Bob Feller in almost every series between the White Sox and the Indians. Edgar would not concede the invincibility of Feller or yield to the power of Cleveland's batters. Often the brilliantly pitched games went on and on into extra innings, hitters returning to dugouts ever so rapidly. Sometimes Smith would endure until the White Sox scratched out the winning run. When that happened, the South Side became a more pleasant place.

In Dykes's first full season as manager, attendance soared to almost 500,000. The boy was bedazzled. Like every other White Sox fan, he worried more about the attendance totals than about the standings. Later there would be a year in which winter lasted into mid-September. Dykes and his White Sox were still in the pennant race along with four other clubs. Then summer returned. The White Sox finished fourth, eight games out.

Much later, when other boys joined the line to emulate their grandfather by picking at fingernails during tense moments in the agonizing history of the White Sox, trades would bring a pitcher named Billy Pierce, a shortstop named Chico Carrasquel, a second baseman named Nellie Fox, a left fielder named Minnie Minoso, a right fielder named Jim Rivera, a catcher named Sherman Lollar. . . .

As would be true of almost every decision that changed professional baseball, no light of inspiration bathed the imaginative pioneers who came up with the idea of exchanging one player for another. They did not intend to collaborate on a stroke of genius. "I'll give you my fella if you'll let me have your fella," one of the two might have said, ever so idly. And the other could have said, "It's a deal."

In their groping search for a way to solve mutual problems, financial or morale, the pioneers contributed much to the mysterious appeal that magnetizes those who are attracted to baseball, bewilders those who are repelled by the most leisurely of the games played by professionals.

This fascinating book gives us The Trade as the stuff of life. The Trade is Hope.

Now if the White Sox could just swing a three-team deal and get a couple of starting pitchers. . . .

It is always winter.

BILL GLEASON
Chicago Sun-Times

TOM KANE
Sportswriter, *Sacramento Bee*

Tom Kane's introduction to baseball was one of the most unusual ever recorded. At an early age Tom worked as the chief usher in Moreing Field—home of the Sacramento Solons in the Triple-A Pacific Coast League. During his forty-two-year tenure with the *Sacramento Bee,* Kane later covered the Solons for many seasons. When baseball used the jet age to deliver two major franchises to the Pacific coast, Kane was available with typewriter in tow to cover the Giants' landing in San Francisco and the A's transfer from Kansas City to Oakland. En route to these assignments, he covered semipro baseball in the Sacramento area and had a press box seat, watching many of these future major leaguers develop into stars. Tom also covered baseball at both the high school and university plateaus.

1/THE A's

Sweat plus Sacrifice
equals Success

Tumult and triumph are synonymous with baseball's three-time World Champion Oakland A's. And complete involvement is the trademark of the AL club's owner, Charles O. Finley, who runs his own show. His engrossment with his A's includes the complete overseeing of the front office and filtering to the clubhouse—and everything in between. And as the ringmaster he does not omit dicta to his managers. General managers, managers, players, office personnel, and radio announcers have felt the sting of Finley's mouthings and actions—sometimes described as fractious behavior. And Charles O. does not susurrate when expounding on the whys and wherefores of the dismissal of one of his underlings.

When Finley obtained approval to make the move from Kansas City and establish the A's in Oakland in 1968, he insisted the team retain the name of the Athletics—the title first made famous by the venerated Connie Mack when the A's were based in Philadelphia. In 1969 Finley ordered his souvenir yearbook dedicated to Mack and his great World Championship team of 1929, which to this day many consider one of the finest baseball clubs ever assembled. Mack ran into financial difficulties in a few years and was forced to sell off some of his stars, who later were to enter baseball's Hall of Fame.

Finley did not escape problems either, but they were not of the financial type which bothered Mack. Owner and operator of a lucrative insurance business, Finley has not found it necessary to dispose of his highly talented and salaried stars to keep the club afloat as was the case with Mack. In fact, Finley has retained the "hard core" of his championship roster since the team's days in Kansas City. There has been an almost constant shuffling of A's personnel since Finley moved West, but it was mostly with those on the fringes. His "hard core" has gained remarkable permanency with the perpetual motion swirling about it.

That "hard core" has triumphed despite fistfights, castigation by the club's owner, bitter arbitration hearings, open criticism by the players of managers—Dick Williams and his successor Alvin Dark—and firings best described as based on personal reasons. The "hard core" is made up of such World Series heroes as Sal Bando, team captain, Bert Campaneris, Gene Tenace, Joe Rudi, Reggie Jackson, Vida Blue, Rollie Fingers, plus comparative newcomers Ray Fosse and a most valuable addition, left-handed Pitcher Ken Holtzman.

The foremost pitcher of the "hard core" group was lost to Finley, but not by design, in the departure of Pitcher Jim ("Catfish") Hunter, now with the Yankees. Hunter won in a breach of contract hearing against Finley, who still is fuming and has threatened to keep trying to void Hunter's contract and future with the Yankees. The ruling in favor of Hunter enabled him to evaluate his services to the highest bidder on the baseball open market. As a result, he signed with New York for more than $3 million.

The sudden and unexpected exit of Catfish didn't create a void in the A's 1975 pitching until the AL championship series. Oakland won 98 games and literally ran away with the Western Division title. Only Kansas City offered anything close to a serious challenge, and still the Royals trailed by seven games at the finish. Against Boston in the fight for the pennant, it was a different story. The Red Sox won the first two games in Boston and clinched a sweep by capturing Game III in Oakland. Manager Alvin Dark was without a stop pitcher of Hunter's established status, and the Oaklands' adopted slogan—"Keep It Alive in '75"—went down the drain. So did the rich postseason spoils the raucous A's had become accustomed to collect.

Catfish's great value is obvious from his record. He was a Cy Young Award winner in 1974 and pitched a perfect game against the Twins in 1968. Although Catfish won 161 games for Finley after a most unusual beginning, he never pitched a single inning in the minors. While the "hard core" did the day-by-day job in 1971, it was Hunter and the sensational Vida Blue, who gave the first indications the A's were on the threshold of greatness—leading to the Western Division championship and the three World Series titles. In the first divisional crown, Hunter won 21 and Blue 24 games. Now The Cat is a member of the A's Alumni Club, which has affiliates on teams, stretching from sea to shining sea.

Although the A's swept through the AL West in 1971, they lost in the championship series to Baltimore. This outcome was most upsetting to the unpredictable Finley, whose dogma is *S* plus *S* equals *S*. Otherwise *Sweat plus Sacrifice equals Success.*

In 1971 a total of fifteen pitchers were manipulated by Manager Dick Williams and Finley. Shortly after the open trading period began, Finley acted to get another pitcher and made a successful trade with the Cubs. He dispatched the personable and talented Rick Monday to Wrigley Field in exchange for Ken Holtzman. Holtzman was an acknowledged pitcher of major league stature in every respect, but he became disenchanted with the Cubs and grumbled over management, managers, etc., and quickly was made available for trade by the Wrigley organization. As things eventuated, the swap turned out to be exceedingly beneficial for both clubs. The trade also made a prophet of Whitey Lockman, ex-Cub manager, who predicted great improvement for Rick after seeing him only a short time during the spring on the Chicago team's training site at Scottsdale Stadium in Arizona.

A few miles away, Holtzman was giving vent to his dislike for anything concerning Chicago before a willing and attentive audience of visiting writers covering the Cubs. Kenny first did his Patrick Henry speech in the clubhouse for a few straggling writers from California. But when the Cub scriveners descended upon him, the conference moved en masse to the players' bench in the open air and sunshine of Rendezvous Park in Mesa. Even the strict disciplinarian Dick Williams did not interfere. He let his left-hander pour it all out—and this was not always the case with the other players. Williams did not want anything or anybody to interfere with his rigid spring schedule—and generally nothing did—except a Finley telephone call.

With his none-too-fond memories of Chicago abolished into limbo, Holtzman responded with 19 victories for the A's en route to the Western Division crown, AL championship, and the culmination in a World Series victory. Ken often complained he was being lifted far too quickly, but with the splendid reliever Rollie Fingers in the wings, it was not without reason.

Against Cincinnati in the 1972 World Series, Ken gained one win, and in 1973 he was a double victor over the NL champion Mets. He added a single series win in 1974 in a duel with the Dodgers. Holtzman also showed his batting muscle with a second inning home run in the fourth game against the Dodgers. It was not the first time in such a circumstance that Holtzman had exerted strong batting punch. Ken had doubled and scored in the first contest with Los Angeles. This even though he had not been to bat during the regular season.

Finley's A's had not reached the World Series pinnacle until Holtzman joined them and became a member of the starting rotation, which included Hunter and Blue as the anchormen. Ken carried a victory total of 133 decisions into the 1975 season, and of this figure 59 were accomplished with the Athletics, proving he was a vital figure in the three straight World Series won by the mustachioed champions.

Besides his pitching prowess, Holtzman's verbal explosions against the Cubs' organization certainly added another qualification for full membership into the inner sanctum of the A's. While Holtzman accepted the trade by the Cubs in a happy manner—anything to get out of Chicago—there were other A's incumbents who expressed not only regrets but bitterness in being shuffled off to the other climes at Finley's direction. Trade talk and constant criticism of one thing or another continually kept the A's occupied off the field as well as on. Festering wounds kept cropping up during postpractice bull sessions in the clubhouse and away from it all.

While baseball players in the main realize the everpresent threat of trades and accept it, Dave Duncan and Mike Epstein were cases in point where personalities surfaced with a resounding crash. Duncan was the cheerleader for the A's, always taking the lead in praising his teammates, and even after his trade to the Indians he maintained that role. He drew unstinted praise from Pitcher Gaylord Perry, one of the greatest competitors in all of baseball.

Dave joined the A's organization in 1963 but really first ran afoul of Finley's policies in 1970 when the Oakland team was under the field management of Johnny McNamara, now filling a similar position with the Padres. Charles O. objected strenuously to Duncan and former A's Coach Charlie Lau rooming together in the east bay city and informed all those willing to listen he would not tolerate it. The matter of money—$10,000—finally sent Duncan to the Indians along with Outfielder George Hendrick during the spring training of 1973. When Williams announced the trade to the press in Mesa just prior to an exhibition game, Reggie Jackson, with a crescendo, gave vent to his feelings, addressing himself to a few sportswriters, who just happened to be present.

"This man is a member of this team!" Jackson shouted. "Why was he traded? There is no good reason. He is a friend to all of us on this team. It is a dirty shame, that's what it is."

Duncan sat in silence and let the volatile Jackson have his say—without benefit of any bleeps. Finally the disconsolate Duncan wandered off to the showers after telling the press corps he would grant them interviews later at the club's motel in Phoenix. To Dave's credit, while he was showered with questions in his Sands' motel room, he did not erupt with diatribes against Finley. True, Duncan was hurt, but he hid his true feelings with a calm which was creditable.

"We were not too far apart in money," Dave disclosed flatly. "But I wanted him to recognize my worth to the club—something he would not do for me or to some of the other members of this team.

"He knew my potential and that I was considered a strong defensive catcher. He also knew I did not like to sit on the bench, and other catchers were brought in, and platooning was inevitable. I had heard talks of trades all winter long and was more or less resigned to the fact I was going to be sent traveling."

Phil Seghi, veteran baseball official, former employee of Finley, and now general manager of the Cleveland club, saw what was going on between Finley and Duncan. The dickering began and Duncan and Hendrick joined the Indians. Seghi knew the A's roster as well as anyone, and in the trade he sent Catcher Ray Fosse and Infielder Jack Heidemann to the A's. Seghi respected Duncan's power and also was aware of the catcher's defensive ability. Seghi was around for part of the time during which Duncan hit 54 HRs for the A's in five seasons. In helping the A's to the World Series title in 1972, Duncan connected for 19 HRs and 59 RBIs.

Ray Fosse definitely has made a contribution to the successes of the A's after he joined them on that spring day in March 1972. He was seriously injured as a not-so-innocent bystander when he tried to break up a fight between Reggie Jackson and Billy North during a clubhouse melee in Detroit. He was on the disabled list from June until late August in 1974 for his protective efforts in that brawl. Ray was extremely pleased with the trade because, as he termed it, "I am happy to be joining a contending club and particularly as strong a club as the A's."

Fosse carted a long list of credentials to Oakland when he greeted the A's. He had led the Indians in batting with a .307 in

1970 and had a total of 42 major league HRs. He was a former Golden Glove winner, despite breaking his right index finger for three seasons in a row, 1968, 1969, and 1970. Ray caught 143 games for the champs in 1973 and batted .256 with seven HRs. His batting mark slipped to .196 the following season. But in both years he had a hand in the A's winning the AL pennant and the World Series.

In the winter of 1972, Finley once more turned to the willing Cubs for outfield help, and he traded veteran Pitcher Bob Locker for Outfielder Billy North, the fleet-footed center fielder and base stealer. Leo Durocher, managing the Cubs at the time, could not say enough in praise of Billy during the spring of 1972 when North was a bright young rookie in the Chicago camp in Scottsdale. North had made up his mind as a youngster to be a baseball player and once deserted his family at the tender age of 12 years to watch a Pacific Coast League game. He was quickly found by the police and happily enveloped by his anxious parents and relatives.

Given a chance to play regularly, North rebounded and batted a robust .285 in 146 games, and stole 53 bases before being felled by an ankle injury. He missed the World Series. The crown coveted by North went to Tommy Harper of Boston by the thinnest of margins—one stolen base. In 1974 Billy reached the 54 plateau in base thefts and a .260 batting figure. Along with Campaneris, he was a constant threat in stealing, and he also provided the A's with a speedy one-two threat on the bases. North's 54 steals was tops in this department and accorded him much personal satisfaction.

During Finley's many changes in personnel, the one trade which caused tempers to flare sans restraint began when Mike Epstein became an Athletic in a major exchange with the old Washington Senators on May 8, 1971. The articulate Epstein, who once started a diet on Thanksgiving Day, became involved in wordy battles with Finley and disagreements with Manager Dick Williams before being cast aside to the Rangers after the 1972 campaign.

Regarded by many as something of a philosopher, Epstein was graduated from the University of California, Berkeley, where he was a baseball and football star. His first affiliation in baseball was with Baltimore, when he was signed off the Berkeley campus by Don McShane, Charles Wallgren, and the late and beloved Freddie Hofmann. Mike was sought by many major league clubs, and it took some fast talking by Hofmann to collar the powerfully built youngster. Epstein ducked in and out of the majors before finally settling with Washington in 1968.

Upon coming to the A's in May 1971, Mike shared first base with Tommy Davis, also a veteran member of the Oakland Alumni Club. For the year Epstein compiled a .237 batting mark but had 60 RBIs and 19 HRs. Minus more than twenty pounds at the start of the 1972 season, Mike could not remain calm, even though the team was winning. He never appeared to be completely at peace with himself, his teammates or Finley or Williams. His attitude is best expressed in his tidy bit of philosophy—"I am the way I am because I am the way I am and nothing is going to change me." This Epstein tenet was told to Finley soon after Mike joined the A's, and he did not change one iota after being banished to the Rangers and eventually to the Angels.

After the World Series victory in 1972, Mike became embroiled in a shouting incident with Manager Williams on a plane trip, and this directly led to his parting with the World Champions.

INTER-LEAGUE MARKETPLACE

Inter-league trading was longtime coming to baseball, but it hit with the speed of a Bob Feller fast ball. The barrier was belatedly lifted November 21, 1959, and two trades were completed that very first historic day. The Cubs traded First Baseman-Outfielder Jim Marshall (later their manager) and Pitcher Dave Hillman to the Red Sox for First Baseman Dick Gernert. Shortly after the news of this deal had cleared on the wire services, the Reds and Athletics (Kansas City based) followed with a joint announcement. The Reds traded Pitcher Tom Acker for Catcher Frank House of the A's.

Altogether nine inter-league trades were completed during a November 21–December 15 period. Of major consequence, the Orioles sent Pitchers Billy O'Dell and Billy Loes to the Giants for Outfielder Jackie Brandt, Pitcher Gordon Jones, and Catcher Roger McCardell.

The Reds were involved in the second biggie, sending longtime star Second Baseman Johnny Temple to the Indians for Pitcher Calvin Coolidge McLish, Infielder Billy Martin, and First Baseman Gordy Coleman.

. . . And that is how it was seventeen years ago. . . .

His objection to being taken out of a series game for defensive purposes was partly due to the brisk exchange with Williams on the plane. But the fact that he fell off at the plate during the classic, with a blank in the hit department in 16 chances, most likely precluded anything else in leading to his departure.

Mike later openly criticized Finley's hiring of pinch runner Herb Washington.

"Some of the management pressure on the A's are ridiculous," Mike exclaimed. "Look at Herb Washington. He is bewildered on the baseball field. Look at some of the guys who struggled in the minor leagues for many years trying to perfect their skills and get to the majors. Then Washington comes along and immediately he is in the majors."

The final salvo fired by Epstein at Finley was direct and only served to further emphasize the bitterness the big athlete felt toward his former employer.

"I see in Finley a man who attempts to generate so much hate against himself by the player that they'll play better," Epstein asserted. "The team with a common enemy has better unity and becomes a more cohesive group. The players then vow to show Finley that they'll win in spite of him."

One of baseball's best designated hitters, the veteran Tommy Davis, spent time with Finley's gang. Tommy was purchased from the Astros the first time around, but subsequently he was signed as a free agent. He was released because of his involvement during Vida Blue's holdout siege, when Tommy introduced the southpaw to Bob Gerst, who handled the negotiations with Finley for Vida. Davis was with several major league clubs, and none of his stops affected his ability to swing a potent bat.

Finley's constant personnel gyrations also brought him another excellent designated hitter in the much traveled and respected Deron Johnson. He also came by purchase from Philadelphia. He was a tremendous performer for the A's during the 1973 drive for the pennant. For lack of a special designated hitter, Deron more than adequately filled the vacancy, destroying AL pitching from May into August. He left the A's via waivers and went on to Milwaukee, thence to Boston, to Chicago with the White Sox, and back to Boston.

Finley made all out efforts to bolster the club when he saw the slightest sign of a faltering step. Even the defunct Seattle Pilots figured in deals with his regime. Finley obtained Catcher Larry Haney for Infielder John Donaldson, but in typical fashion Donaldson was to return to the A's. Also in 1969 Infielder Ted Kubiak and Pitcher George Lazerique were sent to the Pilots for Diego Segui and Shortstop Ray Oyler. Kubiak also was to renew his membership in the club but eventually landed with the Padres in May 1975.

In 1970 the Brewers executed a trade with the A's in which First Baseman Don Mincher and Third Baseman Ron Clark moved to Oakland. Leaving Finley were Catcher Phil Roof, Outfielder Mike Hershberger, and Pitchers Lew Krausse, who also was to return, and Ken Sanders.

Although Finley was busier than a bird dog in an off-limits sanctuary, his 1971 deals didn't include any immediate candidates for the Hall of Fame. Besides Ken Holtzman for Rick Monday, his here-today-gone-tomorrow movements involved mainly fringe players—and some of these were on the far fringe. Reacting like he was playing checkers, Charlie O. moved mainly with the Don Shaws, Ollie Browns, Ron Clarks, and Rob Gardners before getting around to Matty Alou, and Mike Epstein.

The spring of 1972—March 4, to be exact—saw Finley strike for a right-handed pitcher in Denny McLain in a deal with the Rangers for Pitchers Jim Panther and Don Stanhouse. McLain, erstwhile organist and one of the game's tragic figures following his suspension by Commissioner Bowie Kuhn for gambling associations, never came close to achieving the invincible form which brought him fame and the Cy Young Award while with Detroit. Even the wizardry of the A's veteran Pitching Coach Bill Posedel could not restore the form once enjoyed by McLain when he won 31 and 24 games in consecutive seasons for the Tigers. While on the Birmingham roster, Denny was traded to the Braves for slugger Orlando Cepeda. Cepeda saw little duty for the A's—three games—before undergoing surgery for ailing knees. It could not exactly be called a vintage year for the A's in trades, but there were plenty.

In 1973 the A's didn't stand still bidding for a second leg on the World Series trophy. The season started with the Dave Duncan-Ray Fosse exchange and ended with controversy in the key of C. When Mike Andrews made two errors in Game II of the Series, Finley fired him on the spot. When the classic moved to New York for an open date before it was resumed, there were press conferences all over the city. Andrews told his side of the story. Commissioner Bowie Kuhn expressed a few opinions before ordering Finley to reinstate Andrews. This made Mike an instant hero, especially with his teammates. The best 1973 preseason deal for the A's was the North-Locker deal with the Cubs. Proving that nothing is impossible in baseball, at the season's end the Cubs traded Locker back to Oakland for Horacio Pena, another pitcher.

Finley's premier deal for the 1974 club was getting Billy Williams, a longtime Cubs' favorite. After landing Williams for Infielder Manny Trillo and Pitchers Darold Knowles and Locker (lookie-lookie, Locker's a Cub again), the A's owner gave Billy a no-cut, two-year contract for $150,000 a season. This figure made Williams the highest-salaried player in A's history, just like it established him as Oakland's best-paid designated hitter ever.

But Finley did not stop after getting Williams. He again went on to prowl for talent he considered necessary to "keep it alive in '75." John ("Blue Moon") Odom was on his way to Cleveland for Pitchers Jim Perry and Dick Bosman. Once again the astute Phil Seghi figured to get a strong reliever in Odom. Blue Moon had been on the trading block almost every season but somehow managed to escape the Finley swing. Ted Kubiak, who aspired to succeed the classy fielding Dick Green as the A's second baseman, was traded to the Padres for Pitcher Sonny Siebert. Green's threats to retire for several successive springs and also Finley's fetish for platooning second basemen gave Kubiak a chance to stick—not without interruptions. Ted was eligible for three World Series with the Oakland club.

Despite Finley's ceaseless queue of deals, purchases, and releases, somehow he has managed to keep the status quo of the "hard core." Late in 1974 there were rumblings that Reggie Jackson was to leave, but nothing developed. Some of the "hard core" are adding mileage, and the future may force Finley to relegate them to the alumni category.

"I take pride in performance," Finley observed. "I have spent money to obtain the best, and no one can complain over this. I work at my job and that is why I don't have a general manager. Some laughed when I took over as my own general manager. But we have had good players and three World Championships in a row."

A veteran of the A's was greeted during the 1974 World Series with "How are you doing?" His terse reply—"I'm just trying to keep from going crazy." But through all of the tumult, turmoil, stress, and strain, the A's have reveled in success after success. And when it is considered, the three World Series shares and championship series rewards amount to close to $70,000—a lot of sweat and sacrifice did not go to waste. The air of turbulence permeates but does not smother the three-time World Champion Oakland A's.

CLARK NEALON
Sportswriter, *Houston Post*

Clark Nealon is a native Texan who spent forty-five years covering the Texas as well as the national sports' beat. He was a close follower of minor league baseball in Houston for twenty years, and then shifted to the major league level with the birth of the Astros (née Colt .45s) in 1962. In providing first the readerships of the *Houston Press* and then the *Houston Post* with the Best of Nealon, Clark covered nineteen consecutive World Series from Bobby Thomson's historic pennant playoff home run in 1951 to the Miracle Mets in 1969. He flavored this on-the-spot coverage with thirty years of spring training baseball, twenty-four consecutive Kentucky Derbies, and more than a score of Southwest Conference football championship and bowl games. Clark was graduated from Texas A. & M. in 1931.

2/THE ASTROS

Houston's horrible fate: exploding player trades

Severest critics of Houston Astro ventures into baseball's trading marts are inclined to shrug in frustration and comment:

"Oh, well, the Astros are strong contenders in one department: The misfortune, the untimely judgment, or whatever it is that winds up in trades that explode in their faces, almost on the point of release."

It's almost as if the Houston club is hounded by a horrible fate. While the Houston entry struggles on to put it all together just one time, there is all too plain evidence that the Astros have traded away valuable talent, stars-to-be who made key contributions to World Championships, to league titlists, to strong contenders, and to All-Star teams, some with remarkable rejuvenations. Meanwhile the Astrodome's regulars have never mounted a really serious pennant threat.

To stronger clubs eventually have gone stars like Rusty Staub, who performed well in a World Series for the Mets after a stopover at Montreal; Joe Morgan, who became a bulwark for a Cincinnati World Series array; Jimmy Wynn, who found outstanding new baseball life in Los Angeles as a major factor in the Dodgers' drive to the NL title in 1974; Mike Marshall, the out-of-this-world relief pitcher of those same Dodgers; Dave Giusti, a standout relief star for Pittsburgh's World Champions and a perennial contender.

Or Mike Cuellar, a Cy Young Award winner for the Orioles, a series winner, including a World's title season, and immediately a 20-game winner upon departure from the Dome; or Jack Billingham, ordinary for the Astros but a pacesetter on the mound for a Cincinnati World Series aggregation. And John Mayberry, who became an All-Star power hitter for Kansas City after going away for two pitchers no longer on major league rosters.

There have been others, some of them valuable to the Astros, but the above have been enough to cascade criticism down on Astro dealing policy in the 13-plus year history of the expansion club that started building from scratch in 1962. It has never finished higher than second in the Western Division (in 1972 the Astros were 84–69). The club showed strong contention only in 1969 when Houston was 2½ games out of first place in the West in early September but faded fast to fifth. That was the year the Astros were authorized to print World Series tickets that served only to become collector's items.

So, slice it any way you like. Multiply it. Or divide it. The result is that Astro trading fortunes have been predominantly bad. The showcase at the top makes it look even worse because it is on that spotlighted stage that developments have made what looked like reasonable trades in the beginning into horrors in retrospect.

Like most critics, however, the Astro blasters overlook some good trades, such as the one that brought Denis Menke from Atlanta and Fred Gladding from Detroit as key figures in that 1969 charge; and even the oft-maligned deal that sent Morgan and Billingham, among others, to the Reds for Lee May and Tommy Helms, both strong operatives in the 1972s club record season; and a 1973 campaign that was the second best ever for Houston at 82–80 and a fourth place finish in the West. Plus the acquisition of star Shortstop Roger Metzger from the Cubs, made possible by the trade of Joe Pepitone to the Cubs when Chicago was pressing for a pennant in 1970. And obtaining Catcher John Edwards from the Cardinals in 1968 to lend the first touch of respectability to the Astros with his defensive assets.

The jury is still out on the 1974 trade of Lee May to the Orioles for two fine young prospects in Outfielder-Infielder Enos Cabell and Second Baseman Rob Andrews. So all of the Astro trades haven't been bad. And some of the mitigating circumstances have been even historic in the form of Commissioner Bowie Kuhn finally settling a deal far from its original intention and against all precedent.

And where developments out of trades have hurt the Astro image, fate in form of death has been most unfortunate. Tragedy seemed to hound the Colt .45s, which was their founding name, almost from the beginning. Jim Umbricht, a strong and improving relief pitcher in the early years, died of cancer in 1964 at the age of 33. Walter Bond, a Colt power hitter of swaddling years, died of leukemia shortly after moving on to the Twins. And Don Wilson, who had pitched two no-hitters and was a solid man in Astro pitching plans for 1975, was found dead, along with his son, of carbon monoxide poisoning at the family home in Houston on January 5, 1975. Jay Dahl, a promising young pitcher in the Houston organization, was killed in an auto accident in 1963.

As in practically all ventures into baseball bartering field, the background of the Astro trades is significant and interesting. Houston deals must fall into two categories: those made in the Paul Richards regime as vice president in charge of baseball (a position he took over when Gabe Paul, the club's first major league general manager, resigned while the operation was still in its infancy) and the transactions made under the general managership of H. B. ("Spec") Richardson, who succeeded Paul Richards when the present chairman of the board, Roy Hofheinz, fired Richards in 1966.

To make the background complete, the observer must realize that Hofheinz had been a minority stockholder to the late R. E. ("Bob") Smith during the Richards regime. Hofheinz and Smith had come to a bitter parting of the ways after 1965, the result of which was Hofheinz's buying controlling interest from Smith. The final stages of the split were accompanied by a sharply and bitterly defined political struggle in the front office of the Houston club. The lines between "Hofheinz men" and "Smith men" were clearly and plainly drawn. Richardson was a Hofheinz man, Richards a Smith man. It followed that when Richards left, Richardson took over, with a strong right-hand man in Grady Hatton, who has been with the club since Gabe Paul's days.

In reality, a bearing on some of the early trades of the Richardson regime was in the fact that Paul, a strong-player man

---

BEATS WORKING

In 1924 the Houston club paid Fort Smith, Arkansas, $1,000 for Outfielder Chick Hafey. At the end of the season, Houston, after a long and bitter fight, sold Chick to the Cardinals for $20,000 and Catcher Harry McCurdy. Hafey was a .300 plus hitter for eight seasons, winning the NL batting championship with .349 in 1931.

with a firm influence on the kids he had signed in the building years, left with bitterness, as mentioned. The players and the new front office obviously felt carry-overs from the parting of the ways between Richards and Hofheinz, and neither benefited. It was all too obvious.

And there are still many close observers of baseball in Houston who see it as another tragedy of the club that the original organization could not have been maintained longer in the building process.

Smith had been the one indispensable man in Houston's progress to major league status. His immense financial responsibility, his standing in the community, his dedication to making the city's presence felt as an NL contender were strongest factors in two bond elections by Harris County voters that made possible the financing of the Astrodome, or Harris County Domed Stadium, the arena's official name. And the dome has to be one of the great bargains of history at a cost of $31 million, the amount voted in bonds that have yet to cost the citizens of Harris County any tax money.

Hofheinz had the dream, the plans, the tremendous promotional and sales talent, and the drive to make the arena a reality that was part of the reason Houston was granted an NL franchise. And he has excelled at keeping occupied and promoting the dome that Evangelist Billy Graham called "The Eighth Wonder of the World." Yet the pillar that was Smith is too often forgotten. Manifestation of Smith's dedication to building a winner in Houston, regardless of the cost, came during a winter meeting in the early 1960s. The man who had already spent millions in expansion pool players and bonus boys was called about a deal that actually was a product of Richards's fertile imagination, but it would have been historic had it been made.

Richards, trying to help a newspaper friend produce a "live" lead for an early deadline, offered to make a deal with the then strong Milwaukee Braves by which Houston would give its entire major league roster and $5 million for Milwaukee's entire major league roster. Mind you, this was before the confettilike money deals of the inflation 1970s. Checking on such a fantastic proposal, a reporter called Smith in Houston to see if the club would lay out such a tremendous figure. Smith hadn't been informed about the proposal, but, without batting an eye, he was ready to talk on the record:

"We'll make the deal," he said with finality. Of course, the Braves turned down the Richards offer.

In any event, Staub, Morgan, and Wynn had become part of the organization under Richards, never reacted well to the new regime, and were never high in the esteem of the restructured player department. The upshot was player discord that brought on, among other things, the replacing of Hatton, who had succeeded Lum Harris, a Richards man, as field manager in 1966. Hatton was replaced by Harry ("The Hat") Walker in 1968 but has continued as a top executive.

It was after the 1968 season that Staub was traded to the then expansion Montreal for Donn Clendenon, Jesus Alou, and $75,000 in a bombshell of a trade by the Richardson regime, including his top advisers Hatton and Walker, following a meeting with Hofheinz. It was a bombshell in at least two ways, in Houston and in baseball history in its final result. Many fans in Houston sided with Staub, who had been held up as the symbol of the early Colts' youth movement and was a popular player. Rusty had hit .333 in 1967 and twice had been an All-Star.

But the Houston furore was mild in comparison to what followed in a deal in which the new commissioner, Kuhn, actually completed the transaction with a precedent-shattering ruling. Clendenon had seemed satisfied at first, but suddenly decided he would not report to Houston after the Astros had declined to secure a very substantial loan he was seeking for a housing investment. Then Staub was quoted as saying he would not return to Houston. Marvin Miller got into the act as players' organization head. It was the cause célèbre of the 1969 spring training season. The commissioner was caught in the middle of a tactical situation in which his concern was not to offend the new owners of expansion Montreal who had tied a big program to Staub, not to mention the other controversial issues.

The final result was that Commissioner Kuhn turned his back on the historically established trade rule by which the deal would have been nullified and the players involved returned. Instead, Kuhn ruled that the deal would be completed with the Expos sending Pitchers Jack Billingham and Skip Guinn to Houston. The Astros protested to no avail.

The irony of the whole mess was that Montreal sold Clendenon to the Mets, and all he did was key the "Miracle Mets" of 1969 to the World's Championship with his right-handed power and ability to hit left-handers, which is why the Astros wanted him. Clendenon also won the MVP award in the 1969 World Series. He very easily could have performed the same service for the Astros, who were so close to the NL West lead early in September with the aid of two of Richardson's initial deals. Those trades brought Menke and Denny Lemaster from Atlanta for Sonny Jackson and Chuck Harrison, and Gladding from Detroit for Eddie Mathews, who had been acquired from Atlanta with Arnold Umbach for Bob Bruce and Dave Nicholson.

Richardson still says he would make the Staub deal as originally fashioned all over again, and he has supporters in this thinking.

The next big deal—the biggest in Astro history—came after the 1971 season. It was Morgan, Menke, Cesar Geronimo, Billingham, and Ed Armbrister for Tommy Helms, Lee May, and Jim Stewart. May had been the slugging star for Cincinnati's World Series team of 1970, and Helms had been the second baseman and an All-Star selection.

Morgan and Manager Harry Walker had failed to see eye to eye on numerous occasions in a lingering difficulty that spilled over into a charge by Morgan in 1972 that "Walker does not like blacks," a charge vigorously denied by Walker. In any event, Morgan's known speed and other talents fit immediately into the Big Red machine. Billingham improved vastly on his Astro records, Menke was a solid player on a World Series team, and Geronimo developed speedily to bring Houston fans' criticism of the deal. But May and Helms were exceptional performers on the 1–2 winningest Astro teams in history in the next two seasons, so the trade wasn't the loss to Houston as it was later painted.

Again there was some irony because several Cincinnati sportswriters and many Red fans roundly criticized the deal from the Red standpoint at the time it was made.

"It was our feeling that we had to do something to hypo interest after the 1971 season," Richardson looks back now. "Our attendance had fallen off badly in 1971, but we had our third and fourth best years in club history in 1972 and our 1–2 best won–loss records, so the trade had to be good for us, too. We thought, also, that separating Morgan and Wynn might help Wynn."

The trade of Wynn and his rejuvenation with the Dodgers in 1974 may be the worst the Astros have made. Jim was traded for Claude Osteen in what was looked on at the time as a deal involving two players nearing the end. Osteen was less than a success for the Astros; he moved on to the Cardinals, and then on to the White Sox. Wynn at 32 had had a couple of bad years for the Astros after earlier slugging excellence, and he never quite adjusted to giving up his center field job to young Cesar Cedeno. Wynn found marvelous new life with the Dodgers in center field to make the trade look bad from the Astros' standpoint, a bonanza for the Dodgers.

"Most of these guys we've traded didn't play for the Astros like they have for their new clubs," shrugs Richardson.

Which statement is certainly correct in the case of Mike Cuellar, who was traded by the Richardson group to Baltimore with Infielder Elijah Johnson for Curt Blefary mainly, after the 1968 season. Cuellar immediately became a 20-game winner and Cy Young Award recipient for Baltimore (1970) and is still going strong. But as an Astro in 1968 Cuellar had had arm trouble. As a matter of fact, the Orioles were warned of that in negotiations; they sent a man to Puerto Rico to check on Mike that winter and decided to make the deal regardless.

At the 1969 World Series, just before his win over the Mets that was the Orioles' lone victory of that series, Mike was asked: "What happened, Mike? What's the difference between pitching for Baltimore and Houston?"

"Over here," Mike answered with a shrug, "they catch the ball and they hit it." Cuellar had faded from 16–11 with 246 innings pitched in 1967 to an 8–11 record with 171 innings pitched in 1968 as an Astro, and the Houston club had been advised medically that Mike's arm was questionable. During Cuellar's first season at Baltimore, he pitched 291 innings, had a 23–11 record, and won the Cy Young Award.

Giusti was a bonus boy from the Gabe Paul regime. He developed into a 15-game winner in 1966 and an 11-game winner the following season before being traded to the Cardinals with Catcher Dave Adlesh for Edwards and Catcher Tommie Smith after the 1968 season. Dave's route to relief stardom included going to San Diego in the expansion pool from the Cardinals in 1968, being traded back to St. Louis and then sent by the Cardinals to Pittsburgh after the 1969 season. Again ironically, Grady Hatton once discussed with Giusti the idea of becoming a relief specialist, but Dave wanted to stick to starting then.

Marshall actually was purchased by the Astros from Seattle

in 1969 for their AAA farm at Oklahoma City. He was an Astro briefly in 1970 before being sold to Montreal, thence to the Dodgers.

Billingham's case is also interesting. Jack was put in the expansion pool by the Dodgers in 1968, went to Montreal, then to Houston in the final Staub deal. Jack's best year in three at Houston was 13–9 in 1970.

Wynn's rejuvenation matched that of Cuellar. Jim had hit .275 with 24 homers and 90 RBIs in 1972, and his last year as an Astro was down to .220 with 20 homers and 55 RBIs in 1973. As a Dodger in 1974, he hit .271 with 32 homers and 108 RBIs to win Comeback Player of the Year honors. So Richardson had a point when he said: "They didn't play for the Astros like they did for their new clubs." Whatever it means, Wynn is still booed by fans when he comes to Houston.

In the trying building years, the Richards regime signed many fine young players like Staub, Morgan, Larry Dierker, Doug Rader, and acquired Wynn in the draft. And Paul did his customary excellent job of acquiring and developing pitching, like Hal Woode-schick, Bob Bruce, Don Nottebart, and Don McMahon, among others, in deals and work with Ken Johnson and Dick Farrell from the expansion pool. And Eddie Kasko, Nellie Fox, Robin Roberts, Johnny Temple, Don Larsen, and Pete Runnels gave the Colts and Astros some names and production in their closing years.

But even Richards made some poor deals in a Houston fate that started so early. For instance he gave Kansas City $100,000, Pitcher Jess Hickman, and Infielder Ernie Fazio for Jim Gentile, who never cut it for Houston. And Manny Mota, still going strong for the Dodgers as a part-timer and pinch hitter, was a Colt .45 who was sent to Pittsburgh with an estimated $50,000 for Howie Goss in a long search for a center fielder, but Howie never hit and was soon gone. And Richards got in on the trades of a world-series-performer-to-be when he sent Catcher Jerry Grote to the Mets in 1965 for cash and Pitcher Tom Parsons. Grote went on to be the Mets' starting catcher in the World Series of 1969 and 1973.

The lingering feeling about Astro trades is perhaps best bound up in that old dugout adage, to wit:

There's one thing about beating your head against a brick wall. It feels so good when you stop.

But Richardson makes no attempt to hide from old trades and plans to fight on doggedly.

"Trades are by nature gambles," he says. "You try to help your club where you know it needs help, and each time we did, but in some cases it didn't work out that way. We have been in the position of trying to gain contention with just a little help. We'll try again in the same situation."

DON MERRY
Sportswriter, *Long Beach Independent-Press-Telegram*

Don Merry, one of the newer Young Turks on the major league baseball beat, is a native of Winnipeg, Manitoba, Canada. He was graduated from Los Angeles State University in California with a major in journalism. In establishing his versatility, Merry has written sports on both sides of the American-Canadian border. The astute thirty-six-year-old staffer has covered the California Angels for the past seven years for the *Long Beach Independent-Press-Telegram.* Merry is a past president of the Los Angeles-Anaheim chapter of the Baseball Writers' Association of America. He is a frequent contributor to national sports publications.

3/THE ANGELS

A stud becomes
a Phillie overnight

They come and they go in steady profusion. Some are faceless creatures, names long since forgotten because they were hardly ever recognizable to begin with—the Dan Ardells, Frank Lejas, and the Tom Silverios of our times. Who are they? What were they?

Others are more readily remembered, even fondly, because they were different . . . maybe even unique . . . and they did things both on and off the baseball field that triggered a tempest in your typewriter—the Bo Belinskys, the Jimmy Piersalls, and the Dean Chances. You knew who they were. At times zany and mischievous and prone to drive management into uncontrollable fits of rage and, most likely, embarrassment. Only the talent was there—if you could harness it. If you couldn't, well, here today and gone tomorrow.

Baseball is a revolving door and the California Angels, née the Los Angeles Angels, have contributed an infinite number of pushes in their comparatively short 15-year existence. Cast your eyes on the major league rosters of the moment and think about it. There, in abundance, are the names of players who, at one time or another, earned a living in Anaheim—laboring in the immediate shadow of Disneyland, not to mention the one cast by their more successful brethren up the freeway—the Los Angeles Dodgers.

Andy Messersmith . . . Jose Cardenal . . . Pedro Borbon . . . Doug Griffin . . . Frank Robinson . . . Vada Pinson . . . Rudy May. Erstwhile Angels, every one, but long since traded away. Or sold with the promise of something in return. So, too, were Alex Johnson, Jay Johnstone . . . Clyde Wright . . . Tom Murphy . . . Jim Spencer . . . Jim Fregosi.

Ah, Jim Fregosi. Shortstop. Italian. Good looks. The first young player who really developed into something in excess of mediocrity with the Angels in those struggling, unsure years which followed the expansion of 1961. Jim Fregosi—the favorite son of the Angels' resident millionaire and owner, Gene Autry. Wherever big baseball transactions are mentioned, Jim Fregosi's name is guaranteed to surface. Not that Jim Fregosi, albeit a capable performer, is destined for inevitable enshrinement at Cooperstown; it's just that the personage he was traded for almost certainly is.

Since their inception on that November day in 1960, the Angels have been served by three general managers—Fred Haney (1961–1968), Dick Walsh (1968–1971), and Harry Dalton (1971–????). A diversified troika, to be sure, but with a common bond characteristic of most general managers in baseball—an unhesitating willingness to wheel and deal. First, they hope it will improve the team's lot. Secondly, they know it will cause the town to start talking, and talking generally means interest, and interest generally can be translated into profit. Throughout a decade and a half, the Angels have participated in 219 deals of varying magnitude. But, in essence, they have really made only one. The big one.

Harry Dalton had achieved notoriety and acclaim while scaling the administrative ladder within the Orioles' organization in the mid-1960s and ultimately winding up in the general manager's upholstered chair. He was enticed to Orange County by Autry on October 27, 1971, when the Cowboy determined that Dick Walsh had outlived his usefulness to the Angels. Autry had grown impatient with his team's seeming persistence to be an also-ran. He had also become disenchanted with the Walsh administration. That administration had been buffeted and finally broken by turmoil and resultant adverse publicity surrounding the suspension and appeal hearing of Alex Johnson and the sudden, dramatic midyear retirement of Tony Conigliaro.

Johnson was the AL batting champion as an Angel in the surprise season of 1970 when the Angels were to be found loitering no further than three games behind league-leading Minnesota in the Western Division as late as the first week of September. Johnson and Conigliaro, the Boston strong boy, were supposed to bring a pennant to Anaheim in 1971. Instead, although hardly working harmoniously, they collaborated in bringing only disaster in a season replete with guns in the clubhouse and fights in the dugout. This was the year the team became known as Hell's Angels. Walsh was summarily released from his seven-year contract despite the fact he had four years remaining. The distraught Autry, traditionally a scrupulous man with a dollar, was obliged to reach into his saddlebags over the next four summers and present Walsh with nearly $250,000.

It was into these grim surroundings that Dalton found himself deposited in October. The Angel roster was littered with deadwood, malcontents, Good Time Charlies, and a few journeymen, some of whom even performed to the best of their limited capabilities. "We had some real zeroes," Dalton was to acknowledge. Additionally, the farm system was in a state of disarray, and there were very few prospects on the immediate horizon. A pennant seemed as far off as the planet Pluto.

IT GOES FOR UMPIRES, TOO!

There have been many reasons for trades in baseball, but a desire to work nearer home led to the swapping of two umpires in 1965. Dick Phillips, umpiring in the far-flung (Indianapolis to Hawaii in one direction, and San Diego to Vancouver in another) class AAA Pacific Coast League, asked for a transfer so that he would be closer to his off-season home in New England. Phillips directed his first request to A. Rankin Johnson, president of the class AA Eastern League, spanning Massachusetts, New York, and Pennsylvania. Johnson refused, claiming his staff was complete for the season.

Hold the phone!

Johnson remembered a preseason promise he had made to Andy Olsen, one of his younger and better umpires. The prexy had promised Olsen the first promotion available. Because this would be a step up for Andy, Johnson proposed a trade of the two umpires: Phillips for Olsen. Dewey Soriano, the PCL president, approved, and the two umpires switched leagues the following June 6.

Three and a half years later Olsen moved again, this time without benefit of a trade. His contract was purchased by the National League, Friday, September 13, 1968. Now a seven-season veteran in the NL, Andy umpired in the 1971 championship series and the 1974 World Series. When he receives his first All-Star game assignment, Olsen will have completed the cycle for the major league men in blue.

Good reason for Olsen's claim: "The trade was my best break ever."

One has to wonder if Dick Phillips would react in the same manner?

Dalton formulated a game plan whereby he would attempt to stall for time by initiating a series of patchwork trades designed to bring a little depth and a modicum of respectability to the Angels while he went about refurbishing the farm system, knowing the first dividends would not be reaped for three to five years. He cast about for the multiplayer deal, hoping to trade one or two players for three or four.

"Jim Fregosi," who had attained star status, at least in Anaheim, and an $82,000 salary, "was my most marketable product," Dalton told himself. Fortuitously, for the Angels anyway, the miracle of 1969 had worn off for the Mets, and their general manager, Bob Scheffing, finding himself in the delightful position of having a plethora of pitching, was at this very moment shopping about for a bat. Better yet, a bat whose owner could play third base. Fregosi, closely scrutinized the previous summer by Mets' scout Dee Fondy, additionally whetted Scheffing's interest by enjoying a productive season amid the turmoil that surrounded the Angels. Furthermore, the Angels, due to the presence of Ken McMullen, acquired in April 1970 in a trade which sent Aurelio Rodriguez and Rick Reichardt to the Senators, had no intentions of shifting Fregosi to third base.

On November 30, 1971, Dalton cleared the way for Fregosi's departure when he acquired another shortstop. In his first transaction on behalf of the Angels, Dalton peddled left-handed Relief Pitcher Dave LaRoche to the Twins in exchange for Leo Cardenas, the possessor of a gifted glove and a strong throwing arm. It later developed, however, that Cardenas had lost a step afield and his range was diminished. This disturbing fact prompted Dalton to send Cardenas to Cleveland in April 1974, and after that particular move, Dalton remarked cleverly, "I hated to trade a man of his statue."

But with Cardenas on his roster, Dalton was now free to shop around for the best Fregosi offer. Inevitably, Dalton and Scheffing bumped into each other during the winter meetings which were held that year in Phoenix. When Scheffing mentioned he was in the market for a hitter, Dalton said he had one for him by the name of Fregosi.

Dalton was craving a pitcher and the Mets had them in abundance—Tom Seaver, Jerry Koosman, Gary Gentry, Jim McAndrew, and Nolan Ryan on the front line, with Danny Frisella and Tug McGraw in the bullpen, and Jon Matlack, Buzz Capra, and Jim Bibby waiting in the minor league wings. Dalton opted for Gentry and also tossed out the names of Capra and Matlack, but when Scheffing recoiled at this overture, Dalton quickly injected Ryan's name into the conversation.

"I wanted Ryan because I knew he wasn't likely to be a starter with the Mets," Dalton recalled. "We knew he threw as hard as anybody in baseball but, unfortunately, nobody knew whether it was going to be a ball or a strike."

Ryan, the fifth starter for the Mets, was treated like one. He was always yielding to off days or rainouts, and, after four summers, the Mets were beginning to grow weary and impatient waiting for him to harness and control his obviously superior powers.

"Actually," notes Whitey Herzog, now an Angel coach but then director of player development for the Mets, "our other starters threw darn near as hard as Nolie, but they were pitchers and he was still a thrower. He couldn't get his curve over, and he had yet to develop a changeup. I told Harry 'He'll fill your park if you get him,' but I honestly didn't think the Mets would trade Ryan."

Ryan began the 1971 season with a flourish, amassing a 7–2 record, but he faltered in the second half and finished a mediocre 10–14 with a 3.97 ERA. He completed only three of 26 starts and caused Met management to continue wringing their hands in frustration.

On December 10, 1971, the trade was consummated. Jim Fregosi went to the Mets in exchange for four players—Pitchers Nolan Ryan and Don Rose, Catcher Francisco Estrada, and Outfielder Leroy Stanton. Ryan, of course, went on to obliterate all manner of strikeout records, occasionally peppering his performance with a no-hitter—he had four at last count. Stanton continues to patrol the Angel outfield while Dalton turned around and later dealt Rose to San Francisco for Pitcher Ed Figueroa, who can now be observed as a member in good standing of the Angels' starting rotation.

Fregosi only served to remind New York fans of the bad deal the Indians got when they parted with Manhattan Island for assorted trinkets. Eventually he was packaged off to Texas, the catcalls from the frenzied denizens of Shea Stadium still scorching his ears. "I suppose Nolan Ryan can thank me for making him famous," the irrepressible Fregosi is liable to tell anyone who will listen today.

Naturally, not all of Dalton's manipulations have turned out so magnificently for the Angels. Early in 1972 he sent Pitcher Tom Murphy, then struggling along as a borderline starter, to the Royals for Outfielder-First Baseman Bob Oliver. Ollie hit a few home runs over the course of the next two and one-half years before he was bundled off to Baltimore. Murphy, after brief stops at Kansas City and St. Louis, has developed into the stopper in the Milwaukee bullpen.

Another Dalton deal which blew up in his face occurred in May 1973 when he traded First Baseman Jim Spencer and Pitcher Lloyd Allen to Texas for First Baseman Mike Epstein, Pitcher Bill Hands, and Catcher Rick Stelmaszek. Epstein and Dalton had been together in Baltimore, but in the interim Epstein had sampled success with the Oakland A's. When the A's dispatched him to Texas after his celebrated contretemps with Manager Dick Williams aboard an airplane during the 1972 World Series, Epstein was crushed—and moody—and nonproductive. An avid amateur pilot—he was known as Sky King and eagerly monitored all Angel takeoffs and landings—and horse rancher, Epstein simply lost interest in hitting home runs and drew his release early in the 1974 season.

Compared to the Ryan deal, which required an interminable series of conversations spread across six days and nights, Dalton was able to swing another trade of major proportions in a relatively short period of time. During the winter meetings of 1972, the Angels acquired slugger Frank Robinson, Pitchers Bill Singer and Mike Strahler, and Infielders Bobby Valentine and Bill Grabarkewitz from their freeway foes, the Dodgers.

Dalton and his Dodger counterpart, Al Campanis, were candid and straightforward enough to accomplish this business in one mere 13-hour sitting in a Hawaii hotel, a sitting punctuated by only four recesses for things like coffee and doughnuts and throat lozenges. In return, the Angels were obliged to part with a topflight pitcher long coveted by Campanis—Andy Messersmith—and Third Baseman McMullen. Because it involved the two neighbors, the trade triggered a spate of follow-up and reaction stories in the Los Angeles area press and, as an attention-grabber, it was particularly helpful to the Angels. The arrival of Robinson, even though at 37 his most notable seasons were behind him, gave Anaheim viewers their first glimpse at a superstar dressed in the double knits of the home team. Financially, if not artistically, the trade was a success.

During the undistinguished season that was 1972, Angel attendance plummeted to an all-time Anaheim low of 744,190 while the team sank another notch in the standings and finished fifth in a six-team division, five games under .500 and 18 behind pennant-winning Oakland. Rejuvenated by the trade, the Angels went over the million mark in paid admissions in 1973 even though they improved only three games in the standings.

Dalton and Robinson have enjoyed a strange alliance. When Dalton ascended to the position of general manager in Baltimore, succeeding Lee MacPhail in the fall of 1965, his first announcement came one hour after he took on his new title, and it concerned the acquisition of Robinson from the Reds. When Dalton joined the Angels, one of his first overtures was to the Orioles in an attempt to pry Robby away from Baltimore, but the Orioles, still perturbed that Harry would desert them for California, thought they would teach him a lesson in civility. They figured the best way would be to deal Robinson to Dalton's new archrival for the baseball dollar, the Dodgers. The trade with Los Angeles thus marked the second time Dalton succeeded in luring Robby away from an NL team. After two seasons with the Angels, Robinson was sold to Cleveland where he eventually became the game's first black manager, a job he would not likely have attained in conservative Orange County.

Even though General Manager Dick Walsh purchased an eventual American League batting champion in Alex Johnson—not to mention the turbulence which evolved from Johnson's presence—Walsh considers a trade he made the day following the Johnson deal as his most illustrious. Johnson and Chico Ruiz, the latter a personable utility infielder who was the godfather of Johnson's daughter (a fact which did not deter him from pulling a revolver from his locker and pointing it in Alex's direction during a flare-up in June 1971), came to the Angels from Cincinnati on November 25, 1970, for three pitchers—Jim McGlothlin, Pedro Borbon, and Vern Geishert.

It was a trade to be touched by tragedy. Ruiz, the author of that famous statement provoked by the fact he once played several games in succession—"bench me or trade me"—was killed in a one-car freeway crash near San Diego after the Angels released him. McGlothlin was stricken with a mysterious disease which cut short his career and also cost him his life.

On November 26, 1970, Walsh obtained Outfielder Micky Rivers, then nothing more than a minor league prospect from Atlanta, to complete a deal begun in September of that year. At that time California delivered the veteran Relief Pitcher Hoyt Wilhelm to the Braves to assist them in what developed into a successful pursuit of the Western Division pennant. From a publicity stand-point, the Angels frowned on the deal because they were planning a big promotion the following spring when Wilhelm figured to appear in his 1,000th game, thereby becoming the first pitcher in history to attain that figure. Wilhelm achieved that plateau in Atlanta but only after the Dodgers, then embroiled in a pennant fight with the Braves, turned down an offer by Walsh for his services. Rivers, blessed with inordinate speed, emerged as a fixture in the Angel outfield.

Johnson won the batting title by going 3-for-5 on the final day of the 1970 season against the White Sox to shade Carl Yastrzemski by a decimal point. Then Johnson was traded to Cleveland at the end of the tempestuous 1971 season during which he was suspended by the Angels for his lack of hustle, only to appeal the edict and win his case.

That was also the season Tony Conigliaro, a Walsh acquisition from Boston in October 1970, quit the team at a 5 A.M. press conference one June morning after striking out six times in a game at Oakland. Conigliaro, whose Newport Beach apartment was next door to curvaceous actress Raquel Welch, came to the Angels along with Jerry Moses and Ray Jarvis in exchange for Ken Tatum, Doug Griffin, and Jarvis Tatum. The Bosox could have had Messersmith in that one, but opted for K. Tatum, a promising reliever.

When Conigliaro claimed his vision was still impaired due to a 1967 beaning, ironically at the hands of an Angel pitcher—Jack Hamilton—and bolted the club, Walsh went to Commissioner Bowie Kuhn and attempted to have the entire trade revoked. He failed and was also ordered to continue paying Tony's healthy $70,000 salary on the grounds that Conigliaro was a disabled player. Events like that seemed to surround Walsh. Even when he got Outfielder Sweet Lou Johnson from Cleveland for Chuck Hinton in 1969, Johnson arrived with $9,500 still owing on a flashy pink Cadillac which Walsh agreed to pay off—and not out of Sweet Lou's $26,000 salary.

Fred Haney was at the helm during the Angels' formative years, and he made 121 moves during his 1961–1968 tenure as general manager, including signing the unpredictable Jimmy Pier-sall three times—and releasing him the same number. A kindly sort, Haney was always reminding Piersall that if he couldn't get a job somewhere else, he would take him back and overlook Piersall's penchant for creating the bizarre.

Haney had nowhere to build but up after the Angels were born in time for the 1961 season, but he worked some transactions which resulted in the club making an amazing run at the pennant in their second year of existence. Sweet Lou Johnson was with the Angels in 1961, before he discovered a taste for pink Caddies. Haney got him from the Cubs shortly before the season started and two weeks later traded him to Toronto of the International League for slugger Leon Wagner, who went on to hit 28 homers that first year and 37 the next. Wagner, however, was a better hitter than he was a businessman, and his clothing store, which he promoted with the slogan "Buy your rags from Daddy Wags," did not survive.

Haney's most productive deal of that first season came in May when he received Ryne Duren, Lee Thomas, and Johnny James from the Yankees for Bob Cerv and Tex Clevenger. Duren, with a reputation for not only being exceptionally fast but also wild, myopic and, occasionally, under the influence, was a savior in the bullpen while Thomas drove in 104 runs in 1962. Haney was also the man who traded Bo Belinsky to Philadelphia after Belinsky's repeated brushes with the law and management threw him into lasting disfavor with his boss. Bo, who authored the first Angel no-hitter against Baltimore in 1962, was traded for Pitcher Rudy May and a first baseman poetically named Costen Shockley.

"That's the first time," Haney snickered after Belinsky was dealt, "that overnight a stud became a Phillie."

FURMAN BISHER
Sportswriter, *Atlanta Journal*

Furman Bisher learned about trades at an early age. He was born on a farm in North Carolina, where they frequently traded a cow awaiting calf for one that wasn't to continue the family's milk supply. Bisher was graduated from the University of North Carolina after spending two years at a most appropriately named school—you guessed it—Furman University in Greenville, South Carolina. Furman has written seven books, won the Sports Writer of the Year award in Georgia eleven times, and is currently the president of the National Association of Sportscasters and Sportswriters. He is a former president of the Football Writers' Association of America, and twice won national turf writing awards.

4/THE BRAVES

Two Braves
top 1,400 home runs

True, the Braves have moved about our nation's profile like a shifty horse trader trying to beat an angry posse out of town. Also, they have changed names as often as a forger. Known as the Red Stockings first—not to be confused with the latter-day Red Sox—the Red Caps, the Beaneaters, the Nationals, the Doves, the Rustlers, THEN the Braves, the Bees, and finally again the Braves forever, as long as forever lasted in Boston. Later in Milwaukee. Still later in Atlanta.

And so this shall be an accounting of the craftsmanship of baseball barter and player exchange that laps over into three cities, and only the Oakland Athletics can match that. Curiously, the long-sightedness of the Red Stockings—et cetera—Braves at the trading counter has scarcely ever merited such a furtive style, their flight from community, or their preceding string of aliases.

There is one point of uniqueness on which they may never be challenged: They are the only major league baseball club ever involved in deals in which two players representing a production of over 1,400 home runs were featured. They took place forty years and two cities apart. While Owner-Judge Emil Fuchs scrambled about trying to extricate the Braves of Boston from the grip of debtors in 1935, he managed the release of the then bulbous and over-the-hill Babe Ruth from the New York Yankees for the required sum of $100, upon which Ruth hit six more home runs, then threw in the sponge. When Henry Aaron approached the close of his career with the Braves of Atlanta, he was granted his desire to "go home" and finish it off in Milwaukee, where he had started, in exchange for a journeyman outfielder named Dave May and a minor league pitcher. After fifteen years as a Yankee, Ruth finished as a Brave; after twenty-one years as a Brave, Aaron finished as a Brewer.

It cannot be said that the Braves' lack of prowess at barter has been limited to any one of their three locations. Nor can it be said that their record at sameness, while checkered at best, has not produced its telling results. The Braves of the twentieth century have been represented by three quite definite periods of success, all three righteously rewarded with pennants, but neither period being of exciting duration. In each of the eras of riches, a key trade or two can be picked out as the element that developed the chemical reaction.

Shortly after George Tweedy Stallings arrived in Boston to establish his "Miracle Braves," he acquired the services of a big pitcher named ("Seattle") Bill James, so called because that's where he came from. Stallings followed that with the purchase of Dick Rudolph, a left-hander the Giants were giving up on. Even after the season of 1914 began, Stallings was frantically trading about, trying to find the right combinations. A veteran pitcher, Hub Perdue, went to the Cardinals for George Whitted and Ted Cather. Infielder Jack Martin went to the Phillies for Josh Devore. As late as August, Stallings picked up Third Baseman Carlisle Smith from Brooklyn. Meanwhile, Rudolph and James were winning 27 and 26 games, and with a club half of whose members were still unpacking, Stallings made the most historic dash to pennant and World Championship known to man. They emerged from the taint of the cellar after July 4, then wiped out the assumedly impregnable Philadelphia Athletics in four straight games.

Such magnificence was a long time coming again to the Braves, thirty-four years to be exact, also equally as unexpected. Three new owners had taken over the club, starring Lou Perini, all three contractors, and as a threesome eventually known as the "Three Steamshovels." (Sportswriters would plaster a nickname on the Madonna.) They traded first for a few excess Cardinals, surrendering Red Barrett, a pitcher, and cash for the then fading right-hander, Mort Cooper, for openers. Liking this so much, they brashly reached into St. Louis and plucked the manager, Billy Southworth, for themselves, just as they might have bought another steamshovel.

With Billy in command, joy of a supreme nature began to develop around the old Braves' Field. There were other trades that helped to develop the scene. Eddie Stanky was imported from Brooklyn to play second base, exchanged for some excess baggage named Ray Sanders and Bama Rowell, and a nice check. Jeff Heath was taken off the hands of the St. Louis Browns, just to prove that the Three Steamshovels were not totally partial to the Cardinals. But the trade that solidified the Boston Braves of 1948 into champions was basically Billy Herman for Bob Elliott. Pittsburgh also got Infielder Whitey Wietelmann, Pitcher Elmer Singleton, and Outfielder Stan Wentzel, but only Elliott really counted in the long run. Herman didn't have one full season left in him. With Elliott at third base and wearing the mantle of Most Valuable Player, the team's first since Johnny Evers of Stallings's miracle season, the Braves won the pennant.

It was, said a neutral, Eddie Dyer, then manager of the Cardinals, "The greatest trade ever made."

Now, the scene shifts to Milwaukee, where the burghers are going daft over the new sensation that Lou Perini et al. have bestowed upon them. To insist that the surge of the transplanted Braves of 1957 and 1958, followed by galling near misses in 1959 and 1960, was the result of the fine art of maneuvering the flesh market would never stand in court. Lou Burdette had come, it's true, in a trade for Johnny Sain of the 1948 heroes and $50,000 when the Yankees were in dire need a few years previous. But mainly, the Braves of Fred Haney's winners were farm grown.

One particular performer who would not have been from the farm, had the better laid plans of the front office not gone awry, was the intended second baseman, Danny O'Connell. The Braves had just about cleaned out the clubhouse to get the Irishman from Pittsburgh. They were trying to heal a festering wound that had existed at second base since Stanky, plus Shortstop Alvin Dark, had been traded to the Giants, there to develop himself another pennant in 1951. Four players, none who ever distinguished themselves as Braves, came in exchange. It was a fairly dreadful mistake.

The Braves gave the Pirates Pitcher Max Surkont, Outfielders Sid Gordon and Sam Jethroe, three farm system pitchers, AND $75,000 for O'Connell. The best thing the poor fellow ever contributed was ballast when, on the brink of the June 15 deadline in 1957, they traded for the answer. It came six feet, one inch tall, wearing red hair and bearing the name of Albert Fred Schoendienst. Red hit .309 and the Braves won the pennant, and he hit .279 and they won the World Series, Burdette pitching three of the victories. But it wasn't so much what Schoendienst hit as what he fielded. One is loathe to point out that the moment he went, felled by tuberculosis in 1959, it was as if a plague had set in on the Braves at second base, for they haven't won another pennant since.

There was a case of a developing division championship in

1969, by which time franchises had multiplied like rabbits, bringing Atlanta into focus, where the ball bounced as if bred by bunnies. The most significant aspect of this was that it stands today as the only championship of any kind Paul Richards, known as a wily appraiser and trader of material, achieved as a major league leader of men. In this case, the maestro gets credit for two strategic personnel moves that brought glory down around his manager, Luman Harris, with whom he'd had this "brother's keeper" act going for years.

Desperately in need of outfield stability, Richards traded three players as disposable as Kleenex tissues to San Diego for Tony Gonzalez, who drove in 50 runs, hit 10 HRs and 15 doubles in 89 games.

September arrived, the Braves still malingering in fourth place, when Richards went to the marketplace again. He found the aged knuckleballer Hoyt Wilhelm, already 46, available and brought him in for the stretch run. If ever a pitcher turned a pennant race around, it was he. In the drive to the wire, Wilhelm won two games, saved four, allowed only one run, and struck out 14 in 12 innings. So pleased was Harris that he summoned his old hand out of the dugout in the final game for a standing ovation in Atlanta Stadium. In the press, the deal appeared as one of waivers at the time. It turned out, Richards had to slip one of the Braves' giltedged rookies to the Angels for Wilhelm, and if you noticed the name of Mickey Rivers in their lineup before he was traded to the Yankees for Bobby Bonds after the 1975 season, . . . you'll realize the real price that was paid for one moment of ecstasy. The Braves were staggered by the Mets in the Championship Series.

The Braves maintained a considerable traffic in tread-worn immortals at one time, and some not so tread-worn. Ruth was neither the first nor the last, only the most pitiable. He was, however, only slightly more so than the formerly magnificent pitcher, Denton T. ("Cy") Young, whom the then Rustlers took on from Cleveland in 1911. Ruth batted .181 before admitting to despair. Young won four and lost five, then tapped out at spring training the following year at age 45. Thus, the franchise helped ring it down for two of the great greats.

George Sisler also came to them in the course of the season of 1928 at the unbelievable price of $7,500, illustrating how convinced Clark Griffith of Washington was that he was through. This was another of Judge Fuchs's moves, but as against the results of the Young and Ruth plunges, both having only their reputations left, it had some merit. Even with failing vision, Sisler managed to finish out the season batting .340, and had two more left in his system of a better than .300 average.

Johnny Evers was another veteran supposedly beyond his peak who brought something of value with him from the Cubs, who had just fired him as manager. It was his fire and vim that contributed the spark to the drive of 1914.

Of course, Rogers Hornsby was far from through when he arrived in Boston in 1928, excommunicated from New York for alleged sins ranging from betting indebtedness to flagrant defiance of the ownership. It was one of the major deals of the age, Hornsby from the Giants for Outfielder Jimmy Welsh, a lifetime .290 hitter, and Catcher Shanty Hogan, big, strong and worthy. The Braves were Hornsby's third club in three years, and the Cubs were about to become his fourth in the year to come, indicating a certain splenetic indifference to becoming one of the gang. In no time, he was manager, and while the team lost 103 games, this sorry condition made no dent on his personal projects.

Hornsby hit .387 and led the league, which no Brave had done since Hugh Duffy. Nevertheless, he was on his way to the Cubs that winter for five players, Fred Maguire, Doc Leggett, Percy Jones, Harry Seibold, Bruce Cunningham, and a check for $200,000—the most important of which, to Judge Fuchs, was the latter. Hornsby proceeded to lead the Cubs to a pennant, won the Most Valuable Player prize and hit another .380, plus 40 home runs. Meanwhile, the Braves lost five less games, and seemed not to miss their jewel at all, finishing a very convincing last without him.

Later others of Hall of Fame or near Hall of Fame caliber careened through on their way to the last exit, some by trade, some by desperation. Paul Waner collected his 3,000th hit as a Brave. Rabbit Maranville returned and played it out in his old suit. Country Slaughter wrapped it up as a Brave in Milwaukee, and Mickey Vernon had only nine games left in him as he passed through.

At one stage, the Braves took to accumulating antiques without such scintillating pasts and showed a profit from it. It happened in 1937, when close-vested Bob Quinn reached down to the minors and purchased two pitchers, Jim Turner from Indianapolis and Lou Fette from St. Paul. Both were over thirty and both had pitched for more than a dozen years. Both won twenty games as vintage rookies in Boston that season.

When the Braves arrived in Atlanta, they came accompanied by John McHale, the general manager, generously slandered as the man who traded them out of Milwaukee. It was Bill Veeck, no piker of a flesh merchant himself, who made the charge.

"The Braves had fallen apart," he said in *Hustlers' Handbook,* "because of bad trades, the most galling thing of all to baseball fans. . . . John McHale, the general manager who made the bad trades (just as he made the trades that killed Detroit), is a nice man, but dull, dull, dull."

There is evidence that the Braves were already cracking after the crunching failures of 1959—costing Fred Haney his job—and of 1960—costing Chuck Dressen his. However, there is some substance to Veeck's broadside, though there is just as much in the fact that a great slack had not been provided for by its previously abundant farm system. It was indeed McHale who, trying to plug that nagging second base gap, traded off Billy Bruton, the finest center fielder the Braves had had in years, to Detroit for Frank Bolling. Now the gap switched to center field.

But where McHale left the Braves most hideously scarred was in pitching. He could be personally charged with having wrecked the youth of the staff. He traded Joey Jay and Juan Pizarro to Cincinnati for Roy McMillan, who was to give aging brilliance to shortstop. Neither Jay nor Pizarro had had a worthy chance of crashing the rotation in Milwaukee, but in Cincinnati, Jay became a 20-game winner, the Reds won a pennant, and he won their only World Series decision in 1961. Pizarro moved on to the White Sox and became a long established major league winner, both starting and relieving, and pitched nearly 15 more seasons. Don McMahon was peddled purely for cash to Houston in 1962. Presumably, his fast ball was losing its velocity, and besides, he was already 32 years old. Twelve years later he was still pitching.

McHale also disposed of Joe Adcock, first baseman through all the days of splendor, to Cleveland for three players who became lost in time. Lou Burdette went off to St. Louis for Bob Sadowski, who failed, and Gene Oliver, who hit like a catcher, but never caught like one.

Paul Richards also blamed McHale for the deal that somewhat surreptitiously sneaked all-time Brave super Third Baseman Eddie Mathews out of town, it being Atlanta this time. Mathews had a special connection with Atlanta, appearing there as a rookie when the territory was Southern Association in 1950. Besides his having hit 512 home runs, certainly a Hall of Fame ingredient, the fans felt that he had better coming than a summary dismissal to Houston for such hangers-on in the final stages of survival as Bob Bruce and Dave Nicholson. No matter who made the deal, Richards later compounded the felony when he filled in the blank "Player to be Named Later." That player turned out to be Sandy Alomar, who later became an All-Star second baseman with California and played on for many successful seasons in the AL. For Mathews, it was a special kind of break, as it turned out. Houston traded him to Detroit, and he wound up in the 1967 World Series as a bonus.

For a man of his repute, Richards failed considerably to live up to his astute image while guiding the Braves in Atlanta. The Mathews move was his first as he succeeded McHale late in 1966, but he growled later that McHale had already made the agreement with Houston. Some of Richards's later moves left his audience short of conviction. For instance, he gave up Denis Menke and Denver Lemaster to get Sonny Jackson, who was supposed to mend the Braves' rip at shortstop. Instead, it didn't, but Menke handled problems at second, third, or short in Houston for several fruitful seasons, and once made the All-Star Game as well as enjoyed the pleasures of the World Series twice later in Cincinnati.

Richards traded three players to the Reds for Deron Johnson in 1967. Johnson promptly turned in the worst season of his career trying to play first base in Atlanta, as well as giving the traffic court considerable business with his late-hour driving habits. But probably Richards's everlasting worst was the trade that sent Clay Carroll along with another pitcher, Tony Cloninger, and Infielder Woody Woodward to Cincinnati for Pitcher Milt Pappas, another pitcher, Ted Davidson (whose wife had shot him down on a street during spring training), and Bob Johnson, willing bat, no position. It was a virtual bust for the Braves, but all three expendables helped the Reds to pennants. Carroll set records for relief pitching, at which he became the ace of the NL.

When Richards was succeeded by his former disciple, Eddie Robinson, trades' benefits began to resemble a business graph in uncertain times. Some good, some bad, and one, such as Felix Millan and George Stone to the New York Mets for Gary Gentry (bad arm) and Danny Frisella, became a regrettable disaster. The very next season, 1973, Millan, Stone, and the Mets were in a World Series. Gentry was later released. An operation failed to bring the arm around. Frisella was traded off for a fair outfielder named Clarence Gaston.

Robinson did manage to recoup some losses when the Mets offered him a little used right-hander named Buzz Capra for $35,000 the next spring. Robinson took. Capra won 15 games, and the gutty little fellow also led the NL in earned-run average.

Robinson's most robust move took place at his first winter meeting as general manager. In Honolulu, he convinced Earl Weaver, Baltimore's manager, to take Earl Williams, a big catcher who didn't care to catch, in exchange for Pitchers Pat Dobson and Roric Harrison, Catcher Johnny Oates, and Davey Johnson, one-time leading second baseman in the AL. For a season, it was a grand stroke. Johnson hit 43 home runs, more than any second baseman in all time in one season, and more than Rogers Hornsby. Harrison won 11 games. Oates was the first-string catcher. Dobson was traded to the Yankees for four fringe players, and here the trade began to come unraveled.

Johnson eventually jumped to Japan, miffed at utility duty, but the Braves drew $130,000 in the exchange. Oates went along as excess baggage in another deal. Harrison was traded to Cleveland for Blue Moon Odom, a pitcher of receding grandeur. BUT, of all things, Williams came back to the Braves in exchange for an unpromising minor leaguer, and found himself in residence where he'd always wanted to be—at first base in Atlanta. Certainly, something was gone, though. He was not the player he had been.

If all had gone well, first base would not have been open, but would have come into the hands of the widely traveled and controversial Richie Allen, who had hit high and low spots in both leagues. Allen had run out on the Chicago White Sox with two weeks to play the previous September. During the winter meetings in New Orleans, in December 1974, Robinson agreed to pay the White Sox $1,000—that's right, one thousand—for rights to Allen, who let it be known right away he wanted no part of Atlanta or its manager, Clyde King. Racial and sectional undertones seeped through Allen's refusal. Though never wearing a uniform, he became, as the spring and the season merged, the most widely known of the 1975 crop of Braves.

Back home in Pennsylvania, Allen tended a dozen racehorses he owned, all on off-track welfare supplied by him. None was productive at the races. The Phillies made overtures, and finally, Robinson made a deal with Paul Owens, the general manager. For the defending HR champion of the AL, former MVP, and yet only 32 years old, with Oates thrown in, Robinson received a first-year player named Barry Bonnell in a deal that will always be questioned. Allen seemed assured of a Philadelphia flag in the East Division that didn't develop. Bonnell was a kid of 19, an if-come proposition.

That's the way baseball trades go and have gone for the Braves over a run of years. Some you like today. Some you like tomorrow. Some you wouldn't like if you had forever.

BOB WOLF
Sportswriter, *Milwaukee Journal*

Bob Wolf, dean of Milwaukee sportswriters, has covered everything from baseball to automobile racing during his twenty-eight-year association with the *Milwaukee Journal.* He covered the Braves during their thirteen-year stay in Milwaukee, and was national president of the baseball writers in 1963. After the Braves fled to Atlanta, Wolf has covered the Milwaukee Bucks since their inception in NBA competition in 1968. Besides his regular assignments for the *Journal,* Wolf writes a television sports column as well as opinion columns on all phases of sports. Bob is a University of Wisconsin graduate and a Purple Heart veteran of World War II.

5/THE BREWERS

From tennis to trade: Brewers land Aaron

The very existence of the Brewers has often been referred to as the second miracle of Milwaukee. It took five years of constant campaigning by President Allan ("Bud") Selig and his colleagues to restore major league baseball to the city that had captured the imagination of the nation for its miraculous support of the Braves in the 1950s, only to lose the team to Atlanta in 1965.

Somehow, though, the Brewers never really made it big with the fans who had been jilted by the Braves until Henry Aaron came home in 1974 after an absence of nine years. True, the club had topped a million at the gate once in its first five seasons, which wasn't bad considering the fact that it never finished higher than fourth. But it always lacked somebody with whom the burghers could identify, and besides, fan interest was crimped by the bitterness that resulted from the departure of the Braves for what they thought were greener pastures.

Then, one Saturday afternoon in November of 1974, Selig broke into the flood of college football scores with the announcement that made the Brewers as important to Milwaukee as the lamented Braves had been. Confirming rumors that had been swirling about since World Series time, Selig told the world that Aaron had been acquired from the Braves for Outfielder Dave May and a player to be named later. For the record, the player named later was Pitcher Roger Alexander, a minor leaguer at the time and a man who may or may not achieve any fame beyond that which automatically comes to someone who is traded for the all-time home-run king.

Landing Aaron was actually easy compared to the struggle required to give Milwaukee the Brewers. It took a mere two years.

"We made our first attempt in 1972," Selig said. "We were at the winter meetings in Hawaii, and Bill Bartholomay (the Braves' board chairman) and I were playing tennis. After we finished our game, we sat down and had a Coke, and I said to him, 'Let me ask you a stupid question. Would you trade Henry Aaron?'

"Bill was shocked, naturally, but we did discuss it for a couple of days, although not much came of it.

"In the summer of 1974, I had the thought again, but I didn't really take it seriously because Hank had said he was retiring at the end of the year. He had broken Babe Ruth's home run record, and he had supposedly made up his mind to go into the Braves' front office.

"But then on the last day of the 1974 season Hank said he wasn't going to play in Atlanta anymore, and that gave me the idea that he was interested in playing somewhere else. I called Bartholomay on Tuesday, two days after the season ended, and asked him, 'How do we start the process?'

"He finally agreed to discuss a trade, and the day before I left for the World Series, I got permission to talk to Aaron. I left the Series on the morning of the last game, flew from Oakland to Atlanta, and the next day I met with Hank and his attorneys. We reached a contract agreement the Saturday after the Series, so I called Bartholomay on Monday and said, 'I've got an agreement with Aaron. Where do we go from here?'

"At that point it was a matter of determining what we would give up, and as desirous as we were of getting Aaron, we couldn't afford to trade our future away. After eleven days of tossing names around between Jim Baumer and Eddie Robinson (general managers of the Brewers and Braves, respectively), we appeared to be at a very solid impasse.

"Finally, Baumer and Robinson went to the general managers' meeting in Colorado Springs and stayed together all week. They joined Bartholomay and me in Chicago after that, on a Friday; and on Saturday, Bartholomay came up to Milwaukee, and we reached an agreement in my office.

"May had been an important player for us, but we were fortunate—and had been fortunate for some time—to be well stocked with outfielders, so we could afford to give him up.

"It was over at last. We not only had Henry Aaron back in Milwaukee after all those years, but we had ourselves a great designated hitter."

From that memorable moment, Milwaukee couldn't do

enough to welcome back its biggest sports hero. The annual Baseball Writers' Dinner was transformed into the Henry Aaron Homecoming Dinner; the annual Play Ball Luncheon was transformed into the Henry Aaron Homecoming Luncheon, and when the season got under way, opening day was transformed into Welcome Home Henry Day. There was no way of telling for sure, but it seemed safe to say that many of the fans who turned out at County Stadium in record numbers to see the Brewers perform had been lured out of nine years of hibernation by the return of Aaron.

Aaron signed a two-year contract at or above $200,000 a year, and said, "I'm happy to be home. I'll never forget the way Milwaukee's fans stuck by me when I was a rookie making all those mistakes. I might never have had the success I've had if it hadn't been for all these wonderful fans in Milwaukee."

It wasn't immediately determined what Aaron would do after his playing days were over, but there was every reason to believe that he would become a key man in the Brewers' front office. Even as a player in 1975, he sat in on many executive sessions with Selig, Baumer, and Manager Del Crandall.

As big as the Aaron deal was, though, it could not in all honesty be called the most important one the Brewers ever made. That distinction would have to go to a swap made three years earlier with the Boston Red Sox—the one that brought the Brewers their first $100,000 player in First Baseman George Scott. Frank Lane, the master trader himself, was the Brewers' general manager then, and he was never prouder of any other deal than this one in which he sent Pitchers Marty Pattin and Lew Krausse and Outfielders Tommy Harper and Pat Skrable to the Red Sox for Scott, Pitchers Jim Lonborg and Ken Brett, Outfielders Joe Lahoud and Billy Conigliaro and Catcher Don Pavletich.

"This deal gives us instant respectability," said Lane, and how right he was. Until that October day in 1971, even the people in Milwaukee scarcely realized that the Brewers were around. Now, for the first time, the club had some truly big names. Selig looks back on that trade as the turning point in the Brewers' fortunes.

"I'd have to call it the best deal we've made," Selig said. "Considering what we got in the deal, and the ultimate by-products of it, you might say it was the making of the franchise.

"Pattin and Harper were actually the only real talent we had, and we were fortunate enough to market them into something worth a whole lot more. We got Scott, certainly one of the best first basemen in baseball, and we ultimately used Lonborg and Brett to get Don Money, one of the best third basemen in baseball, from Philadelphia.

"We also got Billy Champion from the Phillies with Money, and he has become a very valuable pitcher for us. And we used Lahoud in a trade for Pitcher Clyde Wright, whom we in turn traded for Pete Broberg, who has also been a very fine addition to our pitching staff. All in all, I can't begin to measure the importance of the Boston deal to this ball club."

The trade with the Phillies, made October 31, 1972, sent Lonborg, Brett, and two other pitchers, Ken Sanders and Earl Stephenson, to Philadelphia for Money, Champion and Infielder John Vukovich. Only Lonborg is still with the Phillies, although they used Brett to acquire an outstanding second baseman, Dave Cash, from the Pirates. Unlike the Boston trade, the one with Philadelphia met with a decidedly adverse reaction from the fans of Milwaukee. It was by all odds the least popular in the history of the Brewers.

"You'd have thought we had violated motherhood," said Selig. "People called up and asked us, 'What are you doing, trading for a lousy .222 hitter like Money? And how can you give away all that pitching?'

"But we felt that we knew what we were doing. Jim Wilson had just taken over from Lane as general manager, and this was his first trade. We had finished a dismal last in 1972, and we didn't draw any people. Attendance fell off from a million to 600,000. This was a disaster area, to say the least, and we had to do something.

"I was a little worried about giving up four pitchers, but all of a sudden we had an outstanding first baseman and third baseman, and we were eventually to fill in with Pedro Garcia at second and

---

THE MONEY MART

In 1907 Hall of Famer Tris Speaker's minor league salary with Houston in the Texas League was one hundred dollars a month.

young Robin Yount at shortstop to form one of the best defensive infields in baseball.

"Sanders and Stephenson have since disappeared into the night. Lonborg has done remarkably well, and Brett has done well, too, although he has had recurring arm problems, but Money has been a great player in every way, and Champion had an 11–4 season for us in 1974.

"When I look back on the criticism we got for the Money thing, it's almost unbelievable. We took heat all winter. But even before Money started to hit, he became a fan favorite, and the complaints died down, never to be heard again."

The only other Brewer deal that got the public riled up was the one in which Outfielder Danny Walton was sent away. Walton had been the Brewers' first hero, a guy who hit home runs and had remarkable rapport with the fans. But he was only a journeyman player, and in June 1971 he was dealt to the Yankees for First Baseman Frank Tepedino and Outfielder Bobby Mitchell.

"Walton had been a tremendous favorite for rather strange marketing reasons," Selig said. "He was an engaging type of a kid, and you had to like him. But he wasn't hitting, and his defense was such that we couldn't play him in the outfield unless he did hit. So we traded him, and while Tepedino is gone, Mitchell became a good fill-in player for us."

The Brewers were born as the Seattle Pilots in the expansion of 1969, and when Milwaukee inherited them, they were about as bad a baseball team as the legendary Mets of 1962. Marvin Milkes, their general manager in the one season in Seattle and the first season in Milwaukee, made the mistake of emphasizing experience instead of youth.

Typical was the first trade in Brewer history—the one that sent Roy Foster, a promising outfielder, along with Infielder Frank Coggins to the Indians for two worn-out veterans, Outfielder Russ Snyder and Third Baseman Max Alvis. Foster promptly became Rookie of the Year in the AL, just as had Outfielder Roy Piniella, whom Milkes had dealt a year earlier to the Royals for two unforgettable characters named Steve Whitaker and John Gelnar.

"Those are the kind of deals you shouldn't make," Selig said. "They don't help you; they set you back. They were born out of desperation, and that's the kind of thing the Pilots did. They had no philosophy at all. They knew where they wanted to go, but they didn't have the vaguest idea how to get there.

"We have followed Branch Rickey's precepts to a fanatical level. It takes a lot of gambles. You have to be willing to lose some money along the way, and you have to have patience when it hurts to be patient."

Not all of Milkes' trades were misfires. He picked up interim infield regulars in Second Baseman Ron Theobald and Shortstop Roberto Pena at the cost of nothing more than Outfielder Wayne Comer and Infielder John Donaldson. Milkes also made one of the Brewers' best deals ever when he picked up May, the man who was to be traded for Aaron, for nondescript pitchers named Dick Baney and Lou Stephen.

Trader Lane took over in 1971 and somehow chloroformed the Phillies into giving up Outfielder-First Baseman John Briggs for Catcher Pete Koegel and Pitcher Ray Peters. Lane also rated kudos for acquiring Catcher Ellie Rodriguez from the Royals for utility man Carl Taylor; Outfielder Jose Cardenal and two others from the Cardinals for Infielder Ted Kubiak and a pitcher by the name of Charlie Loseth; Pitcher Jim Colborn and two others from the Cubs for Cardenal; Pitcher Frank Linzy from St. Louis for Pitcher Rich Stonum, and as mentioned earlier, Scott & Co., in the monumental deal with the Red Sox.

Yes, Frantic Frank hit his low points, too. He traded Roric Harrison and Wayne Twitchell, who were to become successful pitchers, for such duds as Pitcher Marcelino Lopez and Outfielder Pat Skrable, and he struck bottom when he dealt Pitcher Al Downing to the Dodgers for utility man Andy Kosco. But the good in Lane's administration far outdid the bad, and as noted by Selig, it was the deal he swung with Boston that actually put the franchise on the map.

Wilson followed up the controversial Money trade with one big deal that didn't amount to much and several small ones that did. He sent Rodriguez, Lahoud, Pitchers Skip Lockwood and Gary Ryerson, and Outfielder Ollie Brown to the Angels for Pitchers Wright and Steve Barber, Catcher Art Kusnyer, and Outfielder Ken Berry in what turned out to be a ho-hum thing. Then he stole Pitcher Ed Sprague from the Cardinals and First Baseman Mike Hegan from the Yankees for cash, and Pitcher Tom Murphy from the Cardinals for Infielder Bob Heise.

When Wilson left to head the major leagues' new scouting combine, Baumer moved up from the ranks and made his trading debut in a big way—by closing the Aaron deal. Then he sent Wright to the Rangers for Broberg, Outfielder Bob Coluccio to the White Sox for Outfielder Bill Sharp, and Briggs to the Twins for Outfielder Bobby Darwin.

The one that brought Murphy to Milwaukee qualifies as the biggest heist involving the Cardinals since they purloined Lou Brock from the Cubs for Ernie Broglio. While Heise has slipped back to the minors, Murphy has become the meal ticket of the Brewers' pitching staff, one of the premier relief specialists in baseball.

"We made that deal strictly by chance, too," said Selig. "We were leaving the 1973 winter meetings in Houston and I said, 'Let's not go through O'Hare. You know how busy it is on a Friday night.' So we went by way of St. Louis, and who was on the plane but Bing Devine, Stan Musial, and Red Schoendienst of the Cardinals.

"Bing said to Jim Wilson, 'We're looking for an infielder. Would you take Murphy for Heise?' We wanted to jump on it right away, but we said we'd call them back by midnight, which was the deadline for interleague trading.

"It was a chance thing. If we had gone home the normal way, we never would have made the deal. And I don't know where this club would be today."

BOB BROEG
Sports Editor, *St. Louis Post-Dispatch*

Bob Broeg was only eight years old when he became a baseball buff and was blessed with immediate heroes: the Cardinals' first World Championship team in 1926. A former U.S. Marine, Broeg is the only sportswriter ever to win the University of Missouri's Journalism Medal. Bob traveled with the Cardinals for thirteen seasons. He is a past president of the Baseball Writers' Association of America and remains a member of the National Baseball Hall of Fame's board of directors and the Veteran Players' committee. Broeg has written four books, two on baseball: *Stan Musial, The Man's Own Story* (Doubleday), and *Super Star of Baseball* (Spink). A master of description, Broeg's favorite one-liner came from watching Ol' Mizzou turning Alabama's Crimson Tide into a Trickle.

6/THE CARDINALS

Tops in superswaps: Hornsby for Frisch

The bases were loaded in the first inning of the annual two-game St. Louis city series between the Cardinals and the old Browns. It was 1927, the best of the Roaring Twenties except for the short, stocky second baseman playing his first game in the uniform of the NL ball club whose shirt insignia of a rampant redbird on a bat carried the additional proud message: "WORLD CHAMPIONS." Frankie Frisch, at twenty-nine a great player at his peak, was a veteran of four pennant-winning ball clubs in his native New York, but in his first game for the Cardinals he hopped gingerly from one foot to the other on the spot marked "X."

In probably the greatest head-to-head trade of superstars, undoubtedly the most dramatic and, yes, the guttiest deal ever, club owner Sam Breadon of the Cardinals had swapped baseball's greatest right-handed hitter, Rogers Hornsby, who had AVERAGE .400 for five seasons through 1925. Not only had Hornsby hit the staggering century-high .424 to win another NL batting title in 1924, but he had been named MVP in 1925 and—this above all—just had player-managed the Cardinals in 1926 to their first pennant and World Championship ever.

The Rajah, as they called the handsome, outspoken Texan, was the dimpled darling of St. Louis. He was given a new automobile in appreciation by a city that had waited thirty-eight years from 1888 to celebrate a pennant. Back there in the 1880s, the old Browns had won four in a row when the American Association was classified short-lived as a major league and their colorful German owner Chris Von der Ahe's manager was an imaginative first baseman named Charley Comiskey.

Comiskey, whose greater fame was as a founding club owner of the Chicago White Sox, was the first man ever to play first base by taking his foot off the bag. He also was smart enough to get the hell out of St. Louis as fast as he could, which seemed to be the thing to do as the old French fur-trading post on the west bank of the Mississippi developed a reputation for good beer and bad ball clubs, hot nights and hotter afternoons.

Some of the best-known names didn't even wait to be traded. John McGraw, sold to the Cardinals in 1900 by Baltimore of the NL, played only one season for the Robison brothers, Stanley and Frank. The brothers were Indiana traction-company men who bought the St. Louis Nationals at courthouse auction and swapped the bums en masse for their good, unappreciated Cleveland NL team, the Spiders.

The Robisons not only brought the great right-handed pitcher, Cy Young, and outstanding offensive outfielder, Jesse Burkett, in their gift to a city that had known nothing except losers since Der Poss Bresident, as saloonkeeper Von der Ahe referred to himself, lost everything except the life-size statue that marks his pauper's grave. To begin this century and their second season in St. Louis— at a time the Browns whom they had foisted off on Cleveland set a record for fewest victories (20) and most defeats (134)—the Robisons changed the St. Louis's colors from that drab brown to a bright red. An early-day baseball writer, one Willie McHale, began to call them "Cardinals," referring to the color and not to the bird that became the club's symbol.

Here, the Robisons peeled off $150,000, a staggering sum in the gaslight era of the horse-drawn trolley, for three members of the swashbuckling Baltimore Orioles of the NL. If the name of Second Baseman Billy Keister isn't exactly a household word— unless you're trying to be vulgar—the third base star, John Mc-Graw, and his catching comrade, Wilbert Robinson, were destined for baseball fame as managers as well as players. But Muggsy and Robby had a bellyful of St. Louis in just one season, 1900, even though McGraw hit .337. Intending to jump in 1901 to the new AL, which invaded Baltimore after the NL evacuated it, they waited until the season-ending train headed east chugged across the Eads Bridge. Then, ceremoniously, McGraw and Robinson dropped their St. Louis uniforms into the river.

Young, who had wheelhorsed the Cleveland pitching staff for nine years en route to 23 big league seasons and astonishing 511 victories, also jumped to the AL with a Cy of relief. "It was too damned hot there," complained the Young who suddenly had felt old. And at Boston he rebounded from 20–18 to a league-leading 33–10 record.

So with a one-way traffic of talent, St. Louis had little to cheer about except for 1908 when Connie Mack, fed up with the thirst and eccentricities of a carefree character, dealt colorful Rube Waddell to the Browns. (Don't be confused, dear reader; when the young AL moved its Milwaukee franchise to St. Louis in 1902, the owners latched onto the nickname of the 1880s tradition.) Thanks in large measure to Waddell's flame-throwing left-handed pitching, at times even more spectacular than Rube's elbow-bending, the Browns finished a close fourth in a four-team race that went down to the last day in 1908. As a result of the box office success of Waddell's 19–14 season, the 32-year-old screwball's last good one, Browns' owner Robert Lee Hedges used the profits to build a new grandstand, the first concrete and steel structure of its kind in the boondocks.

From then until 1926, however, St. Louis baseball sagged to the point that when a wit called it "first in shoes, first in booze, and last in the AL," he was only half-right. He could have made it last in the NL, too. Although neither the Browns nor Cardinals contended for anything except the booby prize, St. Louis was an AL town and an angry one, at that, when the Brownies lost the pennant in 1922 by a game to Babe Ruth and the Yankees. The anger was part frustration, part indignation because at a time when the Brownies had a third-base problem of their own, the Yankees peeled off the bankroll again for a late-season acquisition from the Red Sox of a good third baseman, ("Jumpin'") Joe Dugan.

The deal for Dugan apparently led directly to the recommendation by the first commissioner, Judge Kenesaw Mountain Landis,

---

THE "REAL" MEDWICK

Hall of Famer Joe Medwick used the name of "Mickey King" when he broke into baseball in 1930. His football skills were said to be as outstanding as his baseball talent, and the Cardinals reasoned the alias would keep him out of reach of the collegiate recruiters. Several universities, including Notre Dame, reportedly offered the "real" Medwick scholarships.

to bar trades other than waiver-route, inverted-standings' transactions after June 15, still the annual trading deadline.

If the Irish of Kerry Patch on the city's North Side and the South Side Dutch of Carondelet sorrowed in sentiment for George Sisler and his teammates over the near-miss in 1922, St. Louis erupted in 1926 with a joy unknown since Looie met his tootsie-wootsie at the World's Fair in 1904.

Back in 1920, Branch Rickey, a scholarly former big league catcher, graduate lawyer, and college coach, had moved from the Browns over to the rival Cardinals as manager and—as the role then was called—business manager. He had brought Sisler from the University of Michigan campus to the Browns as a picture-book ballplayer.

The Redbirds were so ragtag that Rickey once had swiped his wife's best rug in her absence to carpet the Cardinals' offices and impress a visitor. But B. R. had a dream. He told it to the Cards' new president, Sam Breadon, a former automobile grease monkey who had become a Pierce Arrow dealer and, as a baseball fan, had invested in the community-owned NL ball club. Because the poor-relation Redbirds couldn't compete in the bidding for minor league players—not even after they had tipped off the bush-league operators about the athletes—Rickey proposed to grow his own talent, i.e., to begin what he stuffily called minor league subsidiaries. More generally, it was called the "farm system" and, at its worst, the baseball "chain gang."

Rickey, the psalm-singing, teetotaling Republican orator, and Breadon, the barbershop-singing, convivial Democrat, who was inclined to stutter nervously when he spoke, made a remarkable front-office combination. It worked especially after Breadon persuaded Phil Ball, a cantankerous ice-company magnate who owned the Browns and the ball park, to accept the Cardinals as tenants at Sportsman's Park. Shrewdly, Breadon sold old Robison Field to the city for a new high school and turned the $300,000 over to Rickey to begin the farm system. B. R. began growing his own, to implement the hard-hitting second baseman, Hornsby. Until 1926 though, the St. Louis story was the annual battle between The Rajah and The Sizzler, between the Cardinals' Hornsby and the Browns' Sisler.

Sisler was graceful, poetry in motion, a swift, slick-fielding, place-hitting first baseman who twice batted over .400 in the early 1920s, getting a record major league high of 257 hits in 154 games in 1920. He became player-manager in 1924, the year after he returned following a serious eye infection that affected his vision. Optimistically, Phil Ball expanded the seating capacity of his ball park from 18,000 to 34,000 in 1926, anticipating a pennant.

Hornsby, a larger man and as hard-nosed as his line drives to all fields, was a good pivot man at second base with just one weakness. He didn't go back too well on fly balls because, as J. Roy Stockton of the *St. Louis Post-Dispatch* put it, he wasn't too familiar with pop-ups himself.

Suddenly, on Memorial Day, 1925, Sam Breadon relieved Branch Rickey of the manager's reins, naming Hornsby to the job and insisting, correctly, that by kicking Rickey upstairs to become general manager, B. R. would become even more valuable. Miffed, Rickey insisted he sell his ball club stock and Breadon arranged for Hornsby to buy it.

To win that first pennant in 1926 and to profit, therefore, from Phil Ball's expansion of Sportsman's Park, the homegrown Cardinals needed a right fielder and another pitcher. Rickey traded a personal favorite, Clarence ("Heinie") Mueller, who ran the bases at times like a circus clown, for the Giants' veteran, Billy Southworth.

One day just past the trading deadline that had produced Southworth's inspirational bat, the waiver list showed the name of Grover Cleveland Alexander, 39 years old. Alexander was an alcoholic, epileptic, and his own worse enemy, but he had been one of the greatest pitchers in baseball history. At Chicago, the final straw had come when, obviously feeling no pain, he laughed through a clubhouse meeting held by the Cubs' new manager, Joe McCarthy. Rickey, the prohibitionist, didn't want to claim Alexander, but Hornsby, though he did not drink and had hit the pitcher hard, insisted that Alex be claimed. So for $7,500 Old Pete, as he was called, became a great bargain and, in the twilight of his career, a great hero. He helped the Cardinals win that precious first pennant in 1926, won two games of a World Series upset over the Yankees, and then saved the last one dramatically by ambling out of the bullpen for a bases-loaded strikeout of Tony Lazzeri.

Alex was the hero of the moment, sure, but the favorite of the crowd, though he had batted only .313 in 1926, was Rogers Hornsby. Why, the field foreman was such a team man that when his mother died during the Series, The Rajah directed that the funeral be delayed until he could grab Catcher Bob O'Farrell's perfect throw to tag Babe Ruth, trying to steal second, for the last out at Yankee Stadium.

But now, though there were rumbles about discord and contractual dissatisfaction, the news hit like a bombshell on December 20, 1926, that Hornsby had been traded to the Giants for another second baseman, Frank Frisch, and a pitching nonentity, Jimmy Ring. Irate St. Louis fans hung black crepe on the door of both Breadon's home and his automobile agency. The St. Louis Chamber of Commerce, in unprecedented action, denounced the club owner in a resolution. One St. Louis sports editor wrote bitterly that he never would cover another Cardinals' game.

Breadon's disenchantment with Mr. Blunt, as someone once labeled Hornsby so accurately, might have begun any place. It ended in an infrequent visit to the clubhouse to break the bad news. Down the stretch in 1926, the weary Cardinals had been saddled with moneymaking exhibitions. Hornsby asked Breadon to cancel one scheduled at New Haven, Connecticut, where George Weiss, then operating an Eastern League ball club, said he had spent money in promoting and advertising the big leaguers' appearance.

Breadon made the mistake of breaking the negative news to Hornsby just after the Cardinals had taken a tough loss. As the clever writer Roy Stockton put it with a facile pen, Hornsby "recommended to Breadon an utterly impossible disposition" of the exhibition game. Nobody talked to Sam Breadon like that, even if he did it with four-letter bluntness rather than literary elegance. The club owner reddened. A former poor boy from the sidewalks of New York and with a fear of ever becoming poor again, Breadon offered Hornsby only a one-year contract at $50,000 a year for 1927 when, railbirds insisted, the stubborn owner knew that the equally stubborn Hornsby wanted three seasons and wouldn't settle for less.

So Breadon, who once had turned down a $300,000 cash offer from the Giants' Charles Stoneham for Hornsby at a time when the Cardinals' bankbook was as bare as Mother Hubbard's cupboard, picked up the telephone to New York:

"If you still want Hornsby, Charley, you can have him for Frisch. . . ."

John McGraw wanted Hornsby. At one time he had envisioned both Frisch and Hornsby in the same infield, being aware that the Fordham Flash, as Frisch was called, could move back to third base, where he was as outstanding as at second base. But now the Flash was in McGraw's doghouse, having jumped the club one series at St. Louis in 1926, when—once too often—the manager used the captain as his whipping boy.

Before Hornsby could play for New York, he had to dispose of his St. Louis stock. After all, it just wouldn't do for a Giants' second baseman to let one go through his legs for an error or to strike out with the bases loaded against a club in which he was a stockholder. Hornsby, who had paid only $40 a share for Rickey's stock in 1925, wanted $100 in 1927. Breadon's best offer was $80. Know something? Before the season opened, the NL had to pony up the difference, some $20,000, and retire the equivalent number of shares in the St. Louis club because the two hardheads wouldn't budge.

Hornsby hit .361 at New York, with 25 HRs and 125 RBIs, but The Rajah lasted just one year with the Giants, and made the rounds—to Boston . . . Chicago . . . back to St. Louis, briefly with the Cardinals and then the Browns.

Frankie Frisch? To get back to where we came in, the Fordham graduate, son of a wealthy German linen manufacturer in New York, had been born with a silver spoon in his mouth, but he must have cut his teeth on a brass cuspidor. He was an intellectual roughneck and, though hurt to leave his home hearth in New Rochelle, forty-five minutes from Broadway, he recognized the challenge that faced him in 1927. That winter Frisch moved up to Lake Placid, to ski, skate, hike, and when inactive, to sit out in the snow and read. Branch Rickey asked him to meet the Mahatma one day at Syracuse, then the Cardinals' top farm club. B. R. wanted to give Frisch a pep talk, but he could have saved the inspirational message for someone else. The Flash was ready.

At spring training in Avon Park, Florida, Hornsby's champions resented Frisch, but only briefly. It was hard not to like the effervescent extrovert, a helluva hustler, a good switch-hitter, brilliant base runner, and a great fielder.

In the city series dress rehearsal against the Browns in 1927, the AL club filled the bases in the first inning as Frisch, keyed up, hopped from one foot to another on the spot marked "X" for him and Breadon. Then George Sisler sent a sharp double-play grounder right at Frisch who reached down and, as Shirley Povich of the

Washington Post might say, "felt nothing." The ball skidded into the outfield for a two-run error, and as Frisch would reconstruct it years later:

"I lowered my head and all I could hear 'em yell was 'We want Hornsby . . . WE WANT HORNSBY'. . . ."

Modestly—and he wasn't exactly a modest man—Frisch never did tell that in the eighth inning of that first game in St. Louis in a Cardinals uniform he hit a home run to give Jesse Haines and the Redbirds a 5–3 victory over the Browns.

The Flash didn't make them forget Hornsby, but he certainly made them remember Frisch. In 1927, a season in which the Cardinals won one game more than in 1926 and yet finished a length and a half behind Pittsburgh, the Flash was positively spectacular. He batted .337, stole 48 bases and, fielding like a whirling dervish on both sides of the bag after Shortstop Tommy Thevenow suffered a broken leg, he established a record of 1,037 chances accepted, the most ever by an infielder other than a first baseman.

Frisch played ten more years in St. Louis and developed an affection for the city and for the fans. He helped spark the ball club to four more pennants and, as pilot light of the old Gashouse Gang in the depression era of playing managers, the old clutch-hitting money player broke up the final game of the 1934 World Series with a three-run double at Detroit.

Years later when Sam Breadon was dying of cancer, two years after having sold the Cardinals to Bob Hannegan and Fred Saigh in the fall of 1947, Breadon was asked to pick an all-time team of Cardinal all-stars.

"I couldn't do it," Breadon begged off. "Just take left field alone. In succession, virtually, we had Chick Hafey, Joe Medwick and Stan Musial. . . ." The dying man's dull eyes brightened. "But I'll tell you," he said, "the greatest single-season player I ever had—or saw—was Frank Frisch. He saved us both. And once we drew more that year and the year after than we had the year before, I knew that it was the ball club that counted, not the individual performer. I no longer was afraid to trade a player."

Indeed, Breadon and Rickey, or vice versa, if you prefer, wheeled and dealed over the years, often selling off farm system surplus to help balance the books and frequently to line their own pockets. Rickey had a contract that called for a 10 percent of the profits. At the outbreak of World War II, just after the club owner had severed their long association, the Brain that went to Brooklyn was earning about $80,000 a year in St. Louis.

Between 1926 and 1946, the Cardinals won nine pennants, six World Championships, and finished a close second six times. By the time of an informal testimonial dinner on the last night of the 1946 season—one in which Breadon sold Catcher Walker Cooper, First Baseman-Outfielder Johnny Hopp, and Outfielder Danny Litwhiler among others—the favored Redbirds and the Brooklyn Dodgers just had wound up even-Stephen to set up the first pennant playoff. Roy Stockton, called upon to say a few words, praised Breadon, but the sports editor drew a dark look from the club owner and mutters of disapproval from the Irishman's friends when he said, "But, Sam, you sliced the baloney too thin this time. . . ."

The Cardinals finished a close second each of the next three seasons, then blew the pennant to the Dodgers the final week in 1949 after Murry Dickson beat the Redbirds a fifth time. Dickson had been sold to Pittsburgh for $125,000 that reportedly helped new owner Fred Saigh buy out partner Bob Hannegan.

Years later, Stan Musial, reflecting on a career in which he played on four straight pennant winners and then none for 17 seasons, noted that in the 1940s the Cardinals had played nine straight seasons in which they nearly won almost every time.

"If the club hadn't sold Johnny Mize, then Walker Cooper, and finally Murry Dickson, there's no telling how many in a row we would have won," said Musial, "or if Anheuser-Busch had bought the ball club earlier. . . ."

In 1953 the Brewery's purchase of the Cardinals from Saigh, pressed to sell after conviction for income-tax evasion, proved the final nail in the coffin of the rival Browns. The latter had lagged so badly at the box office in what obviously was only a one-team town that they drew just 80,922 in a seventh-place 1935 season with Rogers Hornsby as manager. By the end of the 1941 season, the Brownies lagged so badly that new club owner Don Barnes, a loan-company executive, had persuaded the league to let him make a bold move. The Browns would switch to Los Angeles, where Chicago's Phil Wrigley had agreed to sell his Pacific Coast League ball park and franchise, and the Angels would move to Long Beach.

General Manager Bill DeWitt had even worked out a two-trip western takeoff for each club via the Super Chief, a crack train that operated out of Chicago. There, in Chicago, Barnes was to receive official approval for the first alteration in the baseball map since

Milwaukee moved to St. Louis in 1902. The meeting, scheduled for a Monday, was abruptly canceled because the day before was December 7, 1941.

Thanks to DeWitt's adroitness in fielding a team of castoffs, cutthroats, and 4-Fs, the Browns did win a wartime pennant in 1944, giving St. Louis a novel one-time streetcar World Series. But when Barnes's successor, Dick Muckerman, ran into an inflationary spiral in improving Sportsman's Park and building a new Texas League Park in San Antonio, the Browns' financial embarrassment grew. To keep the wolf from the door, DeWitt, who had given one-armed Outfielder Pete Gray a chance (1945), began to sell off stars out of economic necessity. The deal by which Shortstop Vern Stephens went to the Red Sox for $310,000 and nine players in 1947 was a real blockbuster.

But DeWitt, commenting years later, did put to rest one report, namely that Bill Veeck, operating at Cleveland, almost dealt Lou Boudreau to the Browns. Veeck's version was that public pressure forced the Sport Shirt to reconsider just in time for Boudreau to play brilliantly in 1948 and to lead the Indians to a pennant and World Championship.

"We never discussed Boudreau and didn't want him," said DeWitt flatly. "We needed money, not an expensive player-manager. By then, as I recall, rules had been changed so that if you traded a player-manager, he had to be accepted as exactly that: A player AND manager."

Veeck, buying out the DeWitt brothers, who had bought out Muckerman in 1949, gave it a whirl with the Browns in 1951 and 1952, but not even the midget pinch hitter, Eddie Gaedel, could do more than create a few laughs. Veeck had one club in town, one going, and one coming, but all three were only mediocre, and his financial fellows deserted him.

When Anheuser-Busch bought the Cardinals in February 1953, and Gussie Busch stomped through rusty, rundown Sportsman's Park, insisting that he'd rather have the Cardinals play in a public park than the unsound old Stadium, Veeck threw in his sport shirt. Quietly, he tried to move to Milwaukee, but Lou Perini, whose Braves had starved in Boston, owned the American Association franchise in Milwaukee.

The NL, with Phil Wrigley at Chicago the key man in making the beau geste, granted Perini's hurried request to move from

Boston to Milwaukee. When Veeck then sought to transfer to Baltimore, the AL rebuffed the sport-shirt burr-head, who was forced to operate in St. Louis as a lame duck. He lost heavily on the field and at the box office in 1953. Only after Veeck, as in wreck, sold to Baltimore interests, did the AL approve the move that made the Browns become the Orioles.

Meanwhile, back at the ranch or the western half of the cheek-to-jowl offices occupied on Dodier Street before Busch bought the ball park and refurbished it, the Cardinals experienced an 18-year fallow period. The old magic was gone. In 1930 at the trading deadline, Rickey sent southpaw Bill Sherdel, a longtime favorite, and young right-hander Fred Frankhouse to the Braves for a grizzled, well-traveled right-hander, Burleigh Grimes, last of the legitimate spitball pitchers.

The trade made bedfellows out of oddfellows, Frisch and Grimes. When Frank was a spirited rookie at New York and Burleigh was a hard-boiled pitcher at Brooklyn, the good lowball-hitting switcher had creamed Grimes's spitter until Old Stubble-beard knocked him down a few times. In retaliation, Frisch bunted, and when Grimes covered first, Frank stepped on Burleigh's ankle and almost severed the Achilles tendon. Afterwards, Frisch apologized. The next time, following Grimes's long convalescence, the Brooklyn pitcher plunked the New York second baseman between the shoulder blades with his first pitch.

Groaning, Frisch yelled angrily, "Damnit, I apologized."

"Yes," said Grimes sweetly, "but you didn't smile."

So now they were rooming together in 1930, each contributing considerably as the Cardinals rallied from fourth place in mid-August to win 30 of their last 40 for a pennant. The next year, when Frisch was the NL's MVP, Grimes won two World Series games in an upset of the heavily favored Philadelphia Athletics.

"That Grimes," Frisch would say when the two Hall of Famers were reunited once more at Cooperstown, "he's the only man who ever scared me. Threw at me on a '3-and-0' count."

Interrupted Grimes, smiling, "It wasn't '3-and-0', Frank, it was '3-and-1.' "

Frisch didn't see anything funny in it when the World Champion Cardinals skidded to sixth in 1932 or early in 1933, and Manager Gabby Street asked the Flash to give it a try at shortstop. The Cardinals' star young shortstop Charley Gelbert had shot himself accidentally in the leg while hunting. Hornsby, 37 and fired by the Cubs as manager, had been hired by the Cardinals as a pinch hitter and was installed at second base.

"You never saw second base so well-covered in your life," Frisch remembered years later with amusement. "I couldn't go to my right at shortstop and Rog, because of his heel spurs, couldn't move at all. So we both camped on the bag." Which meant that the sensitive defensive middle was a disaster for a lineup that couldn't win even with the likes of Pepper Martin, Rip Collins, Joe Medwick, Jimmy Wilson, Frisch and Hornsby in the batting order at the same time.

As a result, Rickey stayed up late one night to swing a deal with Cincinnati for a light-hitting, smooth-fielding, chesty shortstop. Rickey traded off—among others—a right-handed pitcher, Paul Derringer, who would help the Reds win pennants in 1939 and 1940. Mr. Rickey, as he was called by all except his oldest friends, hardly had settled down in trencherman's contentment to breakfast in bed when the shortstop he had acquired, Leo Durocher, breezed into the room and said, brassily: "Well, Branch, now that you've guaranteed yourself a pennant, let's talk about tearing up my contract. . . ."

Thus began the unique substitute-father-adversary relationship between Rickey and Durocher, who did indeed help bring a Gashouse Gang pennant to St. Louis in 1934. Rickey made his mistakes in trading as well as his home-run barters. Just before acquiring Durocher, he had sent Gus Mancuso to New York to give the pennant-bound Giants a good defensive lowball catcher. Bill Terry correctly had figured he needed Gus in 1933 to handle Carl Hubbell's screwball in the dirt and Hal Schumacher's low-dipping sinker. A couple of years later when Frisch was running out of flash and fire, Rickey insisted that a graceful gazelle named Burgess Whitehead wasn't durable enough to play regularly but, traded to the Giants, Whitey was sufficiently strong to shore up a New York weakness in two more (1936–1937) New York pennants.

B. R. had his bad breaks, of course. When he dealt Mancuso, he couldn't know that bright catching prospect Bill DeLancey would suffer career-ending tuberculosis within a couple of years. He couldn't know, either, in keeping Paul Dean and selling Bill Lee to the Cubs in 1934 and Fritz Ostermueller to the Red Sox, that Dizzy's younger brother would develop arm trouble after two fine seasons.

But Rickey had good breaks, too. How else, otherwise, could you account for it when Pittsburgh, given a choice of two A-1 Columbus outfield prospects in 1938, took Johnny Rizzo rather than Enos Slaughter? Or when, as the story goes, the Cubs had their pick of a couple of Redbird shortstop farmhands in 1940 and selected Bob Sturgeon over a tall drink of water named Marty Marion?

Rickey was both good and lucky at times. Dizzy Dean was damaged goods, and Phil Wrigley had caveat-emptor notice when the chewing-gum king peeled off $185,000 early in 1938 and sent along a pretty good pitcher, Curt Davis. Dizzy did help the Cubs win in 1938, but Davis was a 20-game winner at St. Louis in a close race in 1939. A year later, Curt accompanied Joe Medwick to Brooklyn in a player-plus-cash transaction that brought $125,000 more into B. R.'s and Sam Breadon's favorite bank account. From then until Anheuser-Busch bought the Cardinals, who really didn't draw well until 1946, if any money was involved in a deal, it was always coming rather than going. Fifty thousand came in the deal by which Mize lugged his home-run bat to the Polo Grounds. The price tag on Dickson was reportedly $125,000 by Hannegan in the final days of his partnership with Saigh. And Breadon sold mule-jawed Walker Cooper to New York for $175,000 before the 1946 season.

The new manager, Eddie Dyer, replacing Southworth, a three-time pennant winner who had fled to Boston for more money and better security, complained to Breadon. But humming a happy tune, Singing Sam told him that, after all, Dyer still had reliable Ken O'Dea and, besides, that highly touted hometown kid, Joe Garagiola, was due out of service any day.

Garagiola, at 20, was thrust into a pressure situation unnecessarily because O'Dea's back forced the old pro to quit, and Del Rice, a good defensive receiver, couldn't hit. Garagiola went from little better than mediocrity as a major leaguer to meteoric success as a television personality and master of mirth. He could have broken in more naturally if the powerful Cooper hadn't been dealt. But, then, big Coop and Frank's batterymate brother, Mort, had had the temerity to argue salary with Breadon. Few could do that and survive.

Batting champion Chick Hafey, docked $2,000 after a hold-out the year he won the hitting crown, 1931, tried to make up the two grand and get $15,000 after hitting .349. Hafey, a rangy right-handed hitter who could really run and field and owned a remarkable throwing arm, was so frustrated that he drove in disgust from Florida back home to California, 90 miles an hour across the desert, a pretty good trick for the time. But he couldn't get the raise he wanted. Opening day, 1932, Hafey was dealt to Cincinnati, then the Siberia of baseball. After all, why worry? Down at Houston, there was that muscular kid named Medwick and. . . . But suddenly the farm-system advantage, lost first to the Yankees and then to the Dodgers and other enterprising clubs willing to spend more in a competitive market, was gone completely.

So Vaughan ("Bing") Devine, a Knothole Gang fan of the Cardinals when they won their first championship in 1926, faced a different task when he returned from general manager's apprenticeship at Rochester in 1955. First off, the frail, pale former basketball star and minor league infielder watched as Frank Lane, brought in from the White Sox at the suggestion of J. G. Taylor Spink, publisher of the *Sporting News,* dealt unwisely and not well in 1956, Frank's first year as general manager.

Lane, one of a kind, came armed with tradition-flouting, chip-on-the-shoulder notions, the first of which was to remove the bat-and-birds' insignia from the uniform shirt front in favor of an English script "Cardinals." Next, at a time his 1956 ball club reacted well to the manager he had named—Fred Hutchinson—Lane dealt a steady shortstop, Alex Grammas, and gave the job to a kid, Don Blasingame, who was better suited for second base. Then Lane sent the 1955 NL Rookie of the Year, Bill Virdon, to Pittsburgh for a good-field, no-hit center fielder, Bobby Del Greco. Bringing the wrath down on the ball club and the brewery, the compulsive wheeler-dealer sent an extremely popular player, Red Schoendienst, to the Giants for a shortstop, Alvin Dark, deemed necessary to fill the position Blasingame couldn't.

Then rumors circulated that Stan Musial was headed to Philadelphia for Robin Roberts. The late Julius ("Biggie") Garagnani, Musial's business partner, called a brewery official, John L. Wilson, and said in fractured English that reflected neither his clout nor his native shrewdness: "I got news for you, John, if the kid is traded, he ain't going." At about this time, Gussie Busch issued a statement that Musial would not be traded—then or ever. Lane was told, quietly, to clear it with Sidney, meaning, for chrissakes, Frank, keep your shirt on before we lose ours.

Lane, under constraint, dealt wisely and well his second season, one in which the Cardinals made a good run for it with Milwaukee, finishing a close second, the club's best finish since 1949. Then, ignored by Busch in a request for an extension of a contract that still had one year to go, Frantic Frank fled to Cleveland.

So Devine, the longtime organization man, stepped in at 40 and, recognizing that the ball club was not as close to a pennant as its brave effort in 1957 had indicated, he set about going for the long haul. With none of Lane's bluster or four-letter words and few of Frantic Frank's catch-phrases, he set the course that finally paid off—after he had gone.

Although he acquired his share of clinkers, Der Bingle made his mark the first time around at Colorado Springs' scenic Broadmoor Hotel in December 1957. He accomplished it (1) by a deal he made and (2) by one he didn't make. First, Devine turned down what he labeled "a very fair" offer from Philadelphia of Center Fielder Richie Ashburn and former Redbird left-hander Harvey Haddix for Ken Boyer, a third baseman who in his third season (1957) had played center field and not well. "I'm banking that Boyer will be a standout and at third base, a championship player," said Devine who was s-o-o right. Boyer was captain, third baseman, and the NL's MVP in 1964, the year the club ended its pennant drouth.

At Colorado Springs, huddling with his manager, Fred Hutchinson, and their Cincinnati counterparts, Gabe Paul and Birdie Tebbetts, Devine then completed his first deal and one which—for some years—he thought was his best. The Cardinals gave up three pitchers, none of whom lingered, for two outfielders of whom one, Curt Flood, was their target. "I give Hutch a lot of credit for our initiating that deal," recalled Devine of the trade by which Joe Taylor also came to the Cards, and Willard Schmidt, Ted Weiand, and Marty Kutyna became Redlegs. Flood, of course, became a brilliant ballhawk, the Cardinals' best glove in center field since Terry Moore and, ultimately, a .300 hitter.

Curiously, after coming as such a bargain, Curt went so expensively when he failed to report to Philadelphia in a controversial, questionable deal thirteen years later. The Cardinals were required to ante up added talent. Funny thing, St. Louis, from which John McGraw, Wilbert Robinson, Cy Young, and others fled years before, had become such a haven for players that Flood, a

$90,000 singles hitter there, turned down $100,000 at Philly. The deal by which Devine gave up Flood, Catcher Tim McCarver, Reliever Joe Hoerner, and a minor league outfielder had a double-barreled disastrous aftermath. The trade followed a disappointing 1969 season, one in which the heavily favored Cardinals failed to compete. First off, Devine didn't keep the chunky second-base veteran, handy Cookie Rojas, who had been obtained from the Phillies. Taking off weight, Rojas became a rejuvenated AL standout at Kansas City.

Next, when Flood decided to test the reserve clause in a case that reached the Supreme Court before Curt wound up polishing the mahogany in a bar in Majorca, the Phillies screamed for compensation. In the last compromise before baseball adopted a buyer-beware policy, Philadelphia accepted St. Louis's first free-agent draft choice, a kid pitcher named Jim Browning, and a convalescing outfielder-first baseman, Willie Montanez, who became a pretty good ballplayer in the City of Brotherly Love.

"The Phillies like to say how they slickered us out of Montanez," said Devine, adding dryly, "What they don't say is that they asked for—and we rejected—their request instead for Santiago Guzman." Which proves that both sides were offsides because Guzman, a promising hard-throwing pitcher, never amounted to a damn.

Devine, learning to take the bitter with the better, built the 1964 pennant-winning ball club by shrewdly trading the pitching the Cardinals could develop for the hitting they couldn't. He learned how lonely a general manager's life can be. One of Frank Lane's second-season (1957) acquisitions, ("Toothpick") Sam Jones, had become so popular in St. Louis that when Devine dealt Jones to the Giants just before the 1959 season, Der Bingle went home for dinner to find his attractive wife and three pretty daughters seated at the table, deadpanned, with toothpicks in their lovely kissers.

"I wouldn't be surprised to see Sam win a pennant for the Giants," said the rebuilding Redbird front-office majordomo, who could have been right in a 21-game season for Jones—if another St. Louis deal hadn't boomeranged.

To get a center fielder, Devine had obtained Gino Cimoli from Los Angeles for Wally Moon, the beetle-browed, rawboned Texas A. & M. graduate. Moon had hit a home run his first time up, opening day of 1954, on the tight spot as right-field replacement for the popular Old War Horse, Enos Slaughter.

Only a Gashouse Gang refugee like Country Slaughter would sit right down and cry when traded to the Yankees, who had won five consecutive World Championships, but that's exactly what old Eno did after acting General Manager Dick Meyer, the brewery wizard, and field foreman Eddie Stanky dealt him. The Yankees gave up a promising outfielder who would become the NL's Rookie of the Year in 1955—Bill Virdon.

Moon, Rookie of the Year in 1954, fell short of expectations in St. Louis, but at Los Angeles, taking aim at the Coliseum's beckoning barrier in left field, the left-handed-hitting lad used an inside-out swing to shank-shot the screen all season. And L.A. nosed out Toothpick Sam Jones and San Francisco.

Undeterred, Devine dealt large left-hander Wilmer ("Vinegar Bend") Mizell to Pittsburgh early in the 1960 season for Columbus Second Baseman Julian Javier, repeating his observation of the year before: "This might win for them (the Pirates) now, but I believe it will help us over the long haul." Provocatively, Devine later would rank Javier ahead of even Frank Frisch, Red Schoendienst, and Rogers Hornsby defensively at second base, though in 11 seasons "Hoolie" couldn't hit with his eminent predecessors.

After the 1962 season, the Cardinals' first full year under Johnny Keane as manager, both the skipper and the general manager agreed that the biggest need was an outfielder and a shortstop. But how to obtain both without breaking up the ball club? Later, after Devine acquired Outfielder George Altman from Chicago and Shortstop Dick Groat from Pittsburgh, Keane would chortle, "I don't know how he did it."

Although Altman was a disappointment in St. Louis, Groat was an integral part of improvement that produced a pennant, but Larry Jackson became a big winner momentarily with the Cubs and Lindy McDaniel a longtime reliable reliever with Chicago and other clubs. The fact is, the strategy came close to utter disaster when Devine became aware that Pittsburgh wanted Don Cardwell, and the general manager acquired the pitcher from Chicago with Altman in the Jackson and McDaniel deal. Devine found his move to obtain Groat for Cardwell suddenly blocked by an unexpected source.

· In his eighties and in his dotage, Branch Rickey had been brought back to St. Louis by Gussie Busch as senior consultant. However, in the scene of his greatest triumph, the old man had shed the years, treated Devine like the glorified office boy he had known a quarter-century earlier and had asserted himself forcefully, stubbornly. Rickey refused to permit the Redbirds to throw rookie Shortstop Julio Gotay into the Groat deal. Finally, cornered by Devine, Keane and two former Redbird managers (Eddie Stanky and Harry Walker) who had been hired by Devine for their ability to teach young players, Rickey relented.

"Very well," B. R. said, menacingly, "I withdraw my veto, but I still don't approve." Julio Who never really made it anywhere. Groat was prominent in a 1963 near-miss and the long-awaited 1964 pennant, one which was bittersweet because Devine was on the outside, canned by Busch in August just as the Redbirds made their pennant move.

Devine's immediate successor, Bob Howsam, brought in from Denver at the recommendation of Rickey, who was playing a cunning Richelieu behind Busch's throne, had nothing to do except lead the applause as the Cardinals, 40–41 at the halfway mark, surged past the floundering Phillies to win. A year later Howsam would unload established veterans such as Groat, Ken Boyer, and Bill White with little in return. But Howsam did swing the 1966 Ray Sadecki-for-Orlando Cepeda deal with San Francisco and the fall trade by which Roger Maris, the wounded home-run hitter, came from the Yankees.

Cepeda and Maris, both bitter and disillusioned when they came to St. Louis, found the tonic to more fun and enjoyment in the carefree one-year general managerial regime of Stan Musial and the cutup atmosphere of the Cardinals' clubhouse. The Redbirds won it all for Musial and his longtime road roommate, Red Schoendienst, in 1967. When Busch found that Devine had been generously helping Musial with the complexities of front-office operation, the sportsman swallowed his pride and asked Der Bingle to give up presidency of the New York Mets in 1968 to return to the club for which he had rooted from boyhood in the Knothole Gang. For a fact, Devine had been commuting from New York because his family just wouldn't leave St. Louis. Curiously, the old river town has sweetened the sour taste of those disenchanted with baseball.

Four players for whom the Cardinals traded became MVPs in the NL, and a fifth deserved the honor. Acquired athletes who won MVP recognition in the uniform of the Redbirds were Bob O'Farrell, 1926; Frank Frisch, 1931; Orlando Cepeda, 1967; Joe Torre, 1971, and. . . .

Said Bing Devine, "Some trades I made were beauts for the other side. Such as maneuvering twice to get Dave Giusti and then dealing him to Pittsburgh (for Carl Taylor) so that he could become the Pirates' Number One man in the bullpen. But the strange thing is that the worst deal I made was hailed as the best—and the best one I made was blasted as the worst."

The one that appeared the best on paper was for Vada Pinson, experienced Cincinnati right fielder, just after Roger Maris retired at the end of the 1968 World Series. Even those of us who hated to see promising young Outfielder Bob Tolan accompany reliever Wayne Granger to the Reds figured that Pinson would help rather than hurt the Cardinals' immediate future, meaning the 1969 season. But Pinson, hobbled by a leg injury, turned out to be Mr. Mediocre in 1969 and then was dealt for a better all-round ballplayer, Jose Cardenal, who in turn was traded not wisely or well to Milwaukee, en route to Chicago. Meanwhile, Tolan and Granger blossomed to help Cincinnati win a pennant in 1970, and Devine caught a lot of what-for.

The Cardinals' best deal—Ernie Broglio for Lou Brock—was approved aboard a bus carrying the club from Dodger Stadium to the Los Angeles airport for a midnight flight to Houston in 1964. General Manager Bing Devine, frowning in defeat, slid into the seat next to Manager Johnny Keane. Der Bingle whispered:

"I can make that deal with the Cubs for Brock, but they still want Broglio."

Looking straight ahead, Keane never changed his expression as he said:

"Make it."

The next day, the last before the trading deadline of June 15, 1964, Devine completed the swap. In the years to come, Brock became King Louie in St. Louie. Especially in 1974, when he stole a record 118 bases after sharing cohero status with Bob Gibson in the 1967 World Series and playing as spectacularly in the Cardinals' loss of the 1968 Series. Ernie Broglio soon was long gone. There is one question springing from this swap which never will be answered: What would have happened to King Louie had Johnny Keane said "Forget it," instead of "Make it?"

HAL LEBOVITZ
Sports Editor, *Cleveland Plain Dealer*

Hal Lebovitz, came into sports with a typewriter and a whistle, plus a ball and strike indicator. A former athlete at Western Reserve University, Lebovitz warmed up for his journalistic duties during an eight-year teacher-coach stint in suburban Euclid, Ohio. Hal umpired baseball for fifteen years, officiated basketball for twenty-five, and football for thirty. A former national president of the Baseball Writers' Association of America, "Lebo" became a football-baseball writer for the *Cleveland News* in 1946. He moved to the *Plain Dealer* after the *News* was sold. Lebovitz combined with Hall of Famer Satchel Paige to write the book, *Pitchin' Man.* He writes two columns for the *Plain Dealer:* "Hal Asks," and "Ask Hal."

7/THE INDIANS

In such ways do trades shape a player's life

An owner who traded with himself. . . . The worst and best deals that weren't made. . . . Trades instigated by sportswriters. . . . A sweatshirt that became enshrined. . . . A deal for a good luck charm. . . . A free agent is a freethinker named Satchel Paige. . . . A general manager hung in effigy. . . . Managers swapped. . . . A general manager who made a big trade and then took over the club he dealt with. . . . A trade that brought the first black manager into the majors. . . .

These are among the unique, intriguing, funny and sometimes sad diamond dealings that have become part of Cleveland's roller-coaster baseball history. Rarely has it been dull on the shores of Lake Erie. Trades, with strange and twisting tales, keep taking place. . . .

The first superstar ever to pitch for Cleveland was a big, strong farmer, Denton True Young, who later became known as "Cy," short for Cyclone, because of the swiftness of his pitches. He was first discovered on the family farm in Tuscarawas County. The Canton team of the Tri-State League signed him for $60 a month. That was in 1890. Later that season he was purchased by the Cleveland Spiders of the NL for $250, and his salary was raised to $75. From then on he blew down hitters with such consistency that a 20-victory season was a poor one for him. Yet, this legendary pitcher who could have—and should have—pitched Cleveland to many championships and stayed close to home while doing so, was gone in perhaps the strangest swap of all after winning 25 games in 1898.

The owner of the Cleveland team, Frank DeHaas Robinson, a streetcar magnate, bought the St. Louis franchise in the NL in

1898, which made him the owner of two teams in the same league. Yes, you read that correctly. He promptly proceeded to send all his good players to St. Louis and the weak ones to Cleveland in exchange, trading with himself—one club for another, the good for the bad. After Cy Young went to St. Louis, the Cleveland Spiders quickly became known as the "Misfits" and soon departed forever from the NL.

It was not until 1909 that Young was brought back where he belonged. By then Cleveland was a charter member in the young AL. Team owner Charley Somers gave two kid pitchers, named Ryan and Chech, and a catcher, named Spencer, to the Red Sox for Cy Young and his personal receiver, Lou Crigar. Young was 42 at the time. Yet he still managed to win 19 games.

General managers are fond of saying, "Sometimes your best deals are the ones you don't make." In 1948 Bill Veeck was stymied from making one that proved to be the epitome of successful nondeals. Conversely in April of 1908 the Cleveland team, then known as the Naps—after Napoleon Lajoie, their fine second baseman and manager—became involved in the worst deal they didn't make. The Naps were training in Macon, Georgia, and the Tigers in nearby Augusta. Owner Charley Somers was with the team. In his hotel room, the phone rang. It was Hughie Jennings, the aggressive manager of the Tigers.

"I'd like to make you this deal," said Jennings. "We'll give you Ty Cobb for Elmer Flick, even up."

Flick, born and raised in the Cleveland area, had been a .300 hitter the past four seasons, a few points above that mark each time. Cobb, who had been with the Tigers only two years, had just batted .350 and had stolen 49 bases. Flick was 31. Cobb was 21.

"Why?" asked the puzzled Somers. "Something wrong physically with Cobb?"

"No," replied the forthright Jennings. "But he can't get along with our players. He's already had two fights this spring."

"We'll keep Flick," said Somers quickly. "He may not be as good a hitter as Cobb, but he's a nice guy."

Cobb hit .324 that season. Flick became ill, scarcely played in 1908, and was never the same in his remaining years. The Tigers won the pennant that season, and many more. That year they won by exactly four percentage points over the Indians. Nice guy Flick eventually made the Hall of Fame. But his greatest claim to fame, he always would say, was that "I'm the guy they wouldn't give up for Ty Cobb."

Under Charley Somers's ownership, the Cleveland Naps made few deals. He was wealthy with extensive holdings in coal and real estate. Mostly he bought players. He had a financial interest in the New Orleans team of the Southern Association as well as full ownership of the Naps. A sportswriter for a New Orleans newspaper told Somers about a player on the team named Joe Jackson, a kid from the deep backwoods of North Carolina who didn't like to wear shoes but who had the "greatest swing I ever saw." Jackson belonged to Connie Mack's Philadelphia Athletics, who had farmed him to New Orleans.

Somers offered Briscoe Lord, an outfielder of promise, in exchange. Mack accepted. Jackson hit .408 the next season for Cleveland and continued to display his "greatest swing" for the team until August 20, 1915. By then Somers had run into terribly hard times. He was in debt and began to sell and trade his best players. He traded Joe Jackson to the White Sox for Bobby Roth, Larry Chappell, Ed Klepfer, AND $15,000.

Four seasons later, ("Shoeless") Joe Jackson, the illiterate with the superswing, became involved in the Black Sox scandal and was banished from baseball for life, never to be named to the Hall of Fame where his talents belonged. Conceivably, had he remained in Cleveland, he would not have been touched by the stigma he was to bear the rest of his years.

In such ways do trades shape a player's life.

A sportswriter started the wheels that brought Joe Jackson to Cleveland. Another, Ed Bang, sports editor of the *Cleveland News*, pushed the button that put Tris Speaker in a Cleveland uniform. It happened a year after Jackson departed. Thus, no one ever will know the greatness of an outfield containing both Speaker and Shoeless Joe.

Somers's financial problems became so acute at the end of the 1915 season that the AL had to find a money man to take over the team, by then known as the Indians. (After Lajoie departed, a newspaper contest was held to determine the new nickname.) James ("Sunny Jim") Dunn, a Chicagoan, agreed to assume the troubled Cleveland franchise. He knew little about baseball, but he was willing to listen, and Bang told him about Tris Speaker.

Speaker had completed six outstanding years with the Red Sox, helping them win the World Series in 1912 and again in 1915. Playing between Duffy Lewis and Harry Hooper, he gave the Red Sox what became known as the "dream outfield." Speaker, dubbed the Gray Eagle because of his premature white hair, was a holdout in the spring of 1916. He wanted $15,000. The Red Sox offered $9,000, and immediately quit counting. Finally Speaker went to spring training, unsigned and unhappy. The club worked out a pay-per-game scale for the exhibition games as owner Joe Lannin threatened to trade Tris.

Bang heard this and the sports editor envisioned Speaker in Cleveland's spacious center field. He immediately passed the information along to Dunn. More than that, he made a strong sales pitch. "Get him. Grab him. Whatever the price, he's worth it," said Bang. Dunn contacted Lannin and negotiations commenced. Meanwhile the unsuspecting Speaker played daily and waited for the final exhibition game against the Dodgers in Brooklyn, where he was to meet Lannin face to face. In the bottom of the ninth, against Rube Marquard, Speaker homered to beat the Dodgers, and among the first to greet him after he circled the bases was Lannin.

"Great, Tris," he said. "Your terms are okay. We'll sign in Boston tomorrow."

Tomorrow never came. The Red Sox traded Speaker to Cleveland for two players, Sam Jones and Chet Thomas, and $50,000. Now Tris had a new idea. He wanted $10,000 of the purchase price. After much bickering he got it, but not until Ban Johnson, the AL president, personally promised the payment.

Three years later, Speaker became manager of the Indians under the most fictionlike circumstances. He was as sparkling for Cleveland as he had been for the Red Sox. Soon he became "assistant manager" to his friend, Lee Fohl. In mid-July of 1919, the Indians were playing the Yankees at League Park. They were ahead, 7–4, in the ninth. But the Yanks had the bases loaded and, with two outs, none other than Babe Ruth was coming to bat. Fohl wanted to change pitchers. Three men were warming up. He looked to Speaker for a prearranged signal. Fohl misunderstood and called in the wrong pitcher. Just as in a story book, Ruth hit a grand slam. The Yankees won, 8–7. Immediately after the game Fohl was fired by Dunn and Speaker was summoned from the clubhouse.

"You're the new manager," said the owner. Speaker vehemently refused until Fohl personally insisted. The following year, 1920, Speaker led the Indians to the World Championship, the first in the team's history.

Things turned less sunny for Sunny Jim Dunn shortly after the World Series. He became ill and died in 1922. His wife took over the unwelcome ownership, and in 1927 she was bought out by a Cleveland syndicate headed by Alva Bradley. He hired an umpire great, Billy Evans, to become general manager.

Evans did make one unforgettable acquisition. He had heard the San Francisco Seals had an outstanding outfield in 1928, composed of Smead Jolley, Earl Averill, and Roy Johnson. He liked the smallest, the 165-pound center fielder, Averill. The Seals of the Pacific Coast League wanted $50,000 for the 25-year-old Averill. Evans settled for $40,000 and two players. Averill asked for $5,000 of the sales price. The Seals wouldn't pay it. Evans did. Bradley was prepared to tell Averill it was a holdup, but when Earl reported, displaying his constant, pleasant smile, Bradley smiled back and said nothing.

Cleveland fans smiled about Averill during the eleven years he played for the Indians. He gave them reason. Batting .316, he played a flawless center field and demonstrated surprising power. In 1975 he was elected to the Hall of Fame, a well-deserved honor.

In the depression years, Evans quit when asked to take a second pay cut. He was replaced by Cy Slapnicka, the superscout who discovered Bob Feller among many others. As general manager, Slap relied mostly on the men he had stocked on the farm and made an occasional trade. Among his first was the one that provided Cleveland sportswriters with their most colorful copy.

At the end of the 1935 season, Slap traded Pitchers Monte Pearson and Steve Sundra to the Yankees for Johnny Allen. When Johnny was around, there wasn't a dull moment—fights with teammates, umpires, rivals, and outbursts against hotel equipment and furniture. Knowing his temper, opposing coaches baited him and Allen often blew his cool. After one stormy game Allen did so much damage to the Brunswick Hotel in Boston, he was slapped with a $300 fine, after which he settled down sufficiently to win 16 games, losing only five, giving him a 20–10 season.

The following year Allen won four straight, then had to go for emergency surgery for a hot appendix. Two weeks later the tough pitcher was back on the mound. He won 11 more in a row, giving him a 15–0 record, one short of the AL mark. He went for the equalizer on the last day of the season, gave up a run in the opening inning on a hard grounder that went through Infielder Sammy Hale for a hit. He lost 1–0.

After the game, Allen berated Hale. Manager Steve O'Neill had to stop a fight. On the train ride back to Cleveland, Allen kept after Hale, with O'Neill constantly trying to serve as peacemaker. Finally the manager said, "If you shut up and forget it, I'll give you gas money for your drive home." Allen lived in St. Petersburg, Florida—$25 worth. He took it and shut up.

The next season O'Neill no longer had to worry about Allen. The Indians had a new manager, Oscar Vitt, also an outspoken individual. In the opening game, Allen was tossed out by Umpire Bill McGowan and fined $25. In early June the Indians were playing in Boston and again McGowan was behind the plate. Allen began to squawk about his calls almost immediately.

In the second inning McGowan called time and told Allen the sleeve of his sweatshirt was dangling and would have to be cut, for it was distracting the batters. Allen vehemently refused to change his shirt or have it trimmed. He stalked off the mound and sat down in the dugout, ignoring the pleas of his teammates and manager. The exasperated Vitt finally said, "That'll cost you $250. No pitcher of mine is going to walk off the mound without my permission." Allen's response is unprintable.

The story of the shirt made headlines and owner Alva Bradley hurried to Boston. In a move worthy of an O. Henry tale, he pacified Allen by purchasing the frayed shirt from him for $250, the price of the fine. It next appeared in the window of the Higbee Company, a large department store in downtown Cleveland. Coincidentally, the president of Higbee's at the time happened to be Alva's brother Charles. Higbee's had paid $250 for the shirt.

Allen never wound up in Cooperstown, but eventually the shirt did. It's still on display there.

It is not surprising that two years later, in 1940, Allen was one of the two ringleaders in a player revolt against Vitt, a rebellion which soon labeled the team "The Cleveland Cry Babies." Despite the friction, or because of it, the Indians lost the pennant to the Tigers in the final week of the season.

Vitt was fired and Allen, no longer effective, also was sent packing—to the St. Louis Browns. Roger Peckinpaugh, a home-grown Cleveland favorite, was named interim manager. The following season the Indians' 24-year-old shortstop applied for the job and got it. Lou Boudreau became the Indians' "Boy Manager." But those were war years and the major problem was to find physically able, draft-exempt players to fill the rosters. It was time for scrounging and little else in an effort to keep the competition alive. Then an ex-Marine, one who eventually had to have a leg amputated because of a war injury, burst upon the Cleveland scene like the fireworks he introduced to the game. Bill Veeck arrived and the deals began to pop.

Once Veeck purchased the club in June 1946, the attention usually centered on the character of the front office rather than the characters on the field, even though some of the latter were personalities of no small stature. Veeck simply was too much. At 33 he was dynamic and indefatigable, spending days and nights romancing the fans. The blond, fuzzy-haired whirlwind knew baseball, having previously owned the Milwaukee franchise in the American Association. And before that he learned from his daddy, Bill Veeck, Sr., who once ran the Cubs.

Veeck was all over town, talking baseball, charming old fans, and making new. Women were his special target. If they came to the ball park, so would hubby and the kids. He gave away nylons and corsages, put roving bands and clowns in the stands. He shot off fireworks. You name it, he did it as he innovatively repackaged the product.

Meanwhile, he worked equally hard to make the product more attractive—the sixth-place team he had taken over—or at least make the fans think it was. Scarcely a week passed, so it seemed, that he didn't contrive some change in playing personnel. He would exchange what he called "cats and dogs," the fringe players, just for publicity and meanwhile try to get a better cat or dog in the attempt, especially if a little extra cash would do it.

Veeck's flamboyance and his iconoclasm—he often irritated the staid baseball establishment—caused many owners and general managers to avoid his trade bait. But he always found two ready listeners, Larry MacPhail, owner of the Yankees and almost as flamboyant as Veeck, and Bill DeWitt, owner of the St. Louis Browns. MacPhail seldom sought what DeWitt did: money to operate with. Veeck's cash was as green as anybody's and often more abundant.

Veeck's first trade of importance revealed his the-hell-with-the-future attitude. He was sitting with MacPhail at Fenway Park during the 1946 World Series between the Red Sox and the Cardinals. Veeck wanted the Yankees' second baseman, Joe Gordon. Gordon had power and he would make a good doubleplay partner with Veeck's player-manager, Shortstop Lou Boudreau. That Gordon was 32 didn't bother Veeck. The second baseman had at least a couple of years left, he figured, even though he had just completed a brutal season. He also knew that MacPhail and Gordon had an argument in the Yankee clubhouse after the last game of the season and nearly came to blows. Gordon surely was available.

"I'll give you Allie Reynolds," said Veeck, "for Gordon and Eddie Bockman. Or, if you prefer, I'll give you Red Embree for Gordon, even up."

Veeck was certain MacPhail would go for the second deal— which is precisely what he was seeking. Bockman had just completed a fine season at third base for the Yankees' Kansas City farm. MacPhail would want to keep him. And Veeck preferred to part with Embree rather than Reynolds. Although Reynolds was only 11–15 that season, he had a poor team behind him, he was mean on the mound, and he could throw hard.

MacPhail was about to take the Embree-for-Gordon offer. Veeck eagerly put out his hand. Just before the handshake Mac-Phail said, "I see Joe DiMaggio sitting over there. Let me ask him." He came back to report, "Joe says I'm nuts if I don't take Reynolds." The two went to a concessions stand, wrote out the deal on a napkin and signed it.

Gordon proved an important man in the Indians' most sensational year, 1948, when they won the pennant and the World Series and broke all attendance records. But from 1949 on, Reynolds helped the Yankees win pennant after pennant after pennant. By then MacPhail had sold the Yankees and Veeck was gone from Cleveland.

The Reynolds-for-Gordon swap triggered another, as they sometimes do, perhaps the luckiest deal Veeck ever made. Knowing the Yankees now needed a second baseman, Veeck offered Ray Mack to his pal MacPhail. Mack, a product of the Cleveland sandlots and the keystone partner of Boudreau from the minors on, was good field, poor hit.

MacPhail had another player Veeck coveted, this one pure fringe: Hal Peck. Peck was what Bill considered "my good luck charm," although there was a time when it appeared otherwise. Peck, a speedy outfielder and good hitter, had played for Veeck at Milwaukee in the early 1940s. He was so promising that Veeck, running the club on a financial shoestring, sought to sell him to the highest bidder. During the season, the White Sox had offered $40,000 for Peck. Veeck was certain he could get much more during the winter.

Then came the bad news. Peck, trying to shoot rats on his chicken ranch, accidentally shot two toes off his left foot. Now nobody wanted him, but Veeck still needed money to continue the Milwaukee operation. What to do? He'd gamble the cost of a train ticket to New York to see his "friend," Larry MacPhail, now the president of the Brooklyn Dodgers.

Buy Peck? Larry merely laughed and said he wasn't interested. Meanwhile Veeck learned MacPhail was going to the racetrack that afternoon. He contrived to be there, shortly "bumping" into MacPhail—and new hope!

"I didn't know you went to the track," said MacPhail. "You don't even know how to bet."

"I've got to win enough money to get home," said Bill.

"Okay," said MacPhail, resignedly. "I'll take Peck. I'll give you $5,000 now and another $18,000 if we keep him opening day."

Veeck, back in the chips, was able to take the train back to Milwaukee.

During the winter of 1946, through the strange twists baseball takes, MacPhail was with the Yankees and had Peck again.

"You need a second baseman," Veeck said to MacPhail. "I'll give you Ray Mack for Peck. But you'll admit that's an unfair deal. You would be stealing. I'll throw in a good young catcher from our minors, Sherman Lollar, if you give me a couple of pitchers."

They agreed on one, Al Gettel, an average right-hander. In addition, Veeck was to get his pick of one of six minor league pitchers. Among the names on the list was Gene Bearden, pitching for Oakland. Managing Oakland was Casey Stengel, who had been Veeck's manager in Milwaukee. Their association, both being fun guys, had been close. He called Stengel for an honest appraisal of Bearden.

"He's your man," said Casey. "Don't hesitate."

Pitching injuries forced Player-Manager Boudreau to give Bearden an emergency start early in the 1948 season. Bearden won. From then on he was unbelievable. His knuckleball was unhittable. He became an instant hero. He won 20 games that year, including the most important one of all, the pennant playoff game against the Red Sox, the only one in AL history. For that game he was Boudreau's choice, after only two days of rest. He also won his World Series start against the Braves, 2–0, and he came in from the bullpen to clinch the final game.

After that season Bearden was nothing and this, too, has a storybook twist. Because the Indians won the 1948 pennant, beating out the Yankees as well as the Red Sox in the close race, the Yanks fired their manager, Bucky Harris. His replacement: Casey Stengel. It could be said, with some logic, that he became the manager of the Yankees because he recommended Gene Bearden to the Indians. It also could be said, and has been by Veeck and other insiders, that it was Stengel who again waved his wand and made Bearden, now an enemy, suddenly ineffective. Having watched Bearden pitch in Oakland, Casey realized his knuckleball, thrown low, dipped below the strike zone.

"Lay off the pitch," he told his Yankees, "until you have two strikes against you." Bearden had to come in higher and he was whomped. With Bearden an 8–8 pitcher in 1949, the Indians fell out of contention. Stengel's Yankees won the pennant—and many more.

As for good-luck charm, Hal Peck, he was the Indians' best pinch hitter in 1948. When Veeck sold the team, Peck retired—permanently.

If Branch Rickey hadn't signed Jackie Robinson in 1946, Bill Veeck possibly would have been the first to break baseball's color line. Once Veeck purchased the Indians, he began to search for an outstanding young black prospect. His scouts told him about Larry Doby, an excollegian playing second base for the Newark Eagles of the Negro League. Rickey had obtained Robinson for nothing. The Negro League couldn't refuse his magnanimous offer of allowing Robinson to play in white company. But Veeck wouldn't have it that way. He offered Mrs. Effa Manley, owner of the Eagles, a trade, $10,000 in cash for Larry's contract. She was delighted. Doby, eventually converted into an outfielder, started slowly, but the first black player in the AL overcame his anxieties, made a major contribution to Cleveland baseball, and helped materially in the 1948 and 1954 pennants.

After Veeck paid Mrs. Manley the $10,000, she offered him Newark's shortstop, who she said was just as good as Doby, for $1,000. Veeck turned it down. The shortstop was Monte Irvin. He later became a star with the Giants.

After Doby had established himself, Veeck had another surprise for the Cleveland fans. Through his friend, Abe Saperstein, owner of the Harlem Globetrotters basketball team, Bill signed freethinker Satchel Paige as a free agent. The legendary pitcher of indeterminate age wasn't so old he couldn't pitch—and win. He also drew fans through the turnstiles, literally thousands of them wherever the Indians played.

In June of 1948 it cost Veeck a player and $100,000 to bolster the Indians' bullpen with a left-handed pitcher: Sam Zoldak. That is what Veeck paid the St. Louis Browns for the apple-cheeked Zoldak. During a victory bash after Cleveland won both the pennant playoff and the World Series, Sam put an arm around Veeck and sobbed: "Bill, you know I'm not worth $100,000." Nevertheless Sam won nine of 15 decisions.

Before the 1948 season Bill Veeck was pleased with his shortstop, but not too impressed with his manager. Because Lou Boudreau filled both jobs, Bill sought to trade Lou, the fans' favorite. He had Al Lopez waiting in the wings to become the new manager, but he couldn't deal for a desired shortstop. The *Cleveland News'* Ed McAuley wrote:

"If Veeck were to trade Bob Feller he might stab some of the fans in their judgments. If he trades Boudreau he will stab many of the fans in their hearts."

Franklin Lewis, sports editor of the rival *Cleveland Press,* sized up the "Trade Lou" situation, writing:

"It is evident Veeck didn't know Boudreau was immortal in Cleveland. Alva Bradley (the former owner) used to say that he hired the managers, and the public fired them. Here's one Alva hired, and only God dare fire him apparently."

Boudreau stayed. The Indians won everything. Lou won the MVP award, and the elated fans eventually named a street surrounding the stadium "Boudreau Boulevard."

Veeck, needing money to settle a divorce, sold the club. Hank Greenberg, Veeck's vice president, pal, and a former slugging great, took over as general manager of the Indians. Hank made some early deals that backfired, and from then on he was ultracon-servative in trades.

Then Greenberg sold his stock in the Indians for a large profit in 1958 and a cyclone hit Cleveland. Enter Frank Lane. He came here fresh from antagonizing Cardinals' fans. There, he had traded away a city favorite, Red Schoendienst, and rumors persist-ed that Stan Musial was about to go. Lane, a dealer, was somewhat like Veeck, only more so. Both would trade fringe players just for headlines. Lane also traded stars, merely for the sake of making trades, or so it seemed. This is not to say he wasn't without ability. He had a genius for revitalizing a team. He immediately proceeded to rebuild the Indians' franchise, just as he had done elsewhere.

Frank Lane discovered a new fan favorite who came close to matching Boudreau's popularity during Veeck's time. It was Rocky Colavito. When Lane became involved in a feud with Colavito, the fans developed a new chant: "Don't Knock the Rock." When Rocky signed his 1960 contract, he was unaware of a clause Lane had inserted. It read: "Player will receive an extra $1,000 if he hits fewer than thirty home runs." Traded to the Tigers before opening day for Harvey Kuenn, a singles hitter, Colavito learned about the secret clause from Bill DeWitt, Lane's counterpart in Detroit. "What do you mean by this?" DeWitt shouted: "One thousand dollars extra NOT to hit home runs? I got him to hit them." Rocky did. Thirty-five HRs. Meanwhile Lane was hung in effigy all over the city.

The next DeWitt-Lane trade was historic because they swapped managers in mid-season. Yes, that is correct: they traded managers. Jimmie Dykes moved from the Tigers to the Indians, and Joe Gordon moved from the Indians—and Lane—to the Tigers. The headlines were bigger than the results.

Lane's stay in Cleveland was unforgettable and brief. At the end of the disappointing 1960 season, the Indians' owners suggest-ed to Charley Finley, new owner of the Athletics, that Lane might be available. Finley jumped at the bait.

Gabe Paul, a solid, experienced baseball man who had spent most of his years at Cincinnati and who had just switched to Houston to get that franchise started, was brought in. He was enticed by the opportunity to buy stock in the club. By now the Indians were undercapitalized and limited in field talent. In September 1964, Paul had to trade Pedro Ramos to the Yankees for Ralph Terry and $75,000. The money was needed to meet the payroll. Ramos's relief pitching won the pennant for the Yankees.

During the winter meetings after the 1972 season, Gabe Paul made what he regarded as his "best ever" deal. The Yankees sought Third Baseman Craig Nettles. Paul, speaking for the Indians, requested plenty in exchange. For Nettles the price was Catcher John Ellis, Infielder Jerry Kenney, Outfielders Charlie Spikes, and Rusty Torres. The Yankees balked on Spikes, a young slugger they had optioned to Syracuse. "No Spikes, no deal," said Paul. Finally the Yankees accepted—if the Indians would throw in a catcher. That was easy: Jerry Moses.

As he walked out of the conference room, Paul told his aide, Phil Seghi: "This is the best deal I ever made in my life." Some six weeks later Gabe Paul became part of a syndicate buying the Yankees. Suddenly he moved to New York on the "wrong" end of "the best deal" he had ever made. Fortunately for him, the deal proved better for the Yankees than his original evaluation—and not quite as good for the Indians.

When Gabe Paul moved from the Indians to the Yankees, Phil Seghi, his longtime assistant with the Reds, became the new Cleveland general manager. Seghi joined the history makers with a single name on the waiver list in September 1974. The name was Frank Robinson, formerly a superstar in both the AL and NL. Robinson's name had been placed there by the Angels. Suddenly the Indians had a new player for the final weeks of the season. The day after the season closed, the Indians had a new manager. It was Frank Robinson, a black man receiving his opportunity to break the color line among major league managers. On October 3, the day after the 1974 season ended, a press conference was called at Cleveland Stadium. TV cameras and movie cameras were present in abundance. Reporters came from everywhere. Commissioner Bowie Kuhn was there. So was Lee MacPhail, president of the American League. So were Frank Robinson and his wife. Making the announcement at a jam-packed press conference, Seghi said simply:

"Frank Robinson is the Indians' new manager."

Seghi's seven words will be remembered as long as baseball is played, and they produced a moment difficult to top. Once again Cleveland had written a major page in baseball history.

JIM ENRIGHT
Sportswriter, *Chicago Today*

Jim Enright missed very few bases during thirty years on the major league baseball beat and thirty-six years of basketball officiating. He made two trips to Europe for United States Air Force basketball clinics and a Good Will Junket to Viet Nam for baseball. This busy pleasure-filled work started in 1928 on *The News-Palladium* in Benton Harbor, Michigan, and continued with the Hearst-owned *Chicago American* in 1937. Jim was one of the official scorers for the 1950 and 1962 All-Star baseball games and returned to Eau Claire, Michigan, for the dedication of the Enright Press Box at Harry Hogue Field on September 23, 1966. Enright, Chicago's Baseball Writer of the Year in 1970, was national president of the basketball writers in 1967–1968.

8/THE CUBS

Big returns on small investments

The story of Lou Brock's baseball life is a tale of two cities. They called him, and not without good reason, a butcher in Chicago. Traded to the Cardinals, Lou became an instant hero in St. Louis. Despite the sudden change in the status of the old and new Brock, this trade automatically became the best or worst depending upon your allegiance to the Cubs or Cardinals.

After Brock was signed out of Southern University in Baton Rouge, Louisiana, for a $30,000 bonus in 1961, his first professional season unfolded just like an unbelievable dream. He did almost everything but drive the team bus for the Cubs' NL farm team in St. Cloud, Minnesota. His Northern league-leading .361 batting average included such impressive items as most hits (181), most runs (117), most doubles (33), and a tip-off of his larceny leanings as evidenced in his stealing 37 bases to share another first.

Almost immediately the fleet-footed youngster—he was 22 at the time—was called up to the Cubs. During a span of 327 games covering two full seasons and part of a third, Brock's day-to-day performance never came close to matching the potential he displayed in drawing the $30,000 bonus or his selection as Rookie of the Year in the NL. The fact is he never really learned to play right field, and this lack of defensive finesse made it easy for the Chicago fans to zing him with the butcher label.

After the Cubs accomplished a minor miracle by posting their best record (82–80 in 1963) since 1946, the hierarchy desired to continue this improvement. The first move was aimed at bolstering the pitching, and in short order it was discovered the Cardinals had declared Ernie Broglio expendable for a price. The price was Brock. Because this was during a time when the Cubs were operated by a committee, the manager-less College of Coaches, it was easy to recall Lou's faulty fielding and frequent spotty hitting. His big plus, speed, seldom was considered because he was playing for a club which seldom strayed away from safety-first book baseball. Now Brock was deemed expendable for a price. The price was Broglio.

Working right to the June 15 trading deadline, they finally completed the deal. It would involve six players. The Cubs sent Brock and two run-of-the-mill pitchers, Jack Spring and Paul Toth, to the Cardinals for Pitchers Broglio and Bobby Shantz, the latter a lionhearted little lefty who was nearing the end of the trail, and Outfielder Doug Clemons, an adequate journeyman outfielder to be used mainly as Brock's replacement. Actually it was a Brock-for-Broglio swap, and the Cubs appeared to have all the best of it on paper. Unfortunately, paper couldn't pitch—and neither could Broglio.

Whereas Brock had been only a .251 hitter with ten stolen bases playing the season's first 52 games with the Cubs, he blossomed rapidly with explosive brillance for the Cardinals. Proving he was more stimulated than shocked over his first deal, Lou batted .348 playing his first 103 games for the Redbirds. Furthermore, the Cardinals' run-run game plan, always daring and frequently reckless, brought out the best of Brock: 33 stolen bases. Manager Johnny Keane made an astute move by assigning Lou to left field, the better-to-forget his unhappy experiences playing right field for the Cubs.

Meanwhile, back in Chicago the Cubs were staggered by a dilemma: Broglio's loss of velocity in throwing his once overpowering fast ball. The big Italian lacked the speed he once possessed to combat the NL's power hitters within the friendly confines of Wrigley Field. There were endless stories to the effect that Broglio "pitched" better at night in the watering spas along Rush Street than he did during the day for the Cubs. Whatever the reason, the BIG pitcher the Wrigleys acquired to become their stop starter, slumped to four scattered victories while losing seven and wondering where the potency vanished to in his bulky 4.05 ERA.

There were other reasons for the almost daily magnifying-glass treatment applied to the now controversial deal. The Cardinals, fighting for their first pennant since 1946, were fused by Brock's ample skills in what was to become the tightest race ever in NL history. Along with turning a last-day-of-the-season 11–5 conquest of the Mets into the pennant clincher, the Redbirds erased the possibility of two postseason playoffs to decide the winner and new champion if the regular season ended in a triple tie.

St. Louis' success in winning a seven-game World Series from the Yankees only added to Lou's laurels as the Cardinals' new Mister Momentum. The classic also produced another historic oddity: the managerial move of Johnny Keane from the "winning" Cardinals to the "losing" Yankees. This surprising swap of sorts was completed when Yogi Berra, the deposed Yankee skipper, became a coach for the Mets. The Cardinals then picked Red Schoendienst as Keane's successor, providing Brock with only his second major league manager—a count which still remains intact.

Brock's success-filled debut with the Cardinals was merely the start of awesome as well as spectacular accomplishments still to come. He would steal 50 or more bases for ten straight seasons, reaching a magnificent record total of 118 in 1974. This enabled the modern boss of base bandits to move 14 up on Maury Wills. In 1962, Lou's first season in the majors, Wills stole 104 bases for the Dodgers. Then it was the general feeling the figure never would be topped. Brock proved the feeling to be wrong with an incredible speed spree. In racing to the charmed 118, the Cub-turned-Cardinal stole second base 112 times, and third six times. All this with only 33 caught stealings—one of them his lone attempt to pilfer home.

Although he was never unhappy over the Chicago to St. Louis move, Brock did enjoy one laugh at the expense of his cousin Cubs during the record run. He stole 15 bases against the Cubs without being thrown out once. Also it is a matter of note that five of his last seven steals were made in games against the Cubs. In this manner Lou became the new runner-up to Hall of Famer Ty Cobb in the all-time stolen base derby when he ran past the ghost of Eddie Collins. Still Brock and Collins share a noteworthy first in World Series traffic. Each has stolen 14 bases, Lou in just two classics, and Eddie in six.

The Redbirds' Mister Fleet started to work on this deadlock in the 1967 World Series against the Red Sox, when he didn't have to psych himself to assure extraordinary effort due to an incident while still a Cub. In 1963 he was a late substitute in a spring exhibition game against the Red Sox in Scottsdale, Arizona. Making the most of this limited opportunity, Lou stole second and third on successive pitches. After his head-first safe slide into third base, Dick Williams, the Red Sox third baseman, bellowed angrily: "That is bush. Who are you trying to impress?" Lou said nothing but filed the incident away for future reference.

Now it's four years later, and the Cardinals are opposing Manager Dick Williams's Red Sox in the World Series. The Brockstyled adrenaline flowed freely as he batted .414 and stole seven bases in the Cardinals' triumph, four games to three. At no time during baseball's rich tournament did Williams ask who Brock was trying to impress. Dick got the message: a painful $3,199.58 poke in the pocketbook—the difference between the winning and losing shares which Brock helped decide. Lou didn't require any memory-dusting to blend a sizzling .464 hitting percentage with seven more stolen bases in the 1968 World Series against the Tigers as the AL champions won a seven-gamer, 4–3.

Still a youthful 36 in 1975, Brock continued to do what he does best: steal bases. If and when he reaches the Hall of Fame in Cooperstown, New York, there should be a line on his plaque reading: The superstar the Cubs had, and let slip away!

There is still another facet in his life-style which proves his exceptional speed isn't limited just to his fleet feet. As an addition to his personal retirement fund, viewers of television commercials frequently see his fingers racing across the yellow pages of the *Redbook* equally as fast as his legs carry him to another stolen base. This outside revenue merely adds to the heavy bread Louis Clark Brock draws as the highest paid base stealer in all baseball history. And whatever became of Ernie Broglio?

Rival clubs would find it difficult to match the Cubs' excellent record in dealing for name players to launch or help continue successful pennant pushes. Before the 1906 season got underway, it was agreed that Doc Casey, the Cubs' 35-year-old third baseman, would be hard pressed to withstand the rigors of another tough season. Doc didn't think so, and he returned to Brooklyn to continue his career with the Dodgers. It mattered not to the Cubs' who sent lefty Pitcher Jake Weimer to the Reds for Third Baseman Harry Steinfeldt. Although Harry was the forgotten man in the Tinker-to-Evers-to-Chance combination afield, his potent bat was a definite factor in the Cubs' unprecedented climb to 116 victories. His .327 average placed him second behind the Pirates' Honus Wagner in the NL batting derby. His 83 RBIs enabled him to tie the Pirates' Jim Nealon for the league lead.

In mid-season Steinfeldt, who remained for the Cubs' Golden Era—four pennants in five years ranging from 1906 through 1910—was reunited with another of his Cincinnati teammates. That would be Pitcher Orval Overall, who promptly won 12 of 15 decisions to help pad the Li'l Bears' 20-game edge over the second-place Giants. With all of its success, the 1906 club still couldn't land the prize it wanted more than any other: the World Championship. The White Sox proved they were Hitless Wonders with ample muscle to beat the Cubs four games to two in the only all-Chicago World Series ever played.

Spurred by the White Sox winning the 1917 World Series from the Giants for what still remains as Chicago's last World Championship, the Cubs returned to the trade marts trying to improve their faded fortunes. The first deal was a blockbuster, with Grover Cleveland Alexander coming to the Cubs from the Phillies along with his battery mate, Bill Killefer, for Pitcher Mike Prendergast, Catcher Pickles Dilhoefer, and $60,000. Alexander pitched three games for his new club, and then enlisted in the army, answering the nation's Work-or-Fight call.

When baseball closed shop on Labor Day, the Cubs owned another pennant with a 10½ game lead over the second-place Giants. Jim Vaughn and Claude Hendrix were 20-game winners, and ("Lefty") George Tyler chipped in with 19. Rookie Shortstop Charlie Hollocher batted a surprising .316 and led the club with 26 stolen bases. Fred Merkle, who came to the Cubs from the Giants via the Dodgers, was the club's best power hitter with .297. This was the season football's supergreat Paddy Driscoll proved he could also play major league baseball during a 23-game tour of duty. In the World Series the pennant luster faded rapidly. Babe Ruth and Carl Mays won two games apiece to carry the Red Sox to a 4–2 edge in the earliest finish ever because it was all over by September 11 as Ruth (1–0) and Vaughn (3–0) exchanged shutouts.

The Cubs' and William Wrigley, Jr.'s first major trade after the 1924 season was strictly a fence-mending job, and the immediate results were far from favorable. The Cubs sent Pitcher Vic Aldridge, Infielder George Grantham, and Albert Niehaus, a nothing first baseman, to the Pirates for Pitcher Wilbur Cooper, First Baseman Charlie Grimm, and Shortstop Rabbit Maranville. During his farewell handshake with Grimm, Pirate President Barney Dreyfuss explained sympathetically:

"You and your damn banjo playing and singing. You finally did it: singing yourself all the way to Chicago. You play good, but that singing. I just can't stand it."

Fun and frolic was the Cubs' main theme in 1925. So much so, the team finished last for its first time in history. Try as they might, three different managers took turns trying to halt the skid.

Bill Killefer, the incumbent, was the first to go with a 33–42 record. Rabbit Maranville followed with a 23–30 log. Finally George Gibson finished with 12–14.

Vowing this "never would happen again," owner William Wrigley, Jr., dispatched Bill Veeck, Sr., his chief aide, to "go out and get the best damn manager and players available, and forget the cost." Veeck came home with Joe McCarthy. Joe had never played a single inning in the majors, but he possessed an outstanding managerial record in the minors. McCarthy also had good book on players he had watched in the minors plus inside information that the Giants had erred in trying to cover up Hack Wilson, assigned to Toledo, Ohio. The Cubs' last place finish finally paid a dividend: first call in the majors' draft of minor league personnel.

In this manner the Cubs obtained Wilson for $5,000, a buy equally as incredible as the Louisiana Purchase. Marse Joe also advised the purchase of Jimmy Cooney, a good-glove shortstop, to fill the gap left by Rabbit Maranville's exit. The Cubs put in a bid for Riggs Stephenson, but the "Ol' Hoss" wasn't immediately available. Later it was said the Indianapolis operators stalled the deal waiting for a better offer. Fifty-one games into the American Association season, the deal was finally approved. Stephenson came to the Cubs with Infielder Henry Schreiber for Outfielder Joe Munson and Infielder Maurice Shannon plus $50,000—double the Cubs' original offer.

The Cubs finished fourth, winning 82 games for a 10-game bulge over .500. Some of their loyalists will forever wonder where they might have finished if McCarthy hadn't been so hasty in unloading Lefty O'Doul, part-time pitcher, sometime outfielder, and full-time slugger. Wrigley paid $15,000 to the Salt Lake City club of the Pacific Coast League for O'Doul on a look-see basis. More, much more, to be paid if the future two-time NL batting champion was retained. An introductory handshake was as close as the two Irishmen got all spring. In fact, O'Doul was gone before the club opened the new NL season. It wasn't too much longer before Grover Cleveland Alexander was sold to the Cardinals for the waiver price because McCarthy didn't cotton to Old Pete's personal conditioning habits.

The conveyor belt into Wrigley's vault remained in high gear as Woody English came up from Toledo, Ohio, at the reported price of $50,000—and here we go again: two players to be named later. Earl Webb was another costly addition. Ditto handyman Infielder

Clyde Beck as the Cubs repeated their fourth place finish in 1927. New faces continued to find their way to Wrigley Field in 1928 when Freddie Maguire, Kiki Cuyler, and Pat Malone checked in. Cuyler came from the Pirates and played very well. After a third-place finish in 1928, the word spread throughout the entire NL: Watch out for the Cubs! This was anything but idle gossip. Especially when Wrigley tapped his own till for $200,000 in cash plus a package of five players to get Rogers Hornsby from the Boston Braves.

An 11-year wait had ended. The Cubs had the 1929 pennant. There would be more to come. Three to be exact, on a three-year basis in 1932, 1935, and 1938. Billy Jurges, Billy Herman, Mark Koenig, Lon Warneke, Burleigh Grimes, and Bobo Newsom were the newcomers in 1932. Charlie Grimm answered the first of three

PLAYING FOR TWO CLUBS IN ONE DAY

Max Flack went home for lunch and missed the news! What news? The news that he had been involved in a record trade. The Cubs and Cardinals played a morning-afternoon doubleheader in Chicago on Memorial Day, May 30, 1922. In the first game Flack played right field for the Cubs, and Cliff Heathcote was the Cardinals' right fielder. After the game Flack was traded to the Cardinals for Heathcote. They became starters for their new clubs immediately: Flack in right for the Cardinals, Heathcote in right for the Cubs in Game Two.

Why did Flack go home for lunch?

"We had a two-hour wait between games, and I figured the three-block walk home for a sandwich would enable me to relax more than if I loafed around the clubhouse. When I returned somebody said: 'Max, you don't live here anymore. You'll find your equipment in the Cardinals' clubhouse.' I felt they were joshing, but I went along with the act. When I got there, Manager Branch Rickey was changing the signs, and then I realized it happened."

Flack and Heathcote are the only two players who share this entry in the baseball record book:

Most Clubs Played, One Day—Two, National League: Max Flack, Chicago, St. Louis, May 30 (AM–PM) 1922; Cliff Heathcote, St. Louis, Chicago, May 30 (AM–PM) 1922.

Both played on pennant-winning teams for the Cubs: Flack in 1918, Heathcote in 1929.

managerial calls, and "Buddy Boy-ed" the club to a pennant with 37 victories in the season's last 57 games. The big deal leading to the 1935 flag was the trading of Pitchers Guy Bush and Jim Weaver, and Outfielder Babe Herman to the Pirates for Fred Lindstrom and lefty Pitcher Larry French.

Possessing mainly right-handed power, the Cubs sought better offensive balance shopping for a lefty hitting slugger. The man they wanted was Chuck Klein. The man they got was Chuck Klein, but it was another till-tapper deal. The man who had hit 180 HRs for the Phillies during the previous five seasons, cost $65,000 and three players—one of them Mark Koenig. Chuck was a .300 hitter for the Cubs in 1934, and batted .293 for the Wrigley pennant winners in 1935. But, the secret was out: Klein couldn't hit left-handers in the same manner he hammered right-handers. Six weeks into the 1936 season he was gone, back to the Phillies with Pitcher Fabian (when was the last time you heard that name in baseball?), Kowalik, and $50,000 for two players. It was a sad story to the tune of $115,000, but it was soon forgotten in the rebuilding for the 1938 pennant.

The cost of the Klein maneuver was peanuts compared to the money involved in the trade for Jerome ("Dizzy") Dean: $185,000 in cash and three players representing another $100,000 in blue book value. Due to an arm injury, the self-established Great One pitched more with his heart than his arm, and still won seven and lost only one. Nevertheless, Dizzy was box office, and it was like Phil Wrigley said: "Going anyplace with Dizzy was like parading behind a brass band."

All the Barrymores put together couldn't have matched the Cubs' drama in 1938. Besides Dean and handyman Tony ("Poosh 'Em Up") Lazzeri, there was Gabby Hartnett's famous homer in the glooming; Big Bill Lee's 22 victories; Stan Hack's .320 average as a lead-off hitter, and aging Carl Reynolds's valuable contributions including an even 150 hits.

The Big Name hunt continued in 1939. The Cubs sent Billy Jurges, Frank Demaree, and Ken O'Dea to the Giants for Hank Leiber, Dick Bartell, and Gus Mancuso. The best the Cubs could do was fourth. Somebody forgot to wind the three-year pennant clock, and it was seven years before they returned to World Series traffic. Phil Cavarretta won the NL batting crown with .355 and possessed an even .500 slugging average, but it remained for a former Yankee, Hank Borowy, to turn the adrenaline on full force. The

Cubs paid $100,000 for Borowy in late July 1945, and he responded with 11 victories and a league-leading 2.14 ERA. Actually it was a steal deal with General Manager Jimmy Gallagher risking his reputation—and winning!

A full fleet of Brinks' trucks was needed to move all the players and the cash figuring in a 1953 blockbuster transfer between the Cubs and Pirates. Six Cubs, Pitcher Bob Schultz, Catcher Toby Atwell, First Baseman Preston Ward, Infielder George Freese, and Outfielders Bob Addis and Gene Hermanski, became Bucs in one sweep. In return the Wrigleys obtained new Hall of Famer Ralph Kiner, Catcher Joe Garagiola, Pitcher Howie Pollet, and Infielder-Outfielder George Metkovich. Is that all there was to it? Would you believe $100,000 in fresh greenbacks came right out of the Cubs' vault? While rushing to the bank with the fresh scratch, Branch Rickey bubbled like champagne, saying: "I'd never made the deal if Preston Ward wasn't included." Ward ended up as he started: a fringe player with no fewer than five clubs.

During his short tenure with the Cubs, Schultz's most note-worthy feat had no association with baseball. From spring training right up until the very moment they locked the horse in the starting gate of the Kentucky Derby, Bob touted something with four legs named Dark Star. What a hunch! Dark Star raced Native Dancer into his first loss, and returned a winning boxcar pay-off of $51.80 for each two dollar investment—and Schultz was down real good. So much so, his semimonthly paycheck of $500 quickly was reduced to mere tip money.

The Cubs returned to the hundred "thou" plateau in 1960 when they signed an 18-year-old high school pitcher-outfielder from Beverly, Massachusetts, for their biggest bonus ever. Danny Murphy never made it big, and oddly enough his best days in the bigs were spent with the Cubs' archrivals: the White Sox.

When it comes to a big return for a small investment, the Cubs' trade for Kiki Cuyler in 1928 is tough to top. They gave up an aging Sparky Adams and Outfielder Floyd Scott, a fringer at best, for Cuyler and seven seasons of stardom timed to Hall of Fame distinction. It was swap shop expertise at its best when Ferguson Jenkins came aboard from the Phillies for two pitchers nearing the end of the line: Larry Jackson and Bob Buhl. When Jenkins asked to be traded, General Manager John Holland got Bill Madlock from the Rangers. Within two years Madlock became the Cubs' fourth NL batting champion in history. The addition of Hank Sauer and

Frankie Baumholtz for Harry Walker and Peanuts Lowrey made Seward's Folly, the deal for Alaska, look like a fire sale. Also it established Jimmy Gallagher, the man who engineered it, as the presiding president of Golden Fleece, Unlimited. Hands, first name Bill, and Hundley, first name Randy, sound like a vaudeville team. Nevertheless, they accomplished far more for the Cubs than Lindy McDaniel and Don Landrum ever did for the Giants.

For the all-time low cash parlay, Hack Wilson for $5,000, and Ernie Banks for $10,000, is diplomatic larceny at its absolute best. Wilson's record of 190 RBIs still stands unchallenged. So does Banks's club record collection of 512 HRs, back-to-back MVP awards, and Golden Glove expert defensive finesse at two positions, shortstop and first base.

And then there is the nightmare to end all nightmares—Lou Brock for Ernie Broglio!

Inasmuch as Burt Hooton opened the 1975 season losing two games for the Cubs, and closed it winning twelve straight—a league-leading streak—for the Dodgers, there could be concern if another Brock for Broglio headache is in the making. Hooton, who finished 18–9 for the season, was traded to the Dodgers for Pitchers Eddie Solomon and Geoffrey Zahn. By the end of 1975 Solomon had been unloaded for the Cardinals' Ken Crosby, and Zahn was on the disabled list.

JOHN F. STEADMAN
Sports Editor, *Baltimore News-American*

John F. Steadman was appointed sports editor of the *Baltimore News-American* at age thirty, which at the time, 1958, made him the youngest man in the country performing such a role on a major newspaper. Steadman had been assistant general manager and publicity director of the Baltimore Colts for almost four years. Coming out of Baltimore City College, he played one season of minor league baseball in the Pittsburgh Pirates' farm system. He says he found out in a hurry that as a future big league catcher, he had a better chance hitting a typewriter in the press box than a breaking pitch with thirty-four inches of ash.

Steadman is the only Maryland writer to ever win the "Best Story of the Year" competition and in 1975 was the recipient of the Dick McCann Memorial Award for long and distinguished reporting in the field of pro football. In addition to a six-day-a-week column since January 6, 1958, he handles a daily sports commentary show on radio station WBAL, the NBC affiliate in Baltimore. He has written three books, the latest being an anthology called *The Best (And Worst) Of Steadman.*

9/THE ORIOLES

"Old 30" catalyst in Orioles' pennant push

It became standard operating procedure for the Baltimore Orioles, in a subtle way, to let some other club worry over the "headaches," with or without a bottle of aspirin to be thrown in later. When a player presented an attitude problem, one who was self-centered, difficult to handle and vocal, they quietly dispatched him to some faraway establishment . . . but always with patience prevailing and no accompanying criticism.

Not all the trades were based on personality. They'd put up with the prima donna types as long as they had ability, but when the opportunity presented itself, they went—like last winter's snow. The Orioles didn't try to assemble all choir boys or young men with impeccable reputations or possessed with tranquil dispositions. But through their outstanding era of accomplishment, the Orioles prided themselves on the kind of individuals they had in uniforms. There was a certain degree of luck but also a definite design to the moves they made.

Their productive farm system kept turning out promising young prospects. Brooks Robinson, John ("Boog") Powell, Dave McNally, Jim Palmer, Andy Etchebarren, Mark Belanger, Bobby Grich, Jerry Adair, Dave Johnson, Don Baylor, and Al Bumbry, among others. They could play.

And what they weren't able to produce individually or collectively, they traded for in the baseball marketplace. The additions complemented what they had and, in one celebrated instance, the deal for Frank Robinson, transformed them from a young, challenging team that was right around the "pennant plate" to one that had a seat at the World Series banquet—not once but four times in the six years Frank was an Oriole.

The man with F. Robinson in block letters on his back came

to Baltimore and meant the difference. No longer a title threat but a championship actuality. The move to obtain Robinson was finalized in December of 1965. During his first season with the Orioles, they immediately won the AL pennant and then wiped out the Dodgers four straight games in the World Series. Robinson was the catalyst. He made it happen.

"He showed us how to win and that we could win," said the other Robinson, first name Brooks, six years later on the day when the Orioles decided they had to make room at the top for young talent that had been retained in a holding pattern with their Rochester Red Wings farm club in the International League. Frank Robinson was then 36 years of age, earning $135,000, and the Orioles felt they were making the proper disposition of a valuable and venerable hitting machine when they sent him to the Dodgers, located in Los Angeles. The Orioles received young chance prospects in return for Robinson, including Doyle Alexander, Bob O'Brien, Royle Stillman, and Sergio Robles. Comparing them to Frank Robinson would be like trying to associate Arthur Rubinstein with Knuckles O'Toole.

The contributions of Robinson cannot be overemphasized. It's difficult to argue with the record book, plus the awareness of the intangibles he brought with him. Frank's first season with the Orioles was immensely productive. When the hit was needed to start a rally or get a run across, it was invariably Robinson making the contribution. That "rookie" season with the Orioles, after ten previous ones with the Cincinnati Reds, meant much to the maturity of Frank Robinson. He earned a true feeling of appreciation from management, his teammates, and the general public. It gave him an absolute awareness that his special talents were finally being recognized and respected.

The day the trade for Robinson was made, Gene Woodling, then a coach for the Orioles, said, "If we don't win the pennant this year with him, then we all ought to be fired. He'll be the best hitter the Orioles ever had."

What prophetic words! The Orioles had a "bat" in their lineup like they never knew before and also one that by its presence added strength to the others that were there. It meant the opposition couldn't afford to make a mistake with either one of the Robinsons or Powell. Consequently, the fear of having to face Robinson, the dangerous threat he represented, added to the psychological as well as physical intimidation of a rival pitcher.

Robinson helped the Orioles to the pennant in 1966 by nine

games and then, decided 8-to-5 underdogs in the Series against the Dodgers, pulled a Don Drysdale pitch into the left field seats in the first inning. Behind that home run came another one by the "other Robinson," and the Orioles were off and winging to a four-game sweep of the Dodgers. Frank was showing them the way. It became a Robinson & Robinson Production.

Earlier in the year, on a Sunday afternoon against the Indians and Luis Tiant, Robinson hit the only ball that was ever driven out of Baltimore Memorial Stadium. It carried over the bleachers in left field, landed on the parking lot, and rolled to a stop under a car, a distance of 540 feet.

"That's still my biggest individual thrill in baseball," says Frank. "The fans wouldn't stop hollering and, honestly, I didn't know the ball had gone that far until I got back to the dugout. Then, out in the outfield, to start the next inning, the applause continued, and then I became more aware of what I had done."

Robinson became probably the most accomplished right-handed hitter in the AL since Joe DiMaggio. And, oddly enough, both of them came from opposite sides of San Francisco Bay, DiMaggio from the North Beach section of the city and Robinson from Oakland. Both of them, when they entered the batter's box, created a case of natural sympathy for the man throwing the ball because of the way they hit with such damaging authority.

The Orioles would have probably won another pennant in 1967, except that Frank Robinson took out Al Weis of the White Sox from making a double play and, at the same instant of contact, removed himself from the active list in mid-season with a concussion and eye injury. Frank ran the bases with deft skill and an incredible sense of timing that never seemed to find him getting thrown out when he made the decision to try to get there.

That injury to Robinson resulted in the Orioles going down the drain. They missed his hitting production and also his leadership. It was a case of the Orioles of 1967 being like the Orioles of pre-Robinson days, when they had good young material at the developing stage but lacking the full resources to assert themselves as winners.

But then came other years and resulting success. Robinson wasn't a "one man" team, but he was the "one man" who made a team. He became the only player in the history of baseball to win the MVP award in the two major leagues, the NL in 1961 and the AL in 1966.

Robinson, by nature, is competitive. He resented it like no

insult he ever heard when Bill DeWitt, president of the Reds, said the main reason he traded him to the Orioles was "because he was an old 30." That comment made Frank bristle. It was almost the same reaction in 1956, his first year with the Reds, when Jackie Robinson was quoted as saying he wanted a longer look at Frank before deciding what kind of a player he was going to be.

And, again, characteristic of his makeup was the realization among the opposition that the worst thing that could happen to them was to "knock Robby down" with one of those things the late Branch Rickey always called a "purpose pitch." Getting up from the dirt, after some pitcher had tried to spin his cap, triggered a boiling reaction in Robinson that made it even more difficult to get him out.

The deal to get Robinson from the Reds found the Orioles giving up Pitcher Milt Pappas, who had been a bonus boy signed in 1957 and acted like one; Pitcher Jack Baldschun, and Outfielder Dick Simpson. The deal was a complete disaster for Cincinnati. Pappas had some physical problems, Baldschun and Simpson never produced, and by June 1 the Reds realized, throughout their organization, that letting Frank Robinson go had been a serious blunder. Meanwhile, in Baltimore, the deal brought instant success.

Preceding the transaction that led to the Orioles acquiring Robinson was a combination of unusual circumstances. It was probably the only time two general managers, outgoing and incoming, for one club, the Orioles, worked to consummate the same deal. Lee MacPhail, now president of the AL, was the general manager when the Baltimore franchise was sold by a group headed by Joseph Iglehart to one directed by Jerry Hoffberger. This brought about a change in command. MacPhail was about to take interim position in the office of Commissioner William D. Eckert where he no doubt spent much time explaining the ABC's of baseball to the highest leader in the game.

MacPhail and scouts Frank Lane and Jim Russo recommended that the Cincinnati transaction be made. But MacPhail, a man of fairness and integrity, didn't want to lock in the Orioles on a deal his successor wouldn't want to make. Harry Dalton, the former farm director who was given the title of director of personnel, was told by Frank Cashen, the new executive vice-president, that the trade was there for him to decide. All he had to do was say "yes" or "no."

Dalton answered in the affirmative. It became what is known in the business as a "steal of a deal." Pappas, after posting years of 12–11 and 16–13 in Cincinnati, moved on to the Braves and, ultimately, to the Cubs. He regained some of his former effectiveness and won a total of 99 games in the NL, including a no-hitter against the Padres. Without having Pappas to trade, the Orioles wouldn't have been able to get Robinson. So, in effect, having him available made all those ultimate pennant conquests possible in Baltimore.

Odd, but Curt Blefary, another player talked about originally in the Reds' deal, was retained by the Orioles long enough to make another momentous trade. That came two years later. Again, at the recommendation of Russo, the Orioles reached out and got Mike Cuellar of the Astros. They gave up Blefary and John Mason for Cuellar, Elijah Johnson, and Enzo Hernandez. It was Dalton's desire, when possible, to try to get a "throw-in" minor leaguer, who maybe had a longshot chance to develop. That time he got Hernandez to come along with Cuellar. Blefary was the bait the Astros went for, but he had only a mediocre performance while Cuellar became an outstanding pitcher for the Orioles, winning 20 or more games in four different campaigns and had 18 wins in two other years.

Then, after another two-year wait, the Orioles needed right-handed pitching help and went knocking on the door of the Padres, who wanted a shortstop. The Orioles had an extra one available. The man who made it possible was the same Hernandez, who had been the "stray" Dalton picked up when he got Cuellar from Houston. The Orioles were, thus, able to use Hernandez to swing the deal for Pat Dobson, who, wouldn't you know, also instantly became a 20-game winner in Baltimore.

The deal was made that time by Cashen, who had succeeded Dalton, when the latter decided to trade himself to the Angels after the World Series of 1971. Dalton left because the direction of the entire Orioles' operation hadn't been given to him. So when the Angels made an offer, he was receptive and suddenly said he had always wanted to live in southern California.

Dalton left and Cashen took over in a transition that was smooth and also effective. Instead of Dalton, Cashen, and Russo putting their heads together on trade possibilities, it became Cashen and Russo. A move to get some right-handed power for the Orioles bombed out when, in retrospect, the club made one of its worst deals ever for Earl Williams of the Braves, giving up Dobson, Roric Harrison, John Oates, and Dave Johnson, who was to hit more home runs—43 in 1973—than any second baseman since Doubleday invented the game.

Two years later, the Orioles handed Williams, who had cost them four players, back to Atlanta for a minor league pitcher named Jim Freeman. They still had an infielder in their farm system, Taylor Duncan, who came in the first Williams swap. The club had little to show for all that maneuvering.

Any time you're evaluating and then trading human beings, there's the chance for looking good or bad, as the performances turn out to be. Every organization has deals it doesn't mind talking or bragging about, but it also has those it would like to eradicate. No doubt, the most shocking deal that ever took place with the Orioles also set a record for numbers. It happened soon after the daring and ingenious Paul Richards came to Baltimore in 1955 as manager and general manager.

What the Orioles had on the field was hardly a reasonable facsimile of a major league team. After all, they were, in the main, the leftovers from the St. Louis Browns who had been transferred to Baltimore only the season before. With no surprise, they had finished in seventh place in an eight-team league brought on by the fact that they lost 100 games and were 57 games behind the first place Indians.

Richards claimed the Orioles needed to look more representative. So he took the team's two hardest-throwing right-handed pitchers, Bob Turley and Don Larsen, and Shortstop Billy Hunter, along with five others, and put them in a package to the Yankees where he got nine—a whole team—in return. Seventeen traded uniforms and addresses.

Maybe the blockbuster deal allowed the Orioles to put more bona fide performers on the field, but it also enabled the Yankees to continue to dominate the AL. Turley became a 20-game winner and, along with Larsen, helped New York to four straight pennants. Larsen produced an unprecedented perfect game in the 1956 World Series. So Baltimore, or rather Richards, had the dubious distinction of trading away a man who was destined for baseball immortality.

The players Richards received from the Yankees, where they had either given their best years of service or else were surplus merchandise, included Gene Woodling, Gus Triandos, Harry Byrd,

Jim McDonald, Bill Miller, Hal Smith, Don Leppert, Kal Segrist, and Willie Miranda.

Odd, but Richards could have saved himself the Larsen embarrassment if he had given the Yankees a veteran right-hander, Joe Coleman, who had been the Orioles' second leading pitcher in 1954. But Richards figured Larsen, who had been 3 and 21, liked the bright lights too much to ever become an imposing figure on a mound, with or without a full windup. The Yankees, according to Richards, would gladly have accepted Coleman over Larsen. That would have been a mistake, from a New York standpoint, because Coleman was near the end of his career. In fact, he never won another game for the Orioles and only two more after he went to the Tigers.

In other ways, over the years, the Orioles are given plus grades in trades for Luis Aparicio, Bob Nieman, Jack Brandt, Hal ("Skinny") Brown, Grant Jackson, Ross Grimsley, Stu Miller, Pete Richert, Don Buford, Lee May, Mike Torrez, and Ken Singleton. They gave up far less for what they obtained in return.

If there was any way to send a general manager to jail for putting over what could be considered "grand larceny," it would be applicable in the Orioles' 1974 deal with the Expos. They gave up Pitcher Bill Kirkpatrick, who didn't report; Pitcher Dave McNally, who retired in early June because he "didn't have it anymore" and refused to accept a salary under false pretenses; and Outfielder Rich Coggins, who was dealt to the Yankees in mid-season.

The two Montreal "rejects," meanwhile, produced powerful credentials in Baltimore. Torrez was only one of five pitchers in the AL who won 20 or more games. He was 20–9, with a 3.06 ERA. Singleton, a switch-hitter, stroked 15 HRs and had an average of .300. So for three players who came through with a minus-pool in Montreal, the Orioles got Torrez and Singleton, two outstanding contributors to the cause.

This became another in a long line of exceptional Baltimore trades. Cashen can take a much deserved bow. Likewise for the May acquisition. He slugged 20 HRs, drove in 99 RBIs, and batted .262. To get May they gave up Enos Cabell, who had only 2 HRs and an average of .264, and Rob Andrews, who didn't hit any more home runs than he was expected to do, which was zero, and batted .238.

So, if the Orioles never make another good trade, they are far ahead of the game in this and other trips to the marketplace. They also benefited handsomely from the draft, picking up such valuable additions as Paul Blair, Myron ("Moe") Drabowsky, Curt Motton, Jim Hardin, Dave May, Gene Brabender, Elrod Hendricks, Chuck Diering, and Bob Boyd. In straight cash deals they came out way ahead with the acquisitions of Jim Gentile, Hal ("Skinny") Brown, George Zuverink, Tommy Davis, and Hoyt Wilhelm. Additionally, they picked up two winning pitchers as free agents in Robin Roberts and Dick Hall, both discarded by the Phillies.

As for talent they possibly let get away through errors of judgment, the Orioles have a remarkable record for minimizing mistakes. They lost Dean Chance and Charley Hinton in expansion drafts and missed retaining Ryne Duren and Dave May via trades.

But it is of considerable importance that in twenty-one years the minor league operation of the Orioles lost only two players, Chuck Cottier and Fred ("Wingy") Whitfield, who ultimately made the majors. Cottier gained his freedom after he changed his home address and his contract was not delivered on time, thus making him an automatic free agent. Whitfield was released in the minor league camp at Thomasville, Georgia, when scouts, manager, and farm department officials became convinced he would never be able to throw good enough to be considered a big league prospect. He fooled them, made the grade, and stayed nine years in the majors as a first baseman.

No discourse or essay pertinent to Baltimore's baseball swap shop would be complete without mentioning what unfortunately happened to them before they even got to play one game in the AL. General Manager Arthur Ehlers, highly qualified and conscientious, read a medical report from the late Dr. George Bennett, who had examined the shoulder of Roy Sievers after he had injured it while playing for the St. Louis Browns. There were, though, two papers Dr. Bennett had written. The first was pessimistic about Sievers's ability to ever throw well enough to play the outfield. But a second examination changed the famed surgeon's opinion somewhat, and he wrote the Browns accordingly.

However, the report Ehlers read, in the compilation of old Browns' correspondence, was the earlier one, and he figured it best to get rid of Sievers because his future was suspect. When the Washington Senators in 1954 offered Gil Coan, he made the move. Coan played only one year in Baltimore, but Sievers, despite a damaged arm, became a standout with the Senators, much to the chagrin of the Orioles. He led the AL with 42 HRs in 1957, became a hero in D.C., and in fact, played twelve years in the majors after the Orioles gave up.

Those early years of the Orioles' existence found them moving players around like the club was a subsidiary of a railroad or an airline. They changed faces continually. They were a "down" team, remember, with not much to look forward to in a then barren farm system, and little talent at the top. It wasn't until Richards had spent literally millions of dollars in signing young bonus players that the Orioles started to see some progress. They acquired such players as Milt Pappas; the late Tom Gastall, who died in an airplane crash; Jim Pyburn, now an assistant football coach at Georgia; Angelo Lagres, Ron Hansen, Steve Dalkowski, Jack Fisher, Dean Chance, Frank Zupo, Bob Saverine, Bruce Swango, Ralph Lairmore, Arnold Thorsland, Bob Nelson, whom Richards's creative mind touted as the "Babe Ruth of Texas"; Chuck Estrada, John Papa, Jerry Adair, Brooks Robinson, Andy Etchebarren, Larry Haney, and hundreds of others.

It was an expensive way, but it paid off. They ultimately had the perfect mix . . . trades and draft claims to go along with good scouts and a farm system that helped structure them from a poor, dog-eared outfit to one that gained universal respectability.

The Frank Robinson acquisition was momentous and meaningful. They didn't get just a right-handed hitting outfielder. They got a man who showed them how to win by dint of his own performance, who drove himself hard and demonstrated by example, not self-proclaiming orations, that the Orioles could and would win. The Baltimore Orioles didn't become a dynasty per se, but they were either a champion or a challenger for ten years after Robinson arrived, which admittedly is sustaining success for longer than the cycle of pennant perpetuity ever intended.

DICK YOUNG
Sports Editor/Columnist, *New York Daily News*

Dick Young wears two hats for the *New York Daily News:* One as sports editor, and another as sports columnist. Dick has no trouble remembering the date of his debut as a major league baseball writer because it was the Dodgers' opening day in 1946. What followed before the Dodgers moved to Los Angeles after the 1957 season Dick describes as the "twelve greatest years of my life." When the Mets were born in 1962, Young was atop the bandwagon to help popularize the fledgling team, stressing the bizarre incidents along with the ineptitude afield. Young thinks and writes as a baseball fan, making himself a favorite with both the box seat holder and the bleacher buff.

10/THE DODGERS

All-worst team saved by tandems and farm clubs

The Brooklyn Dodgers of the 1930s were the clowns of their day. For those not old enough to remember them, maybe you'll recognize them with a comparison to the Pirates of 1952, called by many the worst team in NL history, or to the team that rivaled them for "all-time worst" honors, the 1962 Mets.

There was one similarity between those Dodgers' team and the Mets—Casey Stengel. Casey managed the Dodgers for three years in the 1930s and then was paid not to manage. His replacement, Burleigh Grimes, could not do better. But during Grimes's tenure as manager, the Dodgers obtained Leo Durocher in a trade with the Cardinals; and while they badly needed a shortstop, Leo had other ideas. "I'm here to take your job," he told Grimes. He did. Durocher joined forces in Brooklyn with volatile Larry MacPhail, who had introduced night baseball while general manager in Cincinnati in 1935 and moved to head the Brooklyn front office in 1938. MacPhail's work was cut out for him. Besides being the laughing stock of the entire league, the Dodgers weren't even the best team in their own area. The semipro Bushwicks' team would often outdraw their major league rivals.

The tandem went right to work and the team rose to third place in 1939, Leo's first managerial season, and to second place in 1940. By 1941 all the pieces of the puzzle had fallen into place, and Brooklyn won its first pennant since 1920. Amazingly, the entire starting unit plus the frontline pitchers had all come from outside the organization after MacPhail took over.

Let's take a look at the deals that brought the pennant to Brooklyn.

A few of the key operatives were there before the new regime took over. Third Baseman Harry ("Cookie") Lavagetto came with another player from the Pirates in December 1936 in a trade for Ed Brandt. Cookie batted .277 with 78 RBIs in the pennant-winning season, but will always be best remembered for a double hit six seasons later. It was the third game of the 1947 World Series between the Dodgers and their archrivals, the Yankees. Bill Bevens was one out away from the first no-hitter in World Series history when Cookie slammed a ball off the right-field wall at Ebbetts Field to score two runs and give the Dodgers a 3–2 victory. Ironically, it was the last big league game for Bevens. The New York Giants also gave a big assist to their rivals in a June 1937 trade which sent Pitcher Fred Fitzsimmons to Brooklyn for Tom Baker, a hotshot prospect. Baker turned out to be nothing more than a prospect while Fitzsimmons was 16–2 in 1940 and 6–1 the following year.

Durocher had come after the 1937 season for four players and had been the club's shortstop until a youngster was purchased from the Red Sox' Louisville farm. Harold ("Pee Wee") Reese, a former boys' marble champion, was the heir apparent to Joe Cronin as the Red Sox shortstop. Cronin viewed Reese as a threat to his job. Because of Joe's vanity, the Dodgers were able to obtain the youngster from Louisville, and he went on to remain one of the game's top shortstops for almost 20 seasons.

Another lucky break came when Commissioner Kenesaw Landis declared many Cardinal farmhands free agents after the 1938 season because of illegal actions by the St. Louis club in hiding top prospects. Thus the Dodgers' organization was in a position to sign Pete Reiser, who might have gone down in history as one of the greatest players of all time had it not been for his frequent injuries, most of which were incurred while running into unpadded outfield walls. In the pennant-winning season of 1941, Pete led the NL in batting with .343, runs with 117, 39 doubles, and 17 triples.

Pete, who played center field, was flanked by Dixie Walker in right and Joe Medwick in left. Walker had come up through the Yankee organization while Babe Ruth was still in right field. Dixie had trouble breaking into a veteran outfield that was later augmented by an outstanding rookie from San Francisco named Joe DiMaggio. Dixie drifted to the White Sox and Tigers, hitting over .300 in each place, before undergoing shoulder surgery. Yet, Ted McGrew, one of MacPhail's top scouts, suggested that the Dodgers claim him when he was put on waivers, and the results might have been even better than the Dodgers anticipated. In eight seasons with Brooklyn, Dixie hit .300 or better, in seven seasons and the year that he didn't, he batted .290. In 1941, he hit .311. Besides his accomplishments on the field, he was extremely popular with the fans, earning the nickname of "The Peepul's Cherce."

Rounding out the outfield in 1941 was Joe Medwick, a pal of Durocher's from the Cardinals and a bona fide .300 hitter. In addition to Medwick, the Dodgers also obtained veteran right-hander Curt Davis in the deal which sent four players and $100,000 to St. Louis. Joe hit .318 with 18 HRs and 88 RBIs during 1941, while the throw-in, Davis, was 13–7. The first baseman that year was Dolph Camilli, who came in a deal with the Phillies in March 1938 for Edwin Morgan. The NL's MVP in 1941, the smooth-swinging San Franciscan hit .285 with 34 HRs and 120 RBIs.

The pitching staff was headed by Kirby Higbe and Whitlow Wyatt, both obtained from other organizations. Wyatt, a former sore-armed hurler in the AL, was purchased from Milwaukee of the American Association and at age 32 responded with a 22–10 record. Higbe, obtained in November 1940 from the Phillies for three players and $100,000, tied Wyatt for the league lead in victories with a 22–9 mark. The veteran moundsmen had some help behind the plate from an experienced hand. In the winter of 1940, Mac-Phail went back to the Cardinals and acquired Mickey Owen for two players and $65,000. Still, there was one noticeable hole even after the 1941 season began—second base. In May, MacPhail filled the void by dealing Outfielder Charles Gilbert and Infielder Johnny Hudson to the Cubs for Billy Herman, a new Hall of Famer and ranked as one of the finest second basemen in history. Besides his .285 average and 163 hits, Billy proved to be a big help to his young inexperienced double play partner, Reese.

MacPhail's trades resulted in 100 victories and an NL pennant. But even his genius on the trade market could not bring a World Series title to Ebbetts Field, something that would still be fourteen years away. MacPhail left the Dodgers to join the service during World War II, and he surfaced again as the Yankees' general manager. Meanwhile, his replacement at Brooklyn was Branch Rickey, who came from a similar position with the Cardinals.

The war years saw little trading activity, with the key acquisition being Second Baseman Eddie Stanky from the Cubs for Pitcher Bob Chipman in June 1944. But Rickey moved into full swing after the war. Outside the trade front, he signed Jackie Robinson as pro baseball's first black player in 1946.

Baseball people always insist that a victory at the beginning of the season counts as much as one in the closing weeks. Although the pressure builds up late in the year with a tight pennant race, there's no denying that a win is a win no matter when you get it.

When the Dodgers look back on the 1946 season which saw them finish in the first tie in NL history, they can point to a seemingly insignificant sale to the Giants. Outfielder Goody Rosen was purchased by the Dodgers' crosstown rival on April 27, 1946. The next day the former Dodger contributed to a twin defeat of his ex-team with five hits in a doubleheader: three singles and an RBI in the Giants' 7–3 win in the opening game and a single and 3-run homer in the 10–4 triumph in the nightcap.

Rosen had batted .325 for the Dodgers in the war year of 1945 but lost out when the Brooklyn management decided to go with some outfielders who had returned from the service. The 1946 season was Rosen's last in the major leagues, but the damage he did in one Sunday doubleheader remained for a long time. Brooklyn and St. Louis finished the year with identical 96–58 records, but the Cardinals won two straight in the playoff and then went on to defeat the Red Sox in the World Series. Of course, if Rosen had been sold two days later, the Dodgers might have been in the World Series.

Rickey, who lived by the trading philosophy that it was better to trade a player a year too early than a year too late, unloaded some veterans in May 1947, when Higbe along with Pitchers Hank Behrman and Cal McLish, Catcher Dixie Howell, and Infielder Gene Mauch went to Pittsburgh for seldom-used outfielder, Al Gionfriddo, and an estimated $300,000. At 5–6 Gionfriddo was primarily a defensive specialist and the joke was that Al came to carry the money. Perhaps that was partially true since Rickey owned 25 percent of the team and most of his deals involved money. Nevertheless, the nation became fully aware of the little outfielder's defensive prowess when Gionfriddo robbed Joe DiMaggio of a three-run homer to save the sixth game of the 1947 World Series. But again, the Yankees prevailed in game seven, and the cry of "Wait 'Til Next Year" was echoed throughout Flatbush.

Jackie Robinson's performance as NL Rookie-of-the-Year in 1947, plus the emergence of black Catcher Roy Campanella in the farm system, led to many moves before the 1948 season. Gil Hodges, a muscular right-handed hitter from Princeton, Indiana, had been groomed as the Dodgers' catcher but was shifted to first base because of Campanella. Robinson, who had played first, was then moved to second, and Stanky was dealt to the Braves for Bama Rowell, who never played for the Dodgers.

Walker, a southerner, had vocally objected to Rickey's use of blacks, and though there was no visible conflict between Jackie and Dixie in 1947, Rickey made sure there would be no trouble in the future. After the 1947 season, he dispatched Walker to Pittsburgh with Pitchers Vic Lombardi and Hal Gregg for Pitcher Preacher Roe and Third Baseman Billy Cox—one of Rickey's greatest deals. Cox rounded out an infield with Reese, Robinson, and Hodges which was the NL's best through the mid-fifties. Roe, a southpaw who threw (and got away with) a spitter, combined with Don Newcombe to head the pitching staff. Roe's best season was the ill-fated year of 1951 when he posted a 22–3 record only to see the Dodgers blow a 13½ game lead to the Giants and then lose in a best-of-three playoff on Bobby Thompson's home run off Ralph Branca. In seven seasons with the Dodgers, Roe was 93–37.

During the 1951 season, with Buzzie Bavasi as general manager after Rickey had moved on to Pittsburgh, the Dodgers and Cubs got together in an eight-player deal on the trading deadline. It sent Outfielder Andy Pafko, Pitcher Johnny Schmitz, Infielder Wayne Terwilliger, and Catcher Rube Walker to Brooklyn for Outfielder Gene Hermanski, Pitcher Joe Hatten, Infielder Eddie Miksis, and Catcher Bruce Edwards. Pafko was the key man with the Dodgers needing a left-fielder to round out the outfield of Duke Snider in center and Carl Furillo in right. Andy hit 30 HRs with 93 RBIs in 1951 and also played a key role in the Dodgers' 1952 pennant. As well as the Dodgers made out with that trade, it could have been even better. "This trade could have been made several days ago," said Bavasi when announcing the deal, "but I didn't want that little fat catcher." So Bavasi had turned down Smoky Burgess, who will never go down in history as an outstanding catcher, but who was one of the finest pinch-hitters in baseball history, playing through 1967.

The major acquisition in 1953 was right-hander Russ Meyer, who came from the Phillies in a four-way deal which saw the Dodgers surrender Infielder Rocky Bridges and Outfielder Jim Pendelton. Meyer posted a 15–5 mark that year as the Dodgers won their second straight pennant and third in five years.

Miksis and Bridges were just two of many shortstops who were unable to break into the Brooklyn lineup due to the presence of one man—Pee Wee Reese. Cronin, who viewed the shortstop as a threat to his position with the Red Sox, did not realize at that time how many players would fail to make the grade in Brooklyn because of the same player. From 1941 to 1956, except for four years during World War II, The Captain, as he was affectionately known, played in 140 or more games in a 154-game season. There was little playing time for anyone else at that position.

The Dodgers' scouting system and minor league clubs were the envy of almost every other baseball organization, and when the Dodgers made players available, they had a ready market. During the Reese years, they placed shortstops with several other teams. Bob Ramazzotti was probably the first to go, but not to the team or in the manner that the Dodgers wanted. Cincinnati had a left-handed pitcher named Ken Raffensberger, who had always given them trouble. The southpaw would have rounded out a four-man starting rotation which always seemed to need that one extra starter. Rickey and Warren Giles, then general manager of the Reds, agreed on the deal of Ramazzotti for Raffensberger, but the Dodgers got greedy. Rickey, with his vast scouting system, probably knew the Cincinnati players better than Giles and asked for a minor leaguer as a throw-in. Giles nixed the deal at that point. Ramazzotti ended up with the Cubs for Infielder Hank Schenz, who never played for the Brooklyn Dodgers. The key to the deal for Brooklyn was $25,000.

The second shortstop to leave the Dodgers' organization was Chico Carrasquel, a smooth-fielding Venezuelan, who was literally pilfered by the White Sox before the 1949 World Series. Chico starred for the White Sox for six years. Another shortstop from the Dodgers' organization who wound up in the AL was Billy Hunter, traded by Brooklyn to the St. Louis Browns (remember them?) for three fringe players and $90,000 in October 1952. Two other shortstop candidates ended up with the Phillies in deals less than three years apart. The first was Bobby Morgan, a utility infielder for three years with Brooklyn, before going to Philadelphia in March

---

"BIG POISON" IS REAL POISON

Paul ("Big Poison") Waner, a member of the 3,000 Hit Club, was given his unconditional release five times: twice by the Dodgers, and once by the Pirates, the Braves, and the Yankees.

1954 for Second Baseman Dick Young, another one who never played at Ebbetts Field, and the always present cash: this time $50,000.

When Morgan failed to fill the position, the Phillies went back to the Dodgers for a highly touted Cuban, Chico Fernandez, in an April 1957 deal for Pitcher Ron Negray, First Baseman Tim Harkness, and veteran Outfielder Elmer Valo. Fernandez spent two good seasons in Philadelphia, but he had his finest major league year after being traded to Detroit, where he hit 20 HRs in 1962.

Following form, when Shortstop Reese did retire after the Dodgers moved to Los Angeles, they went to their farm club at Spokane, Washington, in 1959 for Maury Wills. He had just become a switch-hitter under Bobby Bragan's tutelage. And Wills wouldn't have been there if the Tigers, who had purchased him conditionally, hadn't returned him after a spring training trial.

There was no stronger rivalry in baseball than that of the Brooklyn Dodgers and New York Giants, and that rivalry became even stronger when the Dodgers faced Giant right-hander Sal Maglie. So it was somewhat ironical that Maglie came to the Dodgers in May 1956, after going from the Giants to Cleveland the previous year. Sal's contributions to the 1956 pennant were 13–5 mark including a no-hitter. Then he completed the tour of New York's three major league teams when he was sold to the Yankees in September 1957.

The Dodgers left Brooklyn for Los Angeles after the 1957 season and a year later made a swap of outfielders with the Cardinals which drew little attention when completed. It sent right-handed, hitting Outfielder Gino Cimoli to St. Louis for southpaw-swinging Wally Moon. The Dodgers were playing in the Los Angeles Coliseum at this time since the Dodger Stadium had not been completed, and the left-field fence was only 250 feet away. It seemed to be ideal for a right-handed batter, but Moon had other ideas. He developed an inside-out swing and continued to rattle balls off the high, but short, left-field fence so that they were named "Moon Shots." That year Moon hit .302 with 26 doubles, a league-leading 11 triples, 19 HRs and 74 RBIs as the Dodgers won their first pennant on the West Coast.

Sandy Koufax and Don Drysdale will forever be remembered as the Dodgers' Win Twins, the best of the modern lefty-righty tandems. Both settled for just one-team careers, and a popgun was louder than the fanfare heralding their arrival on the big league scene. The Dodgers signed Koufax out of the University of Cincinnati, where he was going to school on a basketball scholarship. Drysdale, meanwhile, pitched 43 games in the farm system at Bakersfield, California, and in Montreal when the bit pitcher was judged ready for the bigs.

Koufax, already enshrined in the Hall of Fame, literally blazed his way to 165 victories while losing only 87. Four of Sandy's victories were no-hit, no-run games—one a perfect performance against the Cubs to climax a 1–0 conquest. During his first three seasons, Koufax was a loser, nine victories to offset ten losses before he reached double digits in the won-and-lost column. At the finish, after four World Series, Mr. K. had 2,396 strikeouts, pitching 2,325 innings. He reached the zenith of his stardom in 1963, winning 25 games and losing five. For this Sandy won the NL's MVP award and the first of three Cy Young awards—the majors' foremost honor for pitchers.

Drysdale was the winner of 209 of 376 NL decisions. In posting a career total of 2,486 strikeouts, Double D established double major league records, pitching six consecutive shutouts, and 58 scoreless innings in a row. A native of Van Nuys, California, Drysdale made the Cy Young Award in 1962 when he won 25 games and lost nine.

At one stage of their careers the two pitchers scored a first you won't find in the record books. They were an entry as holdouts seeking salary increases from the Dodgers—and they won that showdown too! How could they fail with 374 victories and 4,882 strikeouts between them?

After Al Campanis succeeded Bavasi as general manager in 1969, Richie Allen and Frank Robinson were acquired in trades. Allen came from the Cardinals after the 1970 season for Infielder Ted Sizemore and Catcher Bob Stinson. After playing one year with Los Angeles, Allen was dealt to the White Sox for Tommy John. On the same date the Dodgers acquired Robinson from Baltimore in a six-player deal. Like Allen, Robinson played only one season for the Dodgers—going to the Angels in a seven-player deal in December 1972. This is how the Dodgers obtained Andy Messersmith.

But with all the deals, the Dodgers were without a pennant from 1966 as they went to the winter baseball meetings in 1973. They made two bold moves which resulted in the long-awaited flag. First, Outfielder Willie Davis went to Montreal for relief specialist

Mike Marshall. Then Claude Osteen was traded to Houston for Jimmy Wynn, who would become Davis's replacement in center field. Marshall set every relief record with a 15–12 record, 21 saves in a record-shattering 106 appearances. Wynn slammed 32 HRs and had 108 RBIs.

The rivalry between the Giants and Dodgers, with Durocher later switching to manage the Giants while they were both in New York, was unsurpassed in sports history. Few people remember that Jackie Robinson was traded to the Giants. He was dealt after the 1956 season for much-traveled Relief Pitcher Dick Littlefield, but refused to report and retired from baseball. Had he not, it would have renewed one of the strongest pitcher-batter rivalries in baseball: Sal Maglie vs Jackie Robinson. Only this time Maglie would have been the Dodger and Robinson the Giant. That might have been more than even the NL fans in New York could anticipate.

When Walter O'Malley and his associates took control of the Dodgers in 1950, some new type of trading was inserted into the operation. It was O'Malley's philosophy that managerial contracts be limited to season-to-season renewal. This remained the big Irishman's philosophy after Chuck Dressen, who led the Dodgers to back-to-back NL pennants in 1952 and 1953, asked for a new two-year contract. O'Malley stood firm when Dressen said it was: "Two or nothing." In effect the Dodgers traded Dressen for the longest string of one-year contracts since the two M's: John McGraw and Connie Mack. The person who benefited the most from O'Malley's philosophy was Walter Alston, the big man from little Darrtown, Ohio.

When Alston signed his 1976 contract, it was his Number Twenty-Three single-season pact. During this time the Dodgers have won seven pennants and four World Series. In the pennant parade, Alston is marching in outstanding company: Casey Stengel, 10; Joe McCarthy, John McGraw, and Connie Mack, 9. When the astute Ohioan retires, he's assured one big laugh when he thinks back to his original signing on a wintry postseason day in 1953. Then a Brooklyn newspaper headlined his signing to manage the Dodgers in this manner:

WALTER WHO (?) NEW DODGER SKIPPER.

Excellent staying power for a man who had just one time at bat in the major leagues. Then he struck out, but he hasn't since that uneventful day.

MOE SIEGEL
Sportswriter, *Washington Star*

Moe Siegel, a Rhodes Scholar in the delivery of the spoken or written word, took a single course in journalism at Emory University—and flunked it! Never one to stand still, Moe switched to political science and passed easily. A nationally famous raconteur, Siegel refers to himself as "a little boy from Fulton County in Georgia who attended an outstanding Methodist university." In his climb up the journalist ladder, the colorful Word Wizard did stints with the *Atlanta Constitution* and the Richmond (Virginia) *Times-Dispatch* before joining the *Washington Star.* Moe started covering the Washington Senators in 1947, and continued, as he says: "until the club left town in 1971." Opinions in the Siegel Manner are frequently heard on Washington radio-TV sports programs.

11/THE SENATORS/RANGERS

Denny McLain—Bob Short: airborne trade story

The impact of Bob Short's three-year stewardship of the Washington Senators was so great he will not go unremembered in the federal city's celebration of this year's Bicentennial. An empty RFK Stadium, once the scene of major league baseball, or a reasonable facsimile thereof, remains a tragic reminder of Short's ruinous administration.

Until Short shook up the AL's franchise lineup in 1972, Washington fans faithfully survived mediocrity far beyond the call of duty for seventy-one years, but they failed to overcome Short. It was a scandalous display of the stuff patriots are NOT made of. By making the most wretched deal in the city's honorable baseball history, he rewarded more than two million diehards who supported his team's paying the highest prices in baseball. Very coldly, he traded the nation's capital for a hunk of untested fandom on the Dallas-Fort Worth Turnpike, designated by postal authorities as Arlington, Texas.

It was, of course, his last big deal as operator of the late Senators. Ironically, his other big maneuver, bringing Denny McLain in from the Tigers in 1971 for the left half of Washington's infield and the team's best pitcher, eventually forced him to perpetrate the infamy which has left Washington an estranged baseball community.

Because of his fascination for "name" players, Short allowed the Tigers to talk him out of Shortstop Eddie Brinkman, still a sure-handed fielder, Third Baseman Aurelio Rodriguez, plus Pitchers Joe Coleman and Jim Hanna, the latter being usually reserved for the "player to be named later." For this the Senators received the fading McLain, whom the Tigers had been trying to unload, Third Baseman Don Wert, who failed to last out June as a Senator, Outfielder Ellie Maddox, now a Yankee, and Pitcher Norm McRae, of no known baseball address.

It wrecked the Senators, not only as a team, but as a fixture of Washington's summertime entertainment. They have been replaced by a vague promise from Commissioner Bowie Kuhn for the restoration of baseball, which becomes more remote, by the Watergate hearings, and by less frequent student and civil demonstrations. Had baseball not enjoyed a free ride from antitrust laws, Short might have been hauled up before the Federal Trade Commission (the agency which supervises suspect business practices) to explain about the trade which forced him to flee town.

"It wasn't the worst deal in baseball," protests Short in what now amounts to a moot defense of his tragedy. "The guy who sold Babe Ruth to the Yankees, his deal was worse than mine."

Again Short is wrong. The Red Sox, who sold the Bambino to the Yankees, are still in Boston. The Senators, masquerading as the Texas Rangers, are the vicarious love of Texans who don't have tickets to the Dallas Cowboys.

It was not the first time the nation's capital had been sold down the Potomac River for another market. Calvin Griffith, coholder with Short of the Judas Iscariot trophy for civic contributions to Washington, hauled his own Senators out of town to Minneapolis in 1960, but not before the AL ordered an expansion franchise to be named immediately to replace the defecting Griffith. Washington, with only three pennants (1924, 1925, 1933) in its history and only two first division finishes in its last twenty-six years, was not jolted when Griffith announced he was leaving town. When the people later learned he was taking the team with him, however, there was an understandable surge of outrage.

What drove Short to the disastrous McLain trade, the deal which subsequently led to the more disastrous swap of Washington for Texas, is totally academic at this point in time, but some of the explanations are interesting. Perhaps Short's abiding wife, Marion, shed the real light on what makes her peripatetic husband do the things he does. Of course, she was not consulted on the deal, but almost nothing Short does surprises her.

There was a time he was seriously thinking of running for lieutenant governor of Minnesota, a position entirely unbecoming to Short who rarely is caught in the role of a minority stockholder. I phoned Marion, just out of curiosity, to ask why Short, who had only recently resigned as treasurer of the Democratic Party might be interested in a spot so relatively trivial. Besides, wasn't he already busy enough owning a trucking line which grossed $40 million annually, a baseball team, and several Twin Cities hotels?

"It will give him something to do before breakfast," Mrs. Short answered.

Short is a restless devil, cunning, scheming, bright, and with an itch to take charge like I have seen in no other man. Baseball was a new game to him. He was such a novice that he referred to managers as "coaches" and stadiums were no more than "buildings." One thing stood out about Short, however, that his baseball peers were quick to learn. It didn't take him long to catch on, at least that's what he thought. Money also was no object to him, so long as it wasn't his he was spending. He was name conscious. It didn't matter whether the player he wanted was lame or over the hill. Short viewed the "name" as box office.

He didn't mind courting trouble either. He proved that in his second year at Texas when he surrounded himself with front office assistants such as Jimmy Piersall and Frank Lane. Rounding out the unholy alliance was that model of deportment, that shy, self-effacing little Lord Fauntleroyish manager he had yearned for, Billy Martin. This group was his "therapy" after four turbulent years with Ted Williams. Tapes of their meetings, Martin, Lane, Piersall, and Short all in the same room at the same time, would have made the Nixon Watergate tapes sound like a Billy Graham broadcast.

Burton Hawkins, a crackerjack baseball writer for the *Washington Star,* who defected to baseball with the expansion Senators of 1961, points the finger at Manager Ted Williams for the implausible McLain deal.

"Every time we'd lose a game," said Hawkins, the Ranger propaganda minister and road secretary, "Ted would want to trade everybody, anybody. God, how he pressured Short, get rid of this guy, dump that guy, sell him, do something.

"I remember once he gave up on Jeff Burroughs. He wanted to swap him for Roger Repoz. Ted saw Repoz hit a home run for the Angels once and that was enough to convince Williams. Thank God that was one time Short didn't listen to Ted."

Williams developed a sudden distaste for young Pitcher Coleman, scholarshipped to the tune of $75,000 by the Senators.

He wanted his team to be rid of Coleman who, ironically, learned baseball fundamentals from his dad, who pitched for the Philadelphia Athletics, and at Ted Williams's own baseball camp. Old school ties obviously meant nothing to Number Nine. When he turned on a player, he demanded no less than his head.

To be fair, Williams did not set up the Detroit trade involving McLain, but as long as it provided for the departure of the erratic Coleman, it pleased Ted almost as much as catching a bonefish. Short insists he did make every effort to clear his abortive Detroit trade with Williams that October day in 1970, but finding Williams an hour after the last out of the season's last game is a task worthy of Interpol. "He was hiding out, fishing or some damn thing in New Hampshire, God knows where," Short recalled.

For several days after the trade the world still hadn't heard Williams's reaction. Finally, it came, strong, biting, and contemptuous. Any other manager would have been canned on the spot, but Williams didn't give a damn for consequences. "Shitty, shitty as hell. And remember this. That was *his* trade, not mine, *his.*"

Later, in an uncharacteristic display of compassion, Williams softened his displeasure over what still stands as one of baseball's worst trades. "We didn't get enough," he amended his original denunciation. By "enough," it was later learned, Williams, who at first denied any complicity in the Great Hoax deal, insisted on the inclusion of Ike Brown in the deal. Why the Tigers refused to depart with Ike Brown, whom they subsequently permitted to join their alumni with no great sense of loss, remains a mystery this observer is grossly uninterested in probing.

The genesis of the ruinous McLain deal, which ultimately led to the loss of baseball for Washington, was the Washington Baseball Writers' Dinner in January of 1969, the start of Short's administration.

McLain, fresh off of a 31-game season for the Tigers, was a guest. The night before he was honored in Minneapolis by the Twin Cities' writers. He hitched a ride to Washington, along with Frank Howard, with Short on the latter's Lear jet.

"I'd love to play in Washington for an owner like you," McLain, whose repertoire included a private pilot's license, told Short, according to Short.

"I'd love to have you and I'll get you if the Tigers don't demand my whole team in the trade," Short promised in mid-air between Minneapolis and Washington. Unfortunately, it was no idle boast, as disastrous events later proved. It took Short two seasons to acquire McLain. Ironically, Short, almost as stubborn as Manager Williams, does not look back on the flimflam with regret. "If I had to do it over again," he says, "I would."

Somewhere, however, he begs for forgiveness: "It was a phony trade, on Detroit's part. They gave us a sore-armed pitcher. They didn't tell us he was physically a washout. Needed a pain-killing shot almost every day." Short, however, has a way of rationalizing his mistakes. "But I got even. I unloaded him on ("Charlie") Finley." What Short forgot was that the A's dumped him quickly, and even had they kept him, the A's had too much talent for even a McLain to mar their pennant chances.

Years ago, the Chattanooga Lookouts of the Southern Association once swapped a shortstop, Johnny Jones, to the Charlotte Hornets for a turkey, a real live gobbler. The deal was the brain-child of the late Joe Engel, who reasoned he got the best of it.

"I got a meal out of the turkey, that's more than I was getting for Jones," he explained. The McLain trade Short made ranks as a turkey also, but there is a difference. This particular bird was inedible.

I was an eyewitness, once removed, to the unique trade of two major league managers: Joe Gordon of the Indians for Jimmie Dykes of the Tigers in 1960. Frank Lane, then running the Indians, was given credit for a typical Lane stunt, but actually the motivator was Bill DeWitt, general manager of the Tigers. The Indians were in Washington at the time. I recall having a drink on a Saturday night with Bob Neal, the Cleveland broadcaster who tipped me to the story. He said it was his information it would happen the following Tuesday morning.

I checked with Nate Dolan, a major Cleveland stockholder. Dolan's denial was too insincere to be accepted and surely, just as Neal had said, the swap was made—only it came twenty-four hours earlier because of the premature announcement of mine.

Short had not blessed baseball with his presence at this time, but it was the kind of deal to warrant his stamp of approval. He was bold enough one time to propose a territorial swap with Jerry Hoffberger, the Orioles' board chairman. Having decided two clubs could not operate successfully in the Washington-Baltimore area, Short proposed a $1 million payment to Hoffberger if the Orioles would move. Refused, he upped it to $2 million, then $3 million. Rebuffed at every turn, Short then asked Hoffberger to make him the same proposition. Once again it was no dice. "He even voted against my moving to Texas," Short recalled.

If the Short deal for McLain did result in the eventual move of the Senators to Texas, he "rescued" the Rangers' franchise from what he believed to be certain death by another trade. He obtained Ferguson Jenkins from the Cubs in 1974. Jenkins, a consistent 20-game winner for the Cubs who dipped to 14 in 1973, chipped in with 25 wins as a rookie Ranger, enabling the Texans to chase Oakland to the wire for the AL West title and zooming attendance past the one million mark in 1974.

"He saved the franchise for us," said Short. Officially, the trade is listed as Vic Harris and Bill Madlock, but earlier Short had given the Cubs Rico Carty and Mike Paul with an understanding Jenkins would be his after the season. "My record in major trades stands at .500," Short boasts. "I blew the Senators' franchise with the McLain deal and saved Texas with Jenkins. Is that bad?"

JOHN ROBERTSON
Sports Columnist and Radio Broadcaster, *Montreal Star*

John Robertson led the Canadian cheers when Bucky Harris was enshrined in baseball's Hall of Fame in 1975. Harris was the manager of the Washington Senators when Robertson, then a 17-year-old, left-handed pitcher, went to spring training with the club in Orlando, Florida. "Mr. Harris gave me a good look, but I just wasn't fast enough," the man who was named Canada's Sports Writer of the Year in 1973 explained. John learned this definitely when he failed to survive the spring cut of the Fulton, Kentucky, club in the Kitty League the same spring. Besides his radio work, Robertson is a columnist for *Maclean's* magazine, and the *Montreal Gazette*. John is an 11-year veteran on the sports beat.

12/THE EXPOS

One trade akin to leaving monastery

In December 1968, Montreal Expo General Manager Jim Fanning came home from the NL expansion draft and sat down to peruse the motley assortment of zircons discarded from the established teams' hope chests. Much like Diogenes in his fruitless search for an honest man, Fanning was unable to find one established major leaguer young enough and talented enough to begin building a franchise around. So he adopted a pose somewhere between Monte Hall and Frank ("Trader") Lane and howled rather frantically:

"Let's make a deal!"

One month later, 24-year-old Daniel Joseph ("Rusty") Staub was sitting in the office of his close friend and financial adviser, Harry Licata, in downtown Houston—agonizing over his 1968 income tax. Thumbing through a stack of payroll stubs, Rusty discovered a $100 deduction from his Astro salary check that puzzled him. He suspected it was a fine for breaking one of the more than forty club regulations, which covered "crimes" ranging from having the television set on in the club dormitory after midnight during spring training, to using abusive language within earshot of the Houston brass.

He hesitated to call Astro General Manager Spec Richardson; he had returned his 1969 contract to Richardson unsigned, and the next move was up to Spec. So he placed a call directly to the club's payroll department. The girl who answered said she'd have to confirm the information with Richardson's office. Then she came back on the line and said: "Mr. Richardson has been trying to reach you, Rusty, and . . . well, it sure has been nice knowing you."

The impact of what she said was just sinking in when Richardson's voice cut in on the line: "Rusty, I just wanted to let you know that we have traded your contract to the Montreal Expos in return for the contracts of Jesus Alou and Donn Clendenon." Rusty cupped his hand over the mouthpiece and whispered to Harry Licata: "The bastards finally did it. They traded me! I didn't think they'd have the guts to go through with it."

The shock waves would reverberate through Houston within the hour. The Wonder Boy, around whom the Astros had built a franchise and a $60 million Astrodome, had been put up for adoption. For all his differences with Houston management, Rusty had been considered an "untouchable" by all Houston fans except the eligible young damsels. They could both look AND touch, although Rusty used to admonish them severely by saying things such as: "I'll give you an hour to stop that."

The novelty of major league baseball had worn thin in Houston, amid growing suspicion that a goodly number of the one-million-plus fans the Astros were attracting each season were really flocking through the turnstiles just to gaze at the splendor of the $60 million Astrodome. But as one Texas rancher put it: "Why should I pay to see a bunch of horse's asses run around on fake grass, when I can see the real thing for nothing without leaving the ranch."

Rusty was typical of the modern-day breed of young major leaguers, who liked to swing twelve months a year. Thus, getting traded by the Astros was akin to being sprung from a monastery.

"We had players in their thirties, and some even going into their forties," said Rusty. "But at training camp they'd make us be in bed by midnight, with the lights out. You could even be fined for being in bed with your television set on. They came around every night at the stroke of twelve and checked your room by shining a flashlight in your face. They wanted to make sure it was really you.

"To top it off, they locked all but one of the exit doors from the outside. Beside each door they installed boxes with hammers in them, so in case of fire we could break a window and escape. The only time we were allowed out after midnight was if the building was burning."

The Astros had turned down a straight one-for-one swap with Atlanta—Staub for Joe Torre—because Harry Walker preferred Alou and Clendenon. This probably explains why Harry's future as a manager was so short-lived; and it probably helped splinter the plank on which Richardson was eventually to walk.

Torre was dealt to St. Louis instead, for Orlando Cepeda. Joe proceeded to drive in 101 runs for the Cardinals in 1969, 100 in

1970, and won the league's MVP in 1971, after leading the league in average (.363), RBIs (137), and stroking 24 homers.

To make matters worse, the Astros never did get Clendenon, and by the time Commissioner Bowie Kuhn finished sorting out the whole deal, Astro owner Judge Roy Hofheinz was referring to him as "Blewie" Kuhn. "We don't propose," ranted Hofheinz, "to stand idly by and have our franchise destroyed and all of baseball destroyed by a Johnny-come-lately. In less than six weeks on the job, Kuhn has done more to destroy baseball than all of its enemies were able to do in 100 years."

If ever a man fitted the image of the eccentric Texas millionaire, it was the Judge. At a cost of $2 million, he built an ornate seven-story apartment into the Astrodome's right field wall, which overlooks the judge's 55,000-seat rumpus room. The apartment sprawled over twenty-five rooms and resembled the sound stage of a Hollywood movie by Harold Robbins out of Jacqueline Susann. The decor had been described by Bob Hope as "Early King Farouk." Flanking the judge's desk were two six-foot Asian temple dogs. Each room had a gold-plated telephone with the judge's picture in the middle of the dial. The apartment included a private barbershop, beauty parlor, six-hole miniature golf course, bowling alley, shooting gallery, pool hall, and a toyland for his grandchildren, which resembled a miniature Disneyland.

The pièce de résistance was a full-fledged presidential suite which has housed Lyndon Johnson, Frank Sinatra, and other celebrities. The bathtubs are trimmed in purple velvet, and the toilet seats are gold suede. The flush handles are real gold. The judge had a reputation as a renowned practical joker, and visitors who ventured in the washroom suddenly found the whole room moving and numbers flashing to give them the impression they were in the elevator. At the exact moment the facility was used, a siren would go off and everyone outside would have a good laugh at the visitor's expense. The bar included a slanted floor, stools that mysteriously raise and lower themselves, and electrified coins imbedded in the bar, which jolt on command from the bartender.

Understandably, Judge Roy Hofheinz is not the kind of man who likes gazing out his apartment window into ninth place in the NL—especially when directly beneath his window was a vacant space where Rusty Staub used to be, and up the line at first base was another vacant space where Donn Clendenon was supposed to be. Shortly after the Staub for Clendenon and Alou trade was made,

Clendenon had flown into Houston and denied all those ugly rumors started by the press that he was contemplating retirement.

"I thought about it when Montreal first drafted me," said Donn. "But not now. I consider this a challenge, and I'd like to play with a club that's on the way up. I'm really looking forward to spring training. This is when we have to learn to play like a team, to become a unit, to get that winning attitude. I'm here to help Houston win ball games. I guarantee you one thing—we're going to have a club the fans will be proud of."

Standing nearby, at the press conference, Astro General Manager Richardson was grinning from ear to ear. But not for long. Spec made Clendenon an offer and Donn went home to consider it. Then three weeks later, as Spec anxiously awaited the return of the signed contract, he picked up the morning newspaper and read where Clendenon had announced his retirement from baseball to take a job as vice-president of labor relations with Scripto Inc., of Atlanta.

Spec thumbed frantically through baseball's Blue Book, and much to his relief he discovered that under Rule 12-F, if a traded player officially retires from baseball before completing thirty days with his new club, the deal becomes invalid and all players involved revert to their original clubs. This meant that the Astros would get Rusty back and either keep him or make that deal for Joe Torre with Atlanta.

Spec got Clendenon to wire the Houston club and officially request to be placed on the voluntary retired list. Upon receipt of the wire, Spec forwarded it to Commissioner Kuhn's office on February 28. NL President Warren Giles then wired Staub ordering him not to report to the Expos until the matter was resolved. Rusty went down to the Expo camp anyway, and to his surprise the first

---

JUDGE LANDIS ONE UP ON DIZZY DEAN

Judge Landis, the first commissioner of baseball, would not buy Dizzy Dean's bluff when the latter sought free-agent status. Dean claimed he was under 21 when he signed his first professional contract with the Houston Buffs in 1931. Judge Landis accepted Dizzy's marriage certificate introduced by the Buffs to disprove his claim. Case dismissed!

player he met was Jesus Alou, who was supposed to have gone to Houston along with Clendenon in the deal.

Jim Fanning wanted no part of Alou and he got on the phone to Richardson, saying: "We've got one of your ballplayers here."

"Keep him," said Spec. "The deal's off."

"Not in my book it isn't," said Fanning.

It was about then that Commissioner Kuhn began to detect an unsavory aroma to the whole affair. Clendenon, as things turned out, had envisioned a fat $50,000 contract with the Expos, and when he became Houston property and Spec wouldn't come up with even close to this kind of bread, he decided to use the old retirement dodge, to see if he couldn't induce the Astros to trade him. Richardson preferred to scream that the deal was off. Staub, meanwhile, was sitting in civvies at the Expo training camp at West Palm Beach, Florida, vowing to retire if the trade were voided.

The Expo brass were champing at the bit, because they'd built their whole preseason ticket sale in their baptismal year around the arrival of Staub. And Clendenon had written another letter to the commissioner, reiterating that he was indeed retiring. The Expos knew that if Clendenon insisted upon retiring, the commissioner would have no choice but to void the deal. So they took the only avenue left. To prove to everyone that Clendenon was just playing games, the Expos made Clendenon an offer he couldn't refuse—even though he wasn't really their property.

"We could afford to grossly overpay him just to keep him from retiring," said Fanning. "All we were out to prove was that he was insincere about retiring, and this way the deal would not be voided."

Clendenon agreed to terms with the Expos. Then Fanning turned around and said to Richardson, "Look, we got him to agree to a figure. He's all yours. Just pay it." Richardson refused, and told Montreal that if they wanted Clendenon that badly, they could have him themselves. But much to Spec's chagrin, the commissioner ruled that not only was Staub still Montreal property, but Clendenon was still an Expo, too. The Astros would get Alou, plus further player compensation.

It was then that Hofheinz called Kuhn "Blewie" and other assorted unkind names. But it was all to no avail. The Astros finally got right-hander Jack Billingham and southpaw Skip Guinn from Montreal to conclude the deal, but not before sending the Expos three pitchers—Howie Reed, Steve Shea and Leo Marentette. Billingham was a helluva plus, but Spec couldn't resist pushing his luck and dealt him to Cincinnati along with Joe Morgan, Denis Menke, and Ed Armbrister, in return for Lee May (since traded to Baltimore), Jimmy Stewart (now retired), and Tommy Helms (now on the Pirates' bench).

Oh well! Nobody's perfect.

Clendenon, meanwhile, had sent Spec running for the village shrink when he signed with Montreal and told reporters: "I feel I owe it to the game. I don't believe baseball deserves all this confusion. In the interests of baseball I feel I should come back."

At this point in time, Richardson would have gladly offered to perform a frontal lobotomy on Clendenon's headbone with an axe. The moral of the story should be that Clendenon, in his grasping for the almighty buck, got his come-uppance and learned a bitter lesson from it all. After all, solely because of his double-dealing, all the Astros had to show for the departed Staub in 1969 was Jesus Alou, who hit a disappointing .246, Billingham (6–7), and Guinn (1–2) who pitched only 80 innings among them. Meanwhile Staub was hitting a robust .302 at Montreal, with 29 homers and 79 RBIs, as well as leading the league in assists.

Clendenon, unwanted and considered grossly overpaid by the Expos, was used sparingly until June, before being traded to the Mets for Pitcher Steve Renko. And with the Mets, he not only got his just desserts but the whole damned pie, because he elbowed Ed Kranepool off first base and helped lead the Mets to a World Championship. When the World Series had ended, guess who was summoned to stroll front and center to accept a new Corvette Sting Ray from *Sport Magazine* as the MVP in the Series?

None other than the Scripto Kid.

You'd think that Spec Richardson would have learned his lesson about trading with the Expos. But the following year, in 1970, Spec inherited another strong-willed player, who also refused to knuckle under to Houston-type discipline. His name was Mike Marshall. And far from boasting Staub's glowing credentials, Mike had kicked around the minors for five years as a shortstop and pitcher, being rejected by the Phillie, Detroit, and Seattle organizations before landing in Houston.

While Houston Manager Harry Walker was reading the riot act to Marshall, citing all the fines and punishments for breaking club regulations, Marshall interrupted him to ask: "How many times a week will you allow me to have intercourse with my wife?"

Aghast, Harry ordered Marshall to run several laps around the outside of the Astrodome. And Pitching Coach Jim Owens drove Mike outside in a golf cart, with orders to follow him to make sure he did the required laps.

Mike refused. He was dispatched to the minors. Shortly afterward, Spec's assistant, John Mullen, phoned Expo assistant general manager, Danny Menendez, and said:

"You need a pitcher for your farm system? We've got one we want to unload."

"What do you want for him?" asked Menendez.

"Awww, just send us a minor league outfielder," said Mullen.

"I've got just the one for you," said Menendez. "Don Bosch."

The best that could be said about Don Bosch was that one night he faded back into deep center field in Oklahoma City and disappeared right out of organized baseball. Mike Marshall went on to become the best relief pitcher in the NL, and a screwball pitcher in every sense of the word.

It would be nice to say that the Expos capitalized happily ever after on the acquisition of Staub and Marshall. But that would also be in error. After averaging .295, 25 homers, and 90 RBIs in three seasons with the Expos, Rusty was traded to the Mets for three young players—Mike Jorgensen, Tim Foli, and Ken Singleton.

The only one to come close to living up to Staub's credentials was Singleton, who hit .302 in 1973, with 100 runs scored, 103 RBIs, and 26 homers. One season later Singleton was traded, along with Pitcher Mike Torrez—Expos winningest pitcher over the three previous seasons—to Baltimore, in return for Dave McNally and Rich Coggins. McNally retired two months into his first season as an Expo, after getting off to a dismal 3–8 start. Coggins missed the first month with an intestinal ailment, played a handful of games, was sent to the minors, and subsequently dealt back to the AL. In baseball terminology, the Expos went nothing for two—Singleton and Torrez. And all they had left to show for Staub were Foli and Jorgensen—two good-field no-hit infielders.

Marshall, meanwhile, had ascended to greatness with the Expos, earning the NL Fireman of the Year Award in 1973, with a 14–11 mark and a league-leading 31 saves. He set two major league records for most relief appearances (92) and most innings (179), broke the NL record for games finished (92), and was runner-up to Tom Seaver for the Cy Young Award.

But Marshall is an oddball, destined to skulk through life, tormented on all sides by inferior beings. He has no time for children who pester him for autographs. He has no time for awards, voted to him by "unqualified" baseball writers. And he had little respect for his Expo teammates. Ironically it was the latter which proved Marshall's undoing as an Expo. In December 1973, back on the campus of Michigan State University, a young stringer for United Press International made the mistake of asking Mike for a rundown on the Expos. Mike not only ran down the Expos; he backed over teammates Bob Bailey and Ron Hunt, just for good measure.

"Who the hell wants to go back to pitch for that defense anymore," said Marshall.

"Second base was terrible. There's no way I can play another year with Ron Hunt. If I had to, it would be a very strong reason for not going back at all.

"Third base was terrible. We have absolutely no defense with Bob Bailey. You can put a high school kid out there and get the same production out of the defense at third.

"Left field (Ron Fairly) was terrible. Center field, less than average. Right field, less than average.

"When I'm in there pitching in the seventh, eighth, and ninth, and extra innings with a chance of losing the game on one play, I don't want shabby defense behind me. And I can look at my eleven losses and blame eight of them on my defense. I don't want to go back and go through that again without defensive help. That's how I feel. I've made that point clear to the manager and general manager and will continue to do so."

With Ron Hunt and others vowing to extract retribution the next time Marshall walked through the clubhouse door, the Expos had no choice but to trade him. Tragically, they chose to trade him to Los Angeles for Willie Davis. Willie flew up to Montreal to check out the city, was given a courtesy automobile to drive, and immediately rammed a police car. During the season, the only time he didn't loaf was when he was pursued by bailiffs. He led the league in salary advances and unpaid bills. And when he demanded to be traded, the Expos acted with lightning speed. He went to Texas for minor league Infielder Pete MacKanin and minor league Pitcher Don Stanhouse.

Not much to show for Mike Marshall.

To make matters worse, Expos' well of untapped Houston talent dried up with the firing of Spec Richardson. But Montreal still easily has the best baseball team in Canada. Typically, the Expos' best season has been winter.

JOE CASHMAN
Sportswriter, *Boston Record American*

Joe Cashman is known as the "Walter Alston" of the Baseball Writers' Association of America. He served twenty consecutive one-year terms as chairman of the Boston chapter from 1932 to 1951. He was the national president of the writers' organization in 1953. Born in South Boston, Massachusetts, Cashman joined the Hearst-owned *Boston American* when he was seventeen years old and still attending the Boston Latin School. Joe started on the baseball beat in 1928 when both the Braves and the Red Sox called Boston home. From copyboy to his status as one of the nation's foremost baseball writers, Cashman was a Hearst employee for more than fifty years.

13/THE RED SOX

The impossible dream: single season miracle

Thomas A. Yawkey, sole owner and president of the Red Sox, is presently serving his forty-third year in both those capacities, which is a record for longevity as a major league executive. Nor is that Yawkey's only claim to baseball fame. Since buying the Fenway franchise a few weeks before the start of spring training in 1933, he has put his stamp of approval on, or personally engineered, more trades and spent more millions for diamond talent than any other owner in major league history.

When Yawkey first appeared on the Boston scene and began tossing money around as though there would be no tomorrow, Red Sox followers didn't know what to think of him. No wonder, since they had come to look upon the Sox as nothing more than a New York Yankee farm. During the "roaring twenties," virtually every Sox player who had displayed outstanding ability or showed exceptional potential had been shipped to the Bronx Bombers in an exchange for a collection of baseball garbage and large pots of gold.

As a result, in the twelve years before Yawkey showed up, the Sox had finished in the cellar nine times and had never been out of the second division, while the Yanks had won seven flags over those years and had been out of the money only once, thanks mainly to acquisitions from the good old Boston owners. Oddly enough, prior to 1920 the Bosox had been the AL's most successful entry, having captured six pennants and batted .1000 in five World Series since being organized in 1901.

During the club's first eighteen years of existence, it had been involved in only one memorable trade. In 1916 the Sox peddled Tris Speaker to the Indians. Tris was destined to be among the first eight players elected to the Hall of Fame. Spoke, only 28 at the time, had been the Sox hero for seven seasons. He had batted

171

well over .300 each of those years and was rated the finest defensive center fielder of his era. He had signed his Boston contract for 1916 and had gone through spring training with the club. Then, on the weekend before the start of the regular season, while the Sox were in New York for an exhibition series with the Dodgers, came the startling announcement that Tris had been sold to the Indians for $50,000.

The stunned Boston fans, when they got over the initial shock, began to wonder why. The transaction didn't make sense to them. The consensus among the Boston public was that Manager Bill Carrigan had suggested the deal. It was known that the manager and his biggest star didn't care for each other personally. So it was reasoned that the catcher-pilot, who was revered by most of his charges, had instigated the removal of the talented Texan from the Boston roster. Nothing was further from the truth than that allegation, Carrigan told us in an interview some thirty years later.

Here is Carrigan's version.

"When we arrived in New York for those games with the Dodgers, I got a phone call from owner Jim Lannin to meet him at a certain hotel.

" 'I've sold Speaker to the Indians,' he said, almost before I had a chance to sit down in his room.

"I had nothing to do with the deal. It was Lannin's idea. He never told me why. I never asked him. He owned the club. He didn't have to give me the reasons for any of his actions.

"As for my wanting to get rid of Speaker, that's silly. Anybody who thinks I suggested the trade doesn't know Carrigan.

"My one and only goal as a manager was to win as many games as possible. I might hate a player's guts, but if I felt he could help us win games, I wanted him. If I were to get rid of a player because he and I didn't see eye to eye, I'd be cutting off my nose to spite my face.

"It never was any secret that Speaker wasn't one of my favorite persons, and neither was I one of his. But I recognized his talent and was delighted to have him on our side. I hated to lose him.

"I never did find out for sure why Lannin made the deal, but I suspected at the time that he suddenly found himself in need of money to carry on his hotel business and figured there was no easier way for him to raise $50,000 than by cashing in on Spoke."

Speaker was sensational in his first year with the Indians. He won the AL batting crown with .386, thus breaking Ty Cobb's streak of nine stick titles in a row. The best Cleveland could do in the race, though, was to finish sixth. Fortunately for Lannin and Carrigan, the Sox won both the pennant and World Series for the second year in a row in 1916, and the fans forgot all about the Speaker deal. The only deal Lannin made in 1917 was to sell the whole Boston ball club. The new owner turned up in the person of Harry Frazee, a Broadway theatrical producer.

Frazee started off like a dedicated owner. He appointed the smart and popular ex-Athletic Jack Barry, the club's holdover second baseman, as the new manager. He kept intact his famed pitching staff of Babe Ruth, Ernie Shore, Carl Mays, Dutch Leonard, George Foster, and Herb Pennock, and also the star-spangled supporting cast he had inherited. The Sox finished second that season, first year of United States involvement in World War I. The next year saw Barry along with Shore, Duffy Lewis, and others join the navy.

Frazee's next managerial choice was Ed Barrow, the man who was later to create the Yankee dynasty as general manager in New York. Under the new pilot, the Sox bounded back to win another pennant in that abbreviated 1918 season. All seemed serene and the future looked bright at Fenway Park when the war ended a couple of months after the 1918 World Series, wherein the Sox beat the Cubs in six games.

Yet, as it developed, that was but a deceptive calm before the mighty storm that left the AL ball in Boston in a shambles for more than a decade. Following the 1918 Series, Frazee's attitude changed. He ceased to be wrapped up in the Red Sox. His chief concern again became his theatrical enterprises. He needed cash to carry on the latter. To get the money he embarked on a "Wreck the Red Sox" campaign. He surely succeeded.

His initial moves didn't cause any great stir. When Duffy Lewis and Ernie Shore returned from the war, they learned they were going to the Yankees. But the Boston public wasn't unduly upset. After all, the Sox had won the flag without these two players. There was no great uproar, either, when Carl Mays was sent to the Yanks in mid-season. The submarine slinger got fed up with Frazee and asked to be traded. Frazee obliged by sending him to New York over the loud protests of AL President Ban Johnson.

The blockbuster which convinced everybody that Frazee was

bent upon destroying the Red Sox to satisfy his desire for capital to carry out theatrical projects was, of course, the sale of George Herman ("Babe") Ruth to New York for an announced price of $125,000. That was the largest cash sum ever paid for a player up to that time.

If Ruth wasn't the greatest of big leaguers at the time, he was mighty close to it. He was rated the best left-handed pitcher in the league. Dividing his efforts in 1918 between pitching and playing outfield, at Barrow's suggestion, he compiled a 13–6 pitching record, batted an even .300, and tied for the league lead in HRs with 11. Doing the same double duty in 1919, he batted .322 and smashed all major league HR records with 29. Now he was a Yankee, and for the next dozen years semipro clubs around Boston were to outdraw the Red Sox.

The sale of Ruth, while an irreparable blow to the Red Sox, may have been a good thing for baseball in general and the AL in particular. Had he remained in Boston, he might have remained primarily a pitcher instead of becoming a great slugger for the Yankees. His fantastic fence-building as a Bronx Bomber made possible the building of the Yankee Stadium, turned New York from an NL into an AL town, made the fans the country over quickly dismiss from mind the shoddy story of the 1919 Black Sox scandal, and made the Bambino himself the greatest gate attraction in every city in the league.

Nor did Frazee stop with the Ruth sale. By the time he said "good-bye, glad to have met you," to Boston in mid-season of 1923, every Boston player on the defending-champion club he purchased had been sold, most of them to New York. Anyway so much for Frazee.

Now came along a quartet of men from Columbus, Ohio. They were headed by Robert A. ("Bob") Quinn, who, as general manager of the St. Louis Browns, had built up a club which missed tying the Yankees by only one game for the 1922 flag. Quinn was an able, sincere, and highly respected baseball man. After his success with the Browns, who had been AL doormats for the most part before he went to St. Louis, he was confident he could revitalize the Red Sox. He did his darndest, but that was not nearly enough. Actually, he never had much of a chance. Shortly after taking over the club, the wealthiest of the coowners died suddenly, and thereafter the Red Sox treasury was next to barren.

Only a handful of Quinn trades are deserving of recital

nearly a half century later. Clark Griffith, owner of the Senators, had one of his rare brainstorms in 1927. Early in the race he traded sophomore Infielder Buddy Myer to Quinn in exchange for an infielder named Emory Topper Rigney, who at that moment was batting .111. Rigney finished out the season with the Senators and was never heard of again in the majors. Myer did some fine shortstopping for the Red Sox in 1927, and in 1928 he was regular third baseman batting .313. He stood out like a sore thumb among the many misfits he was associated with while in Boston. Griffith finally realized the mistake he had made in giving up on Myer. He rectified it by trading five players to get Buddy back. The quintet of nondescripts which went to Boston was of little help to Quinn.

Myer, on the other hand, on his return to Washington established himself as one of the league's top second sackers, stayed on the job for twelve more years, won a batting title, and finished up with more impressive Hall of Fame credentials than some of those already enshrined at Cooperstown, New York.

The other memorable Quinn deal proved a disaster from a Boston standpoint in the long run. This happened early in the 1930 campaign. Charlie Red Ruffing was in his sixth season with the Sox. He was the losingest pitcher in the AL in 1928 and 1929, being charged with 28 and 22 defeats, respectively. At the same time, he was a most exciting performer. Repeatedly he pitched hitless ball for six or seven innings only to then run out of gas. He hadn't learned to pace himself. The Yankees' mouths watered for him. Quinn satisfied their cravings.

The Quinn blunder was not so much in letting Ruffing go. "Big C" still had to prove himself; he might never do it. It was in not getting more than he did for the young pitcher that Quinn erred. He settled for an outfielder named Cedric Durst, who in six earlier

---

THE SLOW AND THE MIGHTY

They said big Ernie Lombardi was so slow they timed him with an alarm clock instead of a stopwatch during his run to first base. Still, without benefit of one leg hit, The Schnoz stroked 1,298 singles, 277 doubles, 190 HRs, and won two NL batting titles in 1938 (.342), and 1942 (.330).

seasons had never played more than 80 games and never batted as high as .260. He already was 34 years old, and the 1930 season was his last in the majors.

Ruffing, of course, went on to be the Yanks' right-handed ace as well as their Number One right-handed pinch hitter for the next dozen years. He ended up on that lengthy list of Red Sox discards who made it to Cooperstown.

All of this, at long last, brings us to the arrival, in 1933, of the Boston fans' Messiah, alias Thomas Austin Yawkey. It was in mid-January when Bob Quinn, with a sigh of relief and one and one-quarter million of Yawkey money in his pocket, turned over the keys to Fenway Park to the new owner and his closest friend and most trusted adviser, Eddie Collins, who had agreed to fill the general manager's role. There wasn't time for new bosses to make many changes in 1933. Marty McManus already had been signed to a managerial contract by Quinn. The first of the rebuilding moves by the new command was to get Catcher Rick Ferrell from the Browns in exchange for Catcher Merv Shea and CASH. CASH was what every second division club wanted most of all at that time, and only Yawkey was willing to come up with it. If you offered a big league franchise as collateral, the banks wouldn't lend you $1,000 in that brother-can-you-spare-a-dime period.

The next year the Red Sox' renovation began in earnest. Bucky Harris was appointed manager. Moses Grove, Rube Walberg, and Max Bishop came from the Athletics at the cost of $125,000 and a couple of bench warmers. Wes Ferrell and Dick Porter moved from Cleveland to Boston, while the Indians collected a king-size loaf of "bread" and a couple of players of small account.

But so far the Yawkey-Collins combine had done little more than scratch the surface, albeit it had done enough to improve the club to the point where it played .500 ball and climbed to fourth in 1934. The club would have done even better if Grove hadn't come up with a sore arm for the first and only time in his long career. He had to settle for eight victories. He bounded back to win 20 the next year, and in four of the next five seasons he had the lowest ERA in the league.

With the 1934 race over, Yawkey asked Collins: "What player in the league would help the Sox most?"

"Manager Joe Cronin of the Senators," was the reply. "Our big need is a good shortstop with power. But you can't get Cronin."

"How do you know?" snapped Yawkey. "We can at least try."

They tried and they succeeded, though the effort left Yawkey a quarter of a million dollars poorer. Depression still gripped the land. Yet here was Yawkey paying a then record $250,000 for Cronin and throwing in Shortstop Lyn Lary to sweeten the pot. Yawkey couldn't very well demote his most expensive acquisition to private in the ranks. So Cronin was named Boston manager. Where did Harris go? Why, back to Washington to succeed Cronin as Senators' manager.

Nobody was more elated than Collins over the deal for Cronin. He had been miffed because he hadn't been consulted before Yawkey hired Harris a year earlier. Now the Sox had a manager he really admired, and they were rid of a manager he never wanted around.

A fourth-place finish for the second year in a row in 1935 sent Yawkey and Collins back to the marketplace. They started off by luring Jimmy Foxx and Pitcher Johnny ("Footsie") Marcum away from Connie Mack, whose reward this time was $150,000 and change (and a couple of expendable players). Turning back to Mack in a few weeks, they paid another small fortune plus a couple of guys named Joe for Roger ("Doc") Cramer and Eric McNair. And, oh yes, they dropped in on Papa Griffith again. They paid their dues and left with Hall of Famer Heinie Manush in tow.

"Wow," yelled Boston fans in joy. "Can't miss the pennant this year."

Believe it or not, with all the new stars added to the cast, the 1937 Sox ended up in sixth place, 28 games below the roof, as compared to the 1936 outfit which came in fourth and within 15 games of the top. Only Foxx really lived up to expectation. Double X hit .338, collected 41 HRs and 143 RBIs—a performance which would command a half "mill" in dollars today. Opening the 1937 campaign with such illustrious new faces as Mike Higgins, Ben Chapman, and Bobo Newsom, all of whom, naturally, cost plenty, the Sox staggered again most of the way to a fifth-place finish.

The only notable addition to the cast in 1938 was Joe Vosmik, $35,000 acquisition from the Browns. Yet the Sox zoomed all the way up to second place, their highest finish in exactly twenty years or since they had won the World Championship in 1918. Some of the credit for the rise belonged to Vosmik. He batted .324. Foxx had a fabulous year with a million-dollar performance, including a .349 batting mark, 50 HRs and 175 RBIs.

But the man mainly responsible for the Sox beating out

Cleveland for second place was Joe Heving, who had been with the Indians the year before. Learning in the spring that the Indians were asking waivers on him, the 37-year-old Heving begged the Sox to claim him. Cronin wasn't interested. Heving went back to the American Association. In mid-season the Sox bought him from St. Paul. He cost $50,000. Joe could have been claimed on waivers for $15,000 in the spring. Heving got in 16 games. He won eight, saved half a dozen and lost only once. In the next two years he won 21 games and saved a flock more while losing but ten before Cleveland grabbed him back.

The one and only Theodore Samuel Williams made his debut in 1939. He was installed in right field as Ben Chapman was shipped to Cleveland to make room for "The Kid." Chapman had batted a mere .340 as Boston right fielder the year before. Denny Galehouse, who'll long live in Boston memory as the pitcher who lost the playoff game to the Indians in 1948, became a Red Sox in that deal. Another second-place finish took place as rookie Williams broke in with a .327 average, to say nothing of 31 HRs and 145 RBIs.

To digress a bit. Cronin has said Yawkey's biggest mistake was paying $250,000 for him in 1934.

"Griffith would have given me to Yawkey for nothing," Joe will tell you with a straight face. "I had just married the old man's niece-adopted daughter, Mildred Robertson. He wanted the very best for her as a wife and mother. He couldn't afford to give me a salary large enough to enable the Cronins to keep up with the Joneses. All Yawkey had to do was guarantee us that kind of security and Griff would have said 'take him with my blessing.'" Maybe Cronin said that with tongue in cheek. Maybe not.

But Yawkey considers his greatest mistake to have been the sale of Peewee Reese to the Dodgers for $75,000 in 1939.

"We bought the Louisville franchise in the American Association solely to get title to Reese," Yawkey admitted. "I say 'we' because I wasn't the sole owner. Reluctantly, I had let Donie Bush, manager of the club and a close friend of his from Indianapolis, become partners of mine in the purchase.

"Came the Dodgers' offer. I asked Billy Evans, Sox farm director back there, if he'd rate Peewee a 'can't miss' major league prospect.

"'He's a question mark,' said Evans, 'because of his size. He might be too small and frail to make it up here.'

"If I had been sole owner, as I am of the Sox, I would have rejected the offer. But I had to think of my partners also. I debated long. I finally decided to accept the offer."

Most of the smarter baseball minds of that period believed the Sox would have won a flock of pennants instead of only one if Reese's 16 scintillating seasons had been spent in Boston instead of Brooklyn. That one pennant the Sox did win over that stretch was in 1946, the first full season after the end of World War II.

Yawkey hadn't raided the league to assemble that championship machine. The backbone of the club was composed of Williams, Bobby Doerr, Johnny Pesky, Dom DiMaggio, Tex Hughson, Boo Ferriss, Mickey Harris, Earl Johnson, and Jim Bagby, players who had originally come to Boston from the minors.

But the Sox did make one important purchase. The Tigers, believing Rudy York was all washed up at 33, put the veteran on the block. The Sox grabbed him. Rudy played all 54 games at first base. He had 119 RBIs, second only to Williams. "We couldn't have won without York," Cronin has always said.

Eddie Collins had died, Cronin had become general manager, and Joe McCarthy had come out of retirement to become field manager by the time 1948 rolled around. Cronin, armed with Yawkey money, lost no time in establishing himself as a wheeler-dealer second to none. His victim was the Browns, who, as usual, were in a financial bind. The Sox wanted Pitchers Jack Kramer and Ellis Kinder and Shortstop Vern Stephens. They got all three in two separate trades. It cost Yawkey $375,000 in all, and the Browns also received the like of Eddie Pellagrini, Roy Partee, Sam Dente, Al Widmar, Clem Dreiswerd, and a few others.

That swapping almost, but not quite, let the Sox hit two jackpots. Getting off to a very slow start, McCarthy masterminded the club into a first-place tie with Cleveland on the final day of the 1948 race. The Indians won the one-game playoff in Boston. The next year was equally heartbreaking for Yawkey, Cronin, McCarthy & Co. With two games left to play in the 1949 race, the Sox had a one-game lead. They had only to split the two games of the final series of the year in New York to win it all. They were beaten twice by the Yanks, managed for the first time by Casey Stengel.

It was a strange deal in 1951. The Sox purchased Catcher Les Moss from the Browns in May for $50,000 and a player to be named later. When the 1952 season opened, Moss was back with the Browns. Facetiously, some scribes reported that Les was the "player to be named later." That wasn't the case, of course. The Sox had sent a pitcher, Jim McDonald, from Louisville to complete the 1951 deal. But it all boiled down to little more than the Sox paying $50,000 for the loan of Moss for a few months.

Moving on to the expansion era of the sixties, the Sox went through the most agonizing period of any Yawkey club during the first half of the decade. Between 1960 and 1966, they got as high as sixth only once, twice as seventh, twice as eighth, and twice as ninth. Then, would you believe it, they made Dick Williams manager in 1967 and presto! "The Impossible Dream." The pennant. Most startling one-season reversal of form in the annals of baseball.

The infielders and outfielders were erstwhile Boston farmhands who all had been around the season before, but hadn't played for Billy Herman like they did for Williams. But they didn't do the job all by themselves. They were helped tremendously by Catcher Elston Howard, grabbed on waivers in mid-season from the Yankees; Pitcher Gary Bell, another summer addition, who chipped in with 12 victories, and Ken Harrelson, signed as a free agent for a big bonus when Tony Conigliaro went on the disabled list.

Like his predecessors, Dick O'Connell, general manager since the early sixties, has kept busy on the trade mart. In two trades he erased much of the vestige of the 1967 club. First, he traded Jim Lonborg, Ken Brett, George Scott, Joe Lahoud, and Billy Conigliaro to Milwaukee for Tommy Harper, Lew Krausse, and Marty Patton. Only Scott still remains with Milwaukee. None of the trio the Sox got still remain with Boston.

The big trade of 1974 was the one that resulted in Reggie Smith and Pitchers Ken Tatum, John Curtis, Mike Garman, and Lynn McGlothen going to the Cardinals, and Pitchers Rick Wise, Reggie Cleveland, Diego Segiu, and Outfielder Bernie Carbo coming to Boston. The Cards had all the better of that swap. Cleveland was overweight, Wise had a sore arm, and Carbo kept fading after a great start; they were of little help to the Hose. It was different in 1975. The trio of ex-Cards went great guns for the Sox.

"That deal just might turn out to have been the best I've ever made," says O'Connell. His worst trade? No doubt about it, O'Connell confesses. "When I sent Sparky Lyle to the Yankees for Danny Cater and Mario Guerrero."

RED FOLEY
Sportswriter, *New York Daily News*

Red Foley makes no bones about it: He's a self-described baseball nut. Red has been a card-carrying member of the Baseball Writers' Association of America for fifteen of his thirty years with the *New York Daily News.* He has served as chairman of the New York chapter and is the assistant secretary of the writers' national organization. Although assigned to cover such sports as hockey and horse racing, Foley is never out of touch with baseball. His "Ask Red" column, a question and answer segment reserved exclusively to baseball, is published each Sunday in *The News.* In addition to covering both the Mets and the Yankees, Foley has contributed baseball articles to many magazines and *The Sporting News.*

14/THE GIANTS

McGraw's Napoleon rule: addition by subtraction

Baseball's historians have never identified the anonymous sage who coined that chestnut about "the best trades being the ones that aren't made," but it's odds-on he never worked for Horace Stoneham or the Giants. On that you can make book, because whoever has operated the franchise—either in San Francisco or during the Giants' long and checkered existence in New York—has never been indicted for being reluctant to buy, sell, or barter a ballplayer.

Some of their transactions have been bad and more of them have been good. And while others provoked little or no ripple in baseball's meandering mainstream, neither inertia nor indolence were the reasons why. In good times or bad, the Giants have continued to operate in this manner. Stoneham, oblivious to his critics, made all the moves. And while managers as well as players came and went, Horace, in his intractable way, concluded all the deals.

He traded for winners; he traded for losers; and, in more recent times, he even had to stage rent parties in order to stay afloat by selling such longtime Giant favorites as Willie Mays, Willie McCovey, and Juan Marichal. But at no time did Stoneham, like his father before him, ever display an aversion either to voice a proposition or to audit one. Neither, for that matter, did Stoneham's predecessors, John T. Brush or the imperious Andrew Freedman. Each, through the machinations of the fabled John J. McGraw, maneuvered in and out of the marketplace without fear of reprisal or retribution.

McGraw, because of his ponderous success as a manager and innovator, was the game's most dominant figure. A brilliant dugout tactician, the erstwhile Little Napoleon, though salty, sarcastic, and stubborn, possessed a shrewdness and comprehension about players and their latent talents that surpassed those of his prudent partners or frequently prosaic peers. From the time of his unexpected but widely heralded arrival from Baltimore in July 1902, until his retirement in June 1932, the Giants were McGraw and McGraw was the Giants. And for the thirty years that he directed their destinies, few had the temerity to dispute his logic or leadership. Except for perhaps Connie Mack, who just happened to own the Philadelphia A's, no manager possessed McGraw's power in the front office. He called the shots when it came to determining which Giant players would remain and which would go.

It was Freedman, a New York realtor with political connections, who learned that painful lesson shortly after inveigling McGraw to abandon Baltimore for the Polo Grounds. A perennial also-ran during Freedman's administration, the Giants had a succession of managers until McGraw's arrival. And observers, who freely forecast a personality clash between the new manager and Freedman, didn't have long to wait for their prediction to be sustained.

Since the "peace treaty" between the rival National and American Leagues would not be signed until January 1903, the warring factions continued their player raids. As a result, upon leaving Baltimore, McGraw displayed his ability to plunder by stripping the Orioles and the fledgling AL of several players who became the nucleus of the NL pennant he was to win for the Giants in 1904. Along with Pitchers Joe ("Iron Man") McGinnity and Jack Cronin, McGraw pirated Catcher Roger Bresnahan, First Baseman Dan McGann, and Outfielder Steve Brodie from Baltimore. Shortly after arriving in New York, McGraw scanned Freedman's roster and promptly released nine players, none of whom became famous, from the ragtag Giant ball club.

"Those players cost me money," Freedman protested. McGraw, with a perfunctory wave, promptly informed his employer it was addition by subtraction.

"All right, I'll let you run the team to suit yourself," Freedman said.

"You're damn right you will," McGraw retorted, thereby establishing his inalienable right to do as he pleased where the Giants were concerned.

After establishing his authority with Freedman, McGraw did likewise when Brush, an Indianapolis clothier and former stockholder of the Reds, purchased the Giants from Freedman in 1903.

McGraw and the more adaptable Brush enjoyed a profitable association that wasn't terminated until the latter's death in November 1912. Their quinella produced five pennants and a World Series victory in 1905. Following Brush's demise, his son-in-law, Harry Hempstead, served as club president, with the omnipresent McGraw continuing to call the turns that yielded flags in 1913 and again in 1917.

Then, in January 1919, McGraw acquired stock that strengthened his position even more and became linked with the Stonehams, the clan that was to guide the Giants afterwards. Actually, Charles A. Stoneham, a Wall Streeter, prominent racing figure, and a Broadway bon vivant, was the member of the family with whom McGraw was more closely associated. Their alliance, which produced successive pennants in 1921-1924, wasn't severed until February 1934, when McGraw, ravaged by illness, passed away less than two years after resigning as manager to assume a more sedentary post in the front office. When the elder Stoneham succumbed early in 1936, his son, Horace, assumed the presidency.

Under his stewardship the Giants experienced a rollercoaster ride. And while the lows may have endured much longer than the highs during the past forty years, Stoneham continued to operate rather independently from his little corner of the world. Unlike other major league franchises, the Giants were never owned or financed by corporations whose wealth was amassed beyond baseball. The Stonehams, for instance, were never cushioned by monies derived from beer, chewing gum, or other profitable industries. Yet, because of the McGraw influence, the ball club, in good or bad times, was always active in the trade marts. The controversial ex-Oriole established that precedence shortly after assuming command.

Inheriting what had been a chronic second-division club, McGraw immediately began to wheel and deal, making a move with Brooklyn that acquired veteran Shortstop Bill Dahlen. "We can win the pennant with him," McGraw told Brush. A year later, after augmenting his lineup with the acquisition of hard-hitting Mike Donlin from Cincinnati, McGraw's refurbished Giants won a then record 106 games and the NL flag.

After repeating that record in 1905 and then contending for the next few seasons, McGraw astounded the baseball world by paying the Indianapolis club a then record $11,000 for Richard ("Rube") Marquard, a 19-year-old left-hander, in September 1908.

A pitching flop in his early efforts—he was 0–1 in 1908, the year the Giants lost the pennant because of Fred Merkle's infamous failure to touch second base during a Polo Grounds game against the Cubs—Marquard became a winner in 1911, capturing 24 games. Linked with the heroic Christy Mathewson, whom McGraw found upon his arrival in 1902, Marquard won 49 more games in 1912 and 1913 as the Giants, though losing the World Series each time, sewed three straight pennants.

In 1912, McGraw demonstrated his ability as a showman when he signed the immortal Jim Thorpe shortly after the Indian had dominated the Olympics at Stockholm. "I don't really need him," McGraw confessed, "but the fans will pay to see him." Thorpe's diamond career never approached his track and field accomplishments, but his fame was such that the fans did flock to watch him.

When the "outlaw" Federal League, whose two-year war *vs* the majors had cost both sides plenty, disbanded prior to 1916, McGraw paid $30,000 for Benny Kauff, billed as "The Ty Cobb of the Feds." Kauff, however, never cut the mustard, but Eddie Roush, for whom the Giants paid a mere $7,500, did. Unfortunately, Roush, now a Hall of Famer, performed most of his feats for Cincinnati. A Giant briefly in 1916, Roush, along with Bill McKechnie and Mathewson, McGraw's longtime favorite, was dealt to the Reds that season for Infielder Buck Herzog.

Mathewson severed his Giant connection because the Reds wanted him as their manager. As for Herzog, whom Matty replaced as Cincy's skipper, he'd worked for the Giants in 1908–1909 and 1912. Herzog and McGraw were bitter enemies, but each respected the other's skills and, despite his animosity for McGraw, Herzog played pennant-winning baseball for his longtime adversary in 1917.

In the summer of 1919, while waging a losing battle with the pennant-bound Reds, McGraw made a move that had less opulent owners than Stoneham yelling "tilt" when he paid $55,000 to the Boston Braves for Art Nehf, a left-handed pitcher of considerable skill. Two years later, with Nehf winning 20 and Casey Stengel contributing (the latter obtained late that season from Philadelphia), the Giants won the first of four straight flags. Their 1922 pennant was insured when McGraw, again turning to the lowly Braves, wooed right-hander Hughie McQuillen for $100,000. That deal, plus his earlier purchases, so annoyed fellow magnates that the still existing rule prohibiting player trades after June 15 was enacted. But McGraw, as many after him, quickly learned how to circumvent that statute when necessary.

In the spring of 1923, McGraw, after again peeling the rubber band off the senior Stoneham's bankroll, welcomed Outfielder Jimmy O'Connell and left-hander Jack Bentley to the Giants' San Antonio training camp. O'Connell, for whom the Little Napoleon paid $75,000 after the youngster hit .335 in the Pacific Coast League, only lasted until 1924 when his implication in a late-season scandal made him permanently ineligible to remain in the major leagues. Bentley, reported to be the greatest thing to come out of Baltimore since Babe Ruth, lasted several seasons with the Giants, but never justified the $65,000 McGraw had paid for him.

That McGraw was not infallible was evidenced in the winter of 1925 when, through a clerical mixup in the Giants' front office, they failed to reserve the services of Hack Wilson. The muscular slugger, after earlier Polo Grounds tryouts, was being seasoned at Toledo that year. The Giants' failure to exercise their option exposed Wilson to the draft that annually accompanies baseball's winter meetings. As a result, the cellared Cubs obtained his valuable services for a measly $5,000. What Wilson's potent bat accomplished during ensuing seasons in Chicago is a matter of public record.

In August 1926, McGraw's authority was challenged. That's when Frank Frisch, a Giant since 1919, jumped the ball club during an August series in St. Louis. His defection deeply scarred McGraw, who had one day envisioned Frisch as his dugout successor. But such insubordination could not be tolerated and in December of that year, Frisch and Pitcher Jimmy Ring were dispatched to the Cardinals for the great Rogers Hornsby. Though Hornsby, as player-manager, had just directed the Redbirds to their first pen-

---

ALL IN THE FAMILY

The Brothers Meusel, Irish and Bob, hit as close as their family tie. Irish had a career average of .310, and Bob was a point behind at .309.

nant and World Championship, his constant feud with owner Sam Breadon caused a rift that made their relationship untenable.

Actually, McGraw had coveted The Rajah as early as 1919, just prior to Hornsby's succession of six batting titles, many of which he won by batting over .400. The Giants' initial attempt to lure Hornsby was dismissed by Branch Rickey, then general manager of the impoverished Redbirds. In the summer of 1919, McGraw, along with Stoneham, met with Rickey and dazzled him with cash offers that eventually reached $350,000. Rickey, however, realizing Hornsby was en route to becoming an all-time great, spurned the Giants' gold. But by 1926 the situation had changed. Hornsby, like Frisch with McGraw, was persona non grata with Breadon and the deal was consummated.

Though hitting .361 for the Giants in 1927, a year McGraw finally wangled Roush from the Reds, Hornsby's New York stay was brief. His relationship with Stoneham became shattered when the bluntly outspoken Hornsby minced no words telling off his employer. It was to become an enduring problem with The Rajah, one that was later to make him a baseball nomad. Then, in January 1928, Hornsby paid for his remarks when he was dealt to the tail-end Braves for Catcher Frank Hogan and Outfielder Jimmy Welsh. It was not one of the Giants' all-time great transactions. McGraw never approved of Hornsby's dismissal, and when The Rajah stroked .387 for the Braves that season, the critics, realizing the Giants finished just two games behind the pennant-winning Cardinals, ripped the off-season trade.

In fact, shortly after the deal, the New York Baseball Writers, at their annual mid-winter dinner and show, zinged Hornsby's departure in song and story. With the acquisition of Hogan and Welsh, plus the announcement that young Andy Cohen would replace Hornsby at second, the scribes, in their customary off-key style, chanted:

> All your Welshes, Cohens and Hogans
> Won't begin to fill the brogans
> That Rogers Hornsby wore so well
> at second base.

By the time the Giants won another flag in 1933, McGraw was in retirement and Bill Terry was in the dugout. Terry, who was to skipper the club through the 1941 season, won pennants in 1936–1937. After that, it was mostly downhill for the Giants and the youthful Horace Stoneham who had recently succeeded his late father. In 1937 the club made a trade that writers and fans wouldn't let them forget. Terry and Stoneham sent veteran Pitcher Fred Fitzsimmons to the Dodgers for Tom Baker, an obscure right-hander who continued to remain unknown. As for Fat Freddie, who the Giants estimated was washed up at 36, he lasted until 1943 with the Dodgers and was instrumental in the 1941 flag that flew at Ebbetts Field.

Mel Ott, longtime boy wonder of the Polo Grounds, replaced Terry in December 1941. His first move was to relinquish three ballplayers and $50,000 to the Cardinals for power-hitting Johnny Mize. Except for 1942, when they finished a surprising third, the Giants, though attracting a good attendance at the Polo Grounds, spent most of the wartime seasons in the second division. When the war ended, Stoneham, flushed with wartime gate receipts, attempted, as McGraw had done in the old days, to buy a pennant. He paid the Cardinals a massive $175,000 for Catcher Walker Cooper in January 1946, but nothing happened; at least not where pennants were concerned. In 1947, when the club hit a record 221 HRs, Ott was unable to steer them any closer than fourth place.

In July 1948, the Giants made their greatest nonplayer deal since Freedman had acquired McGraw in 1902, when Stoneham dismissed the lovable Ott and replaced him with longtime firebrand, Leo Durocher. Durocher's first move was to inform Stoneham the longballing but lumbering Giant roster "wasn't my kind of ball club." Mize, who was to reach new heights in the AL, was sold to the Yankees in August 1949. Then, in December, the astute Durocher laid the groundwork for the still acclaimed "1951 Miracle Pennant" when he convinced Stoneham to deal with the Braves for Eddie Stanky and Alvin Dark.

The Giants unwillingly parted with Buddy Kerr, Willard Marshall, Sid Gordon, and Sam Webb for the second base-shortstop duo that was to help forge the flag that followed. In May 1951, five months before Bobby Thomson fired "the shot heard 'round the world" in the ninth inning of the final playoff game against the Dodgers, the Giants gained their all-time greatest performer, Willie Mays. Mays, alias The Amazin', was promoted from the club's Minneapolis affiliate, and what he was to accomplish during the next two decades is a book in itself.

Another Giant pennant, the last the Giants were to win in New York, was achieved in 1954, but not before Stoneham, urged by Durocher, made another deal with Boston. This time they obtained left-handers Johnny Antonelli and Don Liddle, plus Infielder Bill Klaus and Ebba St. Claire, a catcher. In exchange the Braves received Sam Calderone, a catcher and the still lionized Bobby Thomson.

Stoneham, ever the sentimentalist, hated to part with Thomson. In fact, he made it a point to reacquire the then fading performer in April 1958. Bringing back old favorites, though their playing skills had already tarnished, was always Stoneham's thing. His managers and their coaching staffs were invariably old Giants. The late Sid Gordon, whom he traded and then recovered, is a perfect example of Stoneham's sympathies toward loyal employees. "Horace takes care of his own" was a baseball statement not without fact.

To make the Stanky-Dark deal in 1949, Stoneham had to relinquish Gordon, a longtime favorite. Then, after the trade was completed, Stoneham recalled how Gordon, who'd been seeking $30,000, had agreed to the owner's offer of $27,500. Though Gordon was now a member of the Braves, who assumed the contract he'd signed prior to the deal, Stoneham made a typical gesture. Rather than have Gordon think he was shortchanged, Stoneham wrote out a check for $2,500 and sent it to Gordon's wife with instructions to buy herself a mink coat.

After Durocher's departure following the 1955 season, Bill Rigney managed the Giants their final two years in New York. He even accompanied them to San Francisco until being dismissed and replaced by Dark in 1961.

However, prior to their California switch, the Giants engineered two more trades, neither of which produced the desired results. In June 1956, Stoneham made a move with the Cardinals, landing Red Schoendienst, Bill Sarni, Jackie Brandt, and Dick Littlefield for Dark, Liddle, Whitey Lockman, and Ray Katt. In December of that year, Stoneham tried to exchange Littlefield and $35,000 to the Dodgers for longtime Giant nemesis Jackie Robinson. But Robby put the kibosh on that one by announcing his retirement from baseball.

Upon arriving in San Francisco, Stoneham celebrated the event by making his first California deal. It wasn't a bell ringer. But just for the record, he sent Ozzie Virgil, now a Giant coach, and Infielder Gail Harris to Detroit for Third Baseman Jim Finigan.

The long-awaited pennant finally came to Candlestick Park

in 1962, and it was a deal made the previous November that clinched it. On that occasion Stoneham sent Pitchers Ed Fisher, Dom Zanni, Verle Tiefenthaler, and Outfielder-First Baseman Bob Farley to the Chicago White Sox for Pitchers Billy Pierce and Don ("Perfect Game") Larsen. Both were instrumental in the pennant that followed. Since then, other deals, none of which produced Giant flags, were made. And while the club occasionally prospered and mostly faltered in the intervening seasons, Stoneham continued to make trades.

Stoneham had two different and very important jobs during recent seasons. One he liked. It involved trading for players. The other he disliked. It was a demanding and never-ending search for dollars to help keep his club afloat in stormy financial seas.

As Trader Stoneham, Horace made the first of two biggie deals in November of 1971. He swapped Gaylord Perry, then a good pitcher, for Cleveland's Sam McDowell, who had all the tools to become a great pitcher. ("Sudden") Sam, however, was involved in two incidents Stoneham had not bargained for. Twice in successive springs McDowell was the party of the first part in brushes with the police in the Phoenix, Arizona, airport before he had an opportunity to claim his luggage after deplaning. The skyscraper southpaw lost both of these decisions, a harbinger of things to come in his brief and not overly successful career as a Giant. Sam lasted until June of his second season before he was on the move again to the Yankees in a straight cash transfer.

Stoneham's next—and last—major move involved trading Bobby Bonds also to the Yankees for Bobby Murcer after the 1974 season. It was a good break for both clubs. Although he was hampered by injuries, Bonds still managed to hit 32 home runs and steal 30 bases for the Yankees. Taking over for Bonds in the Giants' outfield, Murcer collected 91 RBIs to high-spot his .298 batting average in his first National League season.

Because Horace proved a better trader than hunter of dollars trying to bail out his team, the club was sold before the 1976 season. Bob Lurie, a director in Stoneham's organization, headed the San Francisco-Phoenix group purchasing the Giants. The selling price was a reported transaction of eight million and one dollar. Now, for the first time since 1919, the Giants are in operation without a Stoneham at the helm. First it was Horace's father, Charles, and then Horace himself bowing out with a sad Last hurrah!

JOE McGUFF
Sports Editor, *Kansas City Star*

Joe McGuff has carried his trusty Underwood portable typewriter literally thousands of miles since becoming a sports writer in 1951. Joe joined the baseball beat when Kansas City was still a member of the American Association. He started covering the Athletics when they moved from Philadelphia to Kansas City in 1955 and remained on the beat until he was named the *Star*'s sports editor in 1966. Joe has written one book, *Winning It All,* a story of the Kansas City Chiefs' rise to professional football supremacy. Five different times McGuff was named the outstanding sports writer in the state of Missouri by the National Association of Sports Writers and Broadcasters.

15/THE ROYALS

Yankee shuttle bus burns, but trades continue

The history of major league baseball trading in Kansas City is relatively brief, going back only to 1955, but it has been eventful, controversial, scandalous, and in many respects incredible.

To understand the strange developments that have taken place, it is necessary to approach them from a chronological perspective. For the last eighteen years that Kansas City had a minor league team it was a member of the Yankee organization, and players went up and down from New York to Kansas City with something of a yo-yo effect. In 1955 the Philadelphia Athletics franchise was moved to Kansas City, and local baseball fans celebrated what they thought was an end to an era of subservience. The celebration proved to be premature. Over the next five years the Yankees and A's made so many trades that Kansas City was frequently referred to as "a Yankee farm club."

Charles O. Finley purchased the Kansas City franchise in the winter of 1960–1961 and quickly vowed that there would be no more trades with the Yankees. He added a flamboyant touch to the occasion by buying an old school bus and burning it in a parking lot adjacent to Municipal Stadium. With members of the media gathered around him, Finley proclaimed that he was burning the shuttle bus to Yankee Stadium. A little more than four months later he traded Bud Daley, his best pitcher, to the Yankees.

Finley moved the A's to Oakland in 1969, and the following year Kansas City started over with an expansion franchise. In a period of five years Cedric Tallis, the executive vice-president and general manager, compiled what may rank as the greatest trading record in the history of baseball. On June 11, 1974, Tallis was fired by the Royals' owner, Ewing Kauffman, for reasons that have never been fully explained.

In the thirteen years that the A's were in Kansas City a total of 288 different players were members of the team.

The Yankee-farm-club label that was fastened on Kansas City in the period from 1955 through 1959 had considerable justification. At the time the A's were owned by Arnold Johnson, a Chicago businessman with close ties to the Yankees, and the two teams made a total of 16 transactions involving 59 players. Never before or since have two major league teams had such an unusual relationship.

Ten of the players dealt between the Yankees and A's were traded twice. Among those shuffled back and forth were Ralph Terry, Enos Slaughter, Bob Cerv, and Harry ("Suitcase") Simpson.

Typical of the maneuvering that took place between the A's and the Yankees were deals involving Murry Dickson, a veteran pitcher, and Cletis Boyer, signed by the A's as their first bonus boy and later delivered to the Yankees. Dickson was acquired by the A's in the fall of 1957 after being released by the Cardinals. In 1958 the A's were enjoying what at that time was their best season. On August 22, they traded Dickson to the Yankees, who had the pennant race well under control but wanted some insurance plus relief help for the World Series. The details of the trade were astonishing.

On the night the deal was announced, the A's were in sixth place, but they were only two and a half games out of fourth and six and a half out of second. In those days a first-division finish would have led to a civic victory celebration in Kansas City. Dickson was 42, but he had a 9–5 record, a 3.27 ERA, and was the second biggest winner on what was a thin staff. And what did the A's get for Dickson? Well, fans, hang on to your baseball cushion. They got a player to be named later. Moreover, the unnamed player was not to be delivered until the end of the season. When he finally arrived, he was an obscure minor leaguer named Zeke Bella.

The overtones of the Boyer deal were even more disturbing. Boyer was signed May 31, 1955, for a reported bonus of $40,000. As the A's first bonus boy, the public accepted him as a symbol of the club's determination to build for the future. At that time a player who received in excess of $4,000 was obliged to remain with the parent club for at least two seasons before he could be optioned to the minors. As soon as Boyer had completed his two-year period of bench sitting with the A's, he was traded to the Yankees. At the time Kansas City fans angrily asked why the A's would keep a player who was regarded as an excellent prospect on their bench for two years and then trade him to the Yankees as soon as he was eligible to play in the minors.

Years later I learned from what I consider an unimpeachable source that the A's actually signed Boyer for the Yankees, and there was an understanding that he would be turned over to New York as soon as his two-year bonus period expired. The A's actually tried to move Boyer to the Yankees as early as February 19, 1957, but Ford Frick, then the commissioner of baseball, ruled that Boyer would have to stay with the A's until he completed his bonus period.

The biggest deal between the Yankees and the A's, and the one that eventually became the most controversial, was the one in which Roger Maris was sent to the Yankees. Two years after leaving the A's, Maris hit 61 HRs to break Babe Ruth's single-season record.

Before we proceed further in examining the numerous trades between the Yankees and A's, it is important for the reader to understand how this chummy relationship came about. Johnson was a self-made and highly successful businessman. One of his most profitable ventures was the purchase of the holdings of Louis Leverone in Automatic Canteen, a pioneer vending company. Johnson became president of Automatic Canteen and a member of the board of directors. Also on the board was Dan Topping, a coowner of the Yankees along with Del Webb.

Johnson had only a casual interest in sports, but he had a consuming interest in making profitable business deals. After becoming acquainted with Topping, he began to think about the Yankees' real estate holdings in New York and devised a scheme that would produce big tax savings for the Yankees and a profit for himself. Johnson purchased Yankee Stadium and Blues Stadium in Kansas City from Topping and Webb for $6.5 million. He sold the ground under Yankee Stadium to the Knights of Columbus, leased it back and then leased the land and the stadium to the Yankees along with the Kansas City facility.

In 1954 reports spread that the Mack family would have to sell the Athletics. Ernest Mehl, then the sports editor of the *Kansas City Star*, attempted to put together a local group to purchase the team. When this effort was unsuccessful, he began looking for outside interests that might buy the team and move it to Kansas

City. Del Webb recommended that Mehl contact Johnson. When Mehl and Johnson met for the first time, Mehl proposed that he buy the team. Johnson told him, "Not me. I'm a businessman, not a baseball man. I like baseball and I played it as a kid, but I know almost nothing about it."

In time Johnson changed his mind. His motive was profit, and the men who helped to set up the deal for him were Webb and Topping. Johnson purchased the A's franchise after a protracted period of negotiations, and along with it he got Shibe Park in Philadelphia. Johnson himself purchased 51 percent of the stock. Roy Mack, a son of Connie Mack, and some Chicago associates took the remaining 49 percent. Johnson sold Shibe Park to the Phillies, Blues Stadium to the city of Kansas City, and collected a five-year advance on his radio rights in Kansas City. In the end he was able to put the deal together with little or no cash outlay. Hence the warm, friendly feeling for Webb and Topping.

Johnson looked on his Kansas City operation as a business deal and little more. He inserted an escape clause in the lease that provided he could cancel the lease any year that the attendance fell below 850,000. Johnson's critics claimed that he saw Kansas City as little more than a stopping place on his way to the West Coast, but the Dodgers and Giants got there first. What Johnson's long range plans were in Kansas City no one found out because he died in the spring of 1960, suffering a cerebral hemorrhage while driving home from Connie Mack Field in West Palm Beach, Florida.

So much for the background on the A's-Yankees relationship.

Sixteen deals involving more than fifty players highspotted the Yankees' and A's *"Trade Him!"* activity starting in 1955 and continuing for three years and nine months. If nothing else, the volume of this wheeling and dealing between the same two clubs was unusual. Considering the fact that money figured in seven of these transfers, the rival general managers were burdened with almost monthly updating of the blue book values of the traded players.

Enos ("Country") Slaughter, the longtime colorful Cardinal, was traded twice. It was May 11, 1955, when the ageless, spirited Slaughter was sent to Kansas City with Johnny Sain for Sonny Dixon and cash. It wasn't until August 25, 1956, that Country was able to use the second half of his New York to Kansas City to New York flight ticket. It mattered not to Slaughter because he returned to Yankee Stadium in time to be eligible for the 1956 World Series between the Yankees and Dodgers. In this manner he doubled his pleasure: enjoying a left fielder's view of Don Larsen's first-ever-perfect game in the postseason classic and cashing a share of a winning World Series split. For Enos the timing was as perfect as Larsen's historic performance.

Speaking of high stakes, Ralph Terry can tell an even better story. He was traded to the A's on the last day of trading (June 15) in 1957. Within two years he was back, pitching for the Yankees, and had the good fortune of pitching in four straight World Series from 1960 through 1963.

Roger Maris followed Terry to New York some six months later, and still arrived in time to match Ralph's World Series jackpot. Maris's Ruth-topping total of 61 HRs in 1961 proved to be another first. It made him easily available to the endorsement-rich gentry along New York's Madison Avenue—and that isn't straw they bale.

Johnson staunchly defended his Yankee deals, claiming that he was merely seeking the best talent available. Other members of the AL saw the A's-Yankees relationship as an unholy alliance that was helping to keep the Yankees atop the AL standings. In the 10-month period between Johnson's death and the purchase of the Kansas City franchise by Finley, only one other deal was made with the Yankees. It came on May 16, 1960, when Bob Cerv was traded back to the Yankees for Andy Carey.

Finley was a surprise arrival on the Kansas City baseball scene. A group of Kansas City investors was seeking to purchase the A's franchise in the fall of 1960, and they signed a bill of conditional sale with representatives of the Johnson estate. The condition attached to the sale was the approval of the probate court in Chicago. Finley had been seeking to obtain the Los Angeles expansion franchise, but the AL decided to award it to Gene Autry. Finley then went into probate court in Chicago and offered to outbid the Kansas City group for the Johnson holdings. The court was interested only in getting the largest possible price for the Johnson estate, and because of this situation Finley was able to obtain the team.

He arrived in Kansas City with all the blare and fanfare of a circus band. He promised to eventually move his family to Kansas City, he made plans to refurbish the stadium, and he hired Frank Lane as his general manager. In February 1961, he staged his great bus burning and promised there would be no more trades with the Yankees. On June 14 Bud Daley was sent to the Yankees for Art Ditmar and Deron Johnson.

Finley had an interesting explanation ready when asked why he had approved the trade. "Maybe I ought to blame this on my father," he told Mehl. "I guess when I was in high school I was a hard-nosed little punk. I made up my mind to do something, and I was determined I was going to do it. My father told me one day that a wise man changes his mind, but a fool never does. I was thinking of that after I okayed the deal Frank Lane was working on for a week.

"Now I guess I had better tell my thoughts leading up to the thing. I've never gotten into such a business where you make a concrete statement, repeat it a hundred times and then suddenly change your mind.

"Boy, have they been putting the heat on me. Maybe I got out from under. Maybe I didn't. I know I tried. I know I religiously tried to live up to the promise until today. I didn't want to trade with the Yanks. I felt the fans in Kansas City were fed up with that exchange back and forth . . . Put it down to baseball being a screwy business. That's the best I can do."

In reality the trade was orchestrated by Lane, who had clashed repeatedly with Finley and perhaps obtained a degree of satisfaction in seeing Finley pressured into making the deal. Finley was vulnerable to pressure at the time because the team was losing, attendance was smaller than Finley expected, and the mood of the public was turning sour.

Finley was to make two other trades with the Yankees. On May 4, 1965, he sent Doc Edwards to the Yankees for Rollie Sheldon and John Blanchard. On June 10, 1966, Fred Talbot and Bill Bryan were traded to the Yankees for Roger Repoz, Gil Blanco, and Bill Stafford. The two biggest trades Finley made during his seven years in Kansas City came in 1963 and resulted in the acquisition of Rocky Colavito and Jim Gentile. Jerry Lumpe, Ed Rakow, and Dave Wickersham were sent to Detroit for Colavito, Bob Anderson, and $50,000. Nine days later Finley gave up Norm Siebern for Gentile and $25,000.

Many of Finley's deals were made with the profit motive in mind. In a period of three years he made six deals that brought him $425,000 in cash. If this meant that Kansas City was getting the worst of it from a talent standpoint, Charles O. was not overly concerned because he was trying to move the team anyway. In the fall of 1967, the AL allowed Finley to move the A's to Oakland. Kansas City was given an expansion franchise, but it did not start competition until 1969. Ewing Kauffman, founder of a Kansas City pharmaceutical company, was awarded the franchise, and he named Cedric Tallis his executive vice-president and general manager.

From 1969 through June 11, 1974, when he was fired, Tallis made what may rank as the most amazing series of player acquisitions in the history of baseball. His trading record is all the more remarkable because the Royals were an expansion franchise and had little in the way of trading material. When the Royals opened the 1975 season, six of the eight starting positions were being manned on a full-time basis by players acquired in trades.

Tallis made his first important trade in April 1969, when he obtained Lou Piniella from Seattle, also an expansion team, for Steve Whitaker, an outfielder, and John Gelnar, a pitcher. Piniella became a star in Kansas City while Whitaker and Gelnar quickly faded from the major league scene.

Tallis made one of his greatest trades at the winter meetings in December of 1969. He obtained Amos Otis, the Royals' talented center fielder, and Bob Johnson, a hard-throwing pitcher, for Joe Foy. Two seasons later Foy was through in baseball. In June of 1970, Tallis obtained Cookie Rojas from the Cardinals for a minor leaguer, Fred Rico.

The next big trade came at the winter meetings in December 1970. Tallis sent Bob Johnson, Jackie Hernandez, and Jimmy Campanis to the Pirates for Fred Patek, Jerry May, and Bruce Dal Canton. Patek, a shortstop with a high-velocity arm, teamed with Rojas to give the Royals one of the best double-play combinations in the majors. In December 1971, Tallis again made a major acquisition at the winter meetings, obtaining John Mayberry, a power-hitting first baseman, from Houston in exchange for two pitchers, Jim York and Lance Clemons. At the winter meetings in 1972 Tallis obtained Hal McRae from Cincinnati for Roger Nelson, a sore-armed pitcher, and Richie Scheinblum. Fran Healy, the Royals' catcher, was lost to the Giants when he became frozen in the minors, but he was later reacquired for a minor league pitcher, Greg Minton.

Perhaps the trade that Tallis recalls most vividly is the one for Otis. Negotiations started at the time of the World Series in

1969. The Mets wanted a third baseman, and the Royals were offering Foy, but the Mets were more interested in Ken McMullen, who was with Washington. The deal with Washington finally broke down when the Senators kept holding out for two starting pitchers. In the early stages of the talks between the Royals and Mets, Tommie Agee was offered to Tallis, but he declined saying that he wanted Otis. The Royals also wanted Johnson, but the Mets were unwilling to include him. A final meeting was held to discuss the deal, and Tallis told Johnny Murphy, his counterpart with the Mets, that there was no way the Royals could make the deal unless Johnson was included.

"My heart was in my throat when I said it," Tallis recalls. "We sat there a while and finally Murphy said it was a deal."

Tallis is gone, but among Kansas City baseball fans his trades won him a reputation as Cedric The Great.

JACK LANG
Writer-Columnist, *Long Island Press* and *Newark Star Ledger*

Jack Lang, baseball writer-columnist for the *Long Island Press* and *Newark Star Ledger* as well as other Newhouse Newspapers, owns a unique and unchallenged first. He is the only writer who has covered the Mets for all fourteen years of their existence. The Original Met with a typewriter is a thirty-year veteran on the beat, having covered the Dodgers (in Brooklyn) and Yankees earlier. Lang scooped the world on the Giants trading Willie Mays to the Mets (1972), and the selection of Johnny Keane to replace Yogi Berra as Yankee skipper (1964). Jack, national secretary-treasurer of the Baseball Writers' Association of America since 1966 and honorary captain of the writers' World Series charter flights, coauthored Hall of Famer Whitey Ford's book.

16/THE METS

Player to be named later— it's Chiti coming, going

You could sense it that very first year. You just knew that as they continued to grow, the New York Mets—born of expansion in 1962—would make some deals that would turn out to be lulus. And in their brief existence, they have. Most of them they'd prefer to forget.

George Weiss, the master architect who designed and built the great Yankee teams that won ten pennants in a dozen years during the late 1940s and throughout the 1950s, found himself in a strange position in the Mets' first year. Retired against his own wishes by coowners Del Webb and Dan Topping of the Yankees, Weiss was hired by Joan Payson and M. Donald Grant, principal owners of the Mets, to try and build the Mets into a winner. But with the has-beens and never-would-bes George had to start with following the October 1961 expansion draft, he had little recourse but to try and patch up his team in any way he could.

With the Yankees and their vast farm system and unlimited financial resources, Weiss held the reins and could dictate deals that were advantageous to his club. He could peddle off a bundle of Triple-A ballplayers to the have-not clubs like Kansas City and come up with a star like Roger Maris.

It was different with the Mets. George had few players anyone wanted. He found himself going around begging some of his former victims for help . . . any kind of help. And so it was in early 1962 that he made two deals that were doozies. For a change, it was Weiss who got shortchanged. Believing that the cornerstone of any club was a good, solid defensive catcher, Weiss made Hobie Landrith the Mets' first draft pick. When Landrith proved not to be the catcher Weiss thought he was, he sent Hobie off to Washington in exchange for aging former Yankee star Gene Woodling. But he had to have another catcher.

Lo and behold, he came up with Harry Chiti, a burly catcher with some power who had once been a hot prospect with the Cubs. Chiti never made it big with the Wrigleys, and by 1962 he was property of the Indians and playing for their Jacksonville farm club. Weiss decided Chiti would find the short foul lines at the Polo Grounds inviting and arranged for a deal with the Indians.

"We have purchased Harry Chiti for a player to be named later," Weiss happily announced. After Chiti caught a few games for the Mets, it was obvious he was not the answer either. Soon Weiss was ready to unload him. And unload him he did. To complete the purchase of Chiti from Jacksonville he still owed the Indians a player. And who was the player he finally delivered? Why Harry Chiti, of course. So one of the very first deals in Met history was Harry Chiti for Harry Chiti!

If that deal brought guffaws from the veterans in the press box and the New Breed Met fans, they were mild compared to the comments that followed a subsequent deal involving Don Zimmer. Zimmer had been a premium draft pick at the cost of $125,000. He was well known in New York, having played for the Brooklyn Dodgers before they moved west. A fiery player with some power and a penchant for striking out or getting hit in the head with baseballs, Zimmer was installed as the club's third baseman by Manager Casey Stengel.

Zimmer was the first of 49 men tried at that position by the Mets in their first 14 years. No one has held it more than one full season. Zimmer did not hold it for even one month. Tippy—as his teammates nicknamed him—opened the Mets' first season by going 0–for–34 at the plate. It is still a club record. Then one day Zimmer broke out of his slump and got a single. The next day he got another hit. The following day he was traded.

"Weiss wanted to deal Zimmer while he was hot," one baseball writer observed in his story announcing the trade that sent Zimmer to the Reds in exchange for rookie Cliff Cook. It looked like a good deal at the time. Cook had been a third baseman at Indianapolis with a record as a power hitter. Zimmer was old, Cook was young. The Mets were getting a hot prospect for a retread.

The Reds at the time were operated by Bill DeWitt, longtime general manager of the old St. Louis Browns and later an assistant to Weiss with the Yankees. It was one old friend doing another a favor. But DeWitt proved to be less than a friend in this deal. It wasn't until Cook reported that the Mets discovered he couldn't bend over. He had come up with a slipped disk in his back and was useless to the Mets. An operation followed, but Cook never became the player his minor league record promised.

In that very first year Weiss made one deal that did give the Mets some respectability. He purchased Outfielder Frank Thomas from the Milwaukee Braves for cash. The Polo Grounds was an ideal park for Thomas, who because of his size, personality, and demeanor was dubbed "The Big Donkey." Thomas did hit for the Mets. He hit 34 HRs that first year at the Polo Grounds, a club record until Dave Kingman hit 36 in 1975. He also knocked in 94 RBIs, a club record that stood until Donn Clendenon drove in 97 in 1970. But Thomas also had a way of irritating everyone around him.

"He's the only guy I ever met," said one player, "who you want to punch in the nose when he says good morning to you."

Thomas also fancied himself as an airline stewardess. On all the Mets' charter flights that year, Frank insisted on serving the food. He would shove a tray in front of players and say "Gonna eat?" They had no choice the way Frank put it. He lasted with the Mets through 1964 when he was traded to the Phillies for someone named Wayne Graham, one of the many who were tried at third base and found wanting. Wayne lasted just one season.

The continuing and futile search for a third baseman in every year of their existence resulted in the Mets making two infamous deals. They are deals the Mets would prefer to forget, but the outstanding performances of the players they traded away serve as constant reminders to them and their fans. Perhaps the worst deal the Mets ever made was consummated on December 10, 1971, and was made almost out of desperation.

It was just days after the annual baseball meetings were concluded in Phoenix, Arizona, a session which saw a record number of deals completed. Twenty-three of the twenty-four major league clubs had swapped one or more players. Only the Mets stood pat. Aware of the criticism heaped on them for their do-nothing attitude, the Mets were panicked into a deal by Don Grant, who serves as chairman of their board. It was Grant who pushed for the deal that sent Nolan Ryan, Leroy Stanton, Don Rose, and Francisco Estrada to the Angels for aging and injured Jim Fregosi.

It proved to be one of the all-time duds when Fregosi, fat and out of shape, hit only .232 for the Mets while Ryan was winning 19 games for the Angels and leading the AL with 329 strikeouts. A year later, even though Fregosi had finally gotten in shape, he could not play regularly in the NL and was sold for cash to the Rangers.

Ryan, meanwhile, went on to become the premier pitcher in the AL. He won more than 20 games in both 1972 and 1973 and led the league with strikeouts for a third straight year. On the way he also authored three no-hit, no-run games and became a $100,000 a year pitcher. To add to the Mets' embarrassment, Stanton also became a fine hitting outfielder with the Angels. Years later in a moment of pique, Grant blamed a sports writer for the ill-fated Ryan deal.

"You've been knocking us for years because we made that deal," the chairman of the board shouted. "You're responsible for that deal. You criticized us for not making a deal at the winter meetings so we made one."

"I told you to make a deal," the reporter replied, "but not that deal!"

Equally bad was the deal the Mets made on December 3, 1969, two months after they shocked the baseball world by winning the NL Eastern Division title, then knocking off the Atlanta Braves for the league championship, and finally the Orioles for the World Championship.

The Mets had a fairly young and set team and seemed on their way to building a dynasty. They had a pitching staff that included Tom Seaver, Nolan Ryan, Gary Gentry, Jerry Koosman, and Tug McGraw, with Jon Matlack waiting in the wings. They were set everywhere but at the usual trouble spot—third base. So their objective at the winter meetings that year was to land an established third baseman. And they did. They picked up veteran AL Third Baseman Joe Foy in a deal with Kansas City. Foy had hit .262 for KC and was a right-handed hitter with some power. It appeared to be a good deal. In exchange the Mets gave up Amos Otis and Bob Johnson, two players that had tried and were sent back to the minors.

Like so many others they made, this was a deal that was to return and haunt the Mets. Not only did Foy not hit or field the way the Mets expected, he also had personal problems off the field which interfered with his play. After only one year he was gone.

But Otis found a new life in Kansas City. The Mets had made the mistake of trying to make a third baseman out of Amos, but he was unfamiliar and uncomfortable at the position. He flopped badly. The Royals, however, played Amos where he really belonged . . . in center field. And as he developed into one of the AL's best, the Mets were constantly embarrassed because they were unable to come up with a consistently good center fielder. Until Tommie Agee came along and did the job for a couple of years, center field was almost as much of a problem as third base.

So desperate were the Mets for a center fielder that in the winter of 1966 they traded away their most effective pitcher of the previous season—Dennis Ribant—for Center Fielder Don Bosch and veteran Pitcher Don Cardwell. Bosch, who had a fabled minor league career as a premier flychaser, proved to be one of the biggest frauds ever perpetrated on Mets fans. Bosch had come up in the Pittsburgh chain but couldn't dislodge Bill Virdon from center, so the Pirates traded him for Ribant. A constant worrier who had ulcers in his early twenties and premature gray hair, Bosch tried to put up a bravado front. But after taking one look at the smallish ballplayer who was supposed to be the solution to his center field problems, Manager Wes Westrum confided his feelings to intimates.

"My God, they sent me a midget," he observed. "He doesn't even look like a ballplayer."

Bosch played only 44 games that year and hit .140. The next year he played 50 games and hit .171. In October he was sold to Montreal and later figured in a deal for one of the biggest players in the game today. In July 1970, Bosch was traded by Montreal to Houston for an obscure relief pitcher named Mike Marshall. If the Bosch end of the deal did not pan out for the Mets, the other half of it did. Don Cardwell did yeoman work on the mound for four years and contributed eight victories during the 1969 pennant campaign.

Not all Met deals have been bad ones, although the scales do lean heavily to the negative side. One of the all-time good ones, unheralded at the time, was made on October 16, 1965. It brought Catcher Jerry Grote to the Mets from Houston in exchange for Pitchers Tom Parsons and Gary Kroll. Grote has in the years that followed established himself as one of the top defensive catchers in the game, played on two pennant winners, and twice been named to the All-Star team.

Another good deal was the one in November 1972 that

brought Second Baseman Felix Millan and Pitcher George Stone to New York. The Mets sent to the Braves Pitchers Dan Frisella and Gary Gentry, both of whom have since departed the Atlanta scene. Millan has developed into the best second baseman the Mets ever had, an excellent Number Two hitter in the lineup who can move a runner along, and an outstanding pivot man on the double play. In addition, Stone had a fine 12–3 record in the 1973 pennant season.

Two big deals the Mets made with Montreal over the years also led to two pennants. Until they obtained Donn Clendenon on June 15, 1969, the Mets did not have a professional RBI man in their lineup. But Clendenon, who had been traded by the Expos to Houston and failed to report, gave the Mets just what they needed. In the 62 games he played for the Mets that year, he slammed a dozen HRs with 37 RBIs. In the World Series against Baltimore that year, he was a top slugger with three homers and a .357 average.

In 1972 the Mets made another key deal with the Expos that led to their 1973 championship. In that swap they risked three "futures" for one established star. In order to get Rusty Staub, the idol of the Montreal fans, the Mets had to give up Shortstop Tim Foli, First Baseman Mike Jorgensen, and Outfielder Ken Singleton. The gamble paid off. Staub was a perennial RBI leader for the Mets—a big man in the 1973 playoffs with three homers against Cincinnati, and was the top hitter in the World Series against Oakland with .423.

But perhaps the most popular trade in Mets history was made on May 11, 1972, when Grant and Ms. Payson achieved a long cherished dream by bringing Willie Mays back to New York. It was as if Ms. Payson, a patron of the arts, had just purchased a Van Gogh or a Rembrandt. Mays, then 41, was well past his prime but he had long been one of the most popular players ever to appear in New York, and Grant and Ms. Payson felt it only right he should end his career where he began it in 1951.

The Mets paid handsomely for the right to put Willie in a New York uniform once again. They sent debt-ridden Horace Stoneham better than $100,000 in cash as well as a minor league pitcher, Charlie Williams. More importantly, they took over an obligation Stoneham had made to Mays to pay him $50,000 a year for ten years after his retirement from the game.

The deal had been quietly discussed between Grant and Stoneham for some time, with Grant stressing the fact that although they wanted Willie, they hoped to get him while he still had some ability left. They were willing to settle for just a year if that's all it was, but they wanted at least that much.

I was fortunate enough to break the news that created front-page headlines in New York when the wire services picked up the story from my own paper, *The Long Island Press*. The Mets had been in San Francisco ten days earlier, and while I was having dinner with a friend, he remarked to me: "Hey, you guys (the Mets) wouldn't be interested in Willie Mays, would you?" The friend was in a position to know something was in the wind.

"I'm sure they would," was my reply. "Mrs. Payson has always hoped he would play for the Mets some day.

The next day I sought out my friend.

"Were you putting me on last night or were you trying to tell me something?" I inquired.

"I think I've already said too much," was his only reply.

That was all I needed to go to work on the story. The following day when the Mets arrived back in New York, they had the day off. But I didn't. I called Grant at his Wall Street brokerage office and put the question to him.

"Are the Mets negotiating with the Giants for Willie Mays?" I asked him.

At first Grant hedged, stumbled for the right words, and suggested that if anything appeared in print, it might kill any chance of obtaining Mays. His remarks were tantamount to admitting a deal was in the works. He continued to request that I not write anything.

"Look, Don," I said, "no matter what you say I owe my allegiance to my paper, not the Mets. Based on what I know and what you have said, I have to write a story to the effect that negotiations are underway."

In fairness to Grant I must admit he then relented and explained that he had talks with Stoneham and there was a chance of a deal. He still expressed the feeling that publicity would kill the deal. That was not my concern. The eight-column headline across the front page of *The Long Island Press* the next day read: "Shea, Hey! Willie Mays is Coming Home." One week later, on May 11, the deal was announced. That also happened to be my birthday. Confirmation of my "exclusive" was one of the best birthday presents I ever received.

Willie hit .250 his first year as a Met, but he did hit eight home runs, played center for them in the World Series, and got a winning hit in the only game he appeared in against Cincinnati in the playoffs.

Mays's flair for the dramatic was not lost even in his declining years. In his first game as a Met on May 14, 1972, Mays hit a solo homer against his former Giant mates that resulted in a 5–4 victory for the Mets. And on his first visit back to Candlestick Park in San Francisco, it was Willie's two-run homer that produced a 3–1 Met victory.

Ranking right behind the Mays deal in popularity with the Mets fans was the one the club pulled off in October 1967, when Grant and General Manager Bing Devine succeeded in "trading" for a manager.

Wes Westrum, who had sought a renewal of his contract in the waning weeks of the 1967 season and did not get it, up and quit in late September. After several weeks of negotiation, the Mets managed to bring the ever-popular Gil Hodges back to New York. He had managed with success in Washington, to whom the Mets had released him in 1963, and now they wanted him back. But to return him, the Senators insisted on compensation. And so the Mets sent Pitcher Bill Denehy and a reported $200,000 in cash to complete the "deal."

Bringing former Gotham favorites back to Shea Stadium always did sit well with the tradition-minded New York fans. An earlier and equally popular move was the signing of Yogi Berra in 1965 after the Yankees had unceremoniously dumped him following the 1964 season. This was Yogi's reward for leading the Yankees to a pennant and carrying the Cardinals to seven games in the World Series.

"I knew late in the season I was gone," Berra has since admitted. "They never told me but Ralph Houk (then general manager) and the late Dan Topping (then coowner) had made up their minds not to rehire me.

"After they fired me in Topping's apartment the day after the Series ended, I quickly had calls from other clubs. I could have gone to Washington or the White Sox as a player-coach.

"But my old boss, George Weiss, also called me. A few nights later I drove up to his home in Greenwich, Connecticut, and we discussed a contract with the Mets.

"Mr. Weiss hired me as a coach but asked me to work out in

spring training and see if I could play. After all, I hadn't played since 1963. So I tried and late in April 1965 I signed a player contract.

"But I soon knew I couldn't play anymore. I was in four games, went to bat nine times and got two singles. When I couldn't get around on the fastball, I decided to quit just before my fortieth birthday in May."

Berra remained as a coach and in 1972, when Hodges died of a heart attack at the end of spring training, the Mets' hierarchy did not wait long to tap Yogi as his successor. Hodges died in West Palm Beach on Sunday, April 2. Because of the player strike, there were no games and Yogi was down in Miami visiting relatives. The night of Hodges's death, M. Donald Grant, the Mets' chairman of the board, called Berra and asked him to drive up to his Hobe Sound winter home just north of Palm Beach. Berra met with Grant the following morning and agreed to take the job. But no announcement would be made until Hodges's funeral was over.

The Mets were almost callous in their haste to make the announcement. As reporters filed out of the Brooklyn church following the Mass of Resurrection of Hodges, they were button-holed by Public Relations Director Harold Weissman.

"Be at Shea at two o'clock," Weissman informed. "We have a major announcement."

Sure enough, hardly moments after Hodges's casket was lowered into the grave, Grant stood in front of the assembled press and introduced Yogi as Gil's successor. Hodges's loyal coaches, Eddie Yost and Rube Walker stood behind Berra. Yogi had insisted they be retained, but the coaches' eyes were filled with tears. It turned out to be a momentous session. Immediately following the Berra announcement, Grant also informed the press of the deal that brought Rusty Staub from Montreal. Berra had not only inherited Hodges's team but the best lineup in the club's history up to that time.

If the Mays and Hodges deals met with overwhelming approval of Mets fans, one they pulled off in December 1974 did not. That was the trade that sent Tug McGraw, a popular if flaky relief pitcher, to the Phillies in exchange for Center Fielder Del Unser, Catcher Johnny Stearns, and Pitcher Mac Scarce, who in turn was traded for relief Pitcher Tom Hall. The fans did not enjoy seeing McGraw leave the Shea scene, but it did not take them long to forget the deal once they saw the professional way in which Unser played center field. For as in all sports, fans are long on memory and short on patience, and it's "what have you done for me lately" that counts. No matter how popular a player may be in a city one year, he is likely to return in a rival uniform the next year and be razzed. Shea Stadium fans are no different than those anywhere else.

ED BROWALSKI
Sports Editor, *Detroit Polish Daily News*

Ed Browalski learned his baseball as a minor league catcher.
Following retirement as an active player, Ed managed sandlot
baseball teams for more than ten years. On the major league
baseball beat his magic number is twenty-seven, the number of
consecutive years he has covered the Detroit Tigers, All-Star
games, and the World Series. Browalski founded the National
Polish-American Sports Hall of Fame, and still serves as its histori-
an. During the off-season in baseball he is active in city, state, and
national bowling circles. Ed is the immediate past president of the
Greater Detroit Bowling Association.

17/THE TIGERS

Tigers buy a team to get four players!

All or nothing! A befitting description of baseball's initial en masse player trade.

On September 16, 1885, telegraphic reports startled the NL baseball world that the Buffalo franchise was sold to Detroit for $8,000. It was amazing because the season had two weeks remaining.

It was an open secret that the "Detroits" really sought to obtain the "Big Four"—First Baseman Dennis ("Dan") Brouthers, Third Baseman James ("Deacon") White, Second Baseman Harding Richardson, and Shortstop Jack Rowe. They used an infallible method by purchasing the total Buffalo roster, like picking four choice apples from a peck. It was the original mass deal in baseball annals and set in motion a controversial four weeks.

While the Buffalo Bisons fulfilled their baseball calendar, utilizing some of the players Detroit did not want, along with several new signees, the battle of words ensued. The foursome wasted little time joining the Detroit club, but they never donned their new uniforms. NL President Nick Young decreed the quartet could not sign Detroit contracts before October 20. The four players quickly bought return-trip train tickets to Buffalo; upon arrival they declared themselves to be free agents, theorizing they had been released and could not sign with Detroit. The "Big Four Infielders" envisioned $$$ in their pockets coming from the highest bidder for their services.

The press, the fans, and the league players joined in the debate as the "paper war" stormed between the club owners and the "Big Four." The battle clouds subsided, and the players' money dreams were shattered as a later ruling declared that Detroit could place the players on the reserve list. The "Big Four" legally joined the Detroits in the spring of 1886 and sparked the team to immediate improvement. They did not zoom to the top of the circuit but contributed to an interesting race and finished only two and a-half games behind Cap Anson's Chicago White Stockings.

One year hence, Detroit savored its first pennant success with a team that was labeled among the elite of the pre-1900 era. Brouthers, White, Richardson, and Rowe made their presence known as the $8,000 investment paid off substantial dividends. The triumphant year was culminated with postseason success over the St. Louis Browns, champions of the then major league American Association.

This was a novel World Series, a traveling spectacle with 15 games played in ten different cities. It made no difference that the Detroits won their eighth and deciding contest in their eleventh meeting; the tour continued and fulfilled the original 15-game plan.

The 1887 statistics show Brouthers batting .419, Rowe and Richardson at .363—orbit figures over the previous season's averages. The year 1887 was a hitter's heaven on earth. The scoring rules were revised in favor of the batter. Bases on balls were credited as base hits while the hitters were permitted to look at four strikes instead of three. The batters' golden rule lasted only a single season's test, and the three-strike-and-out returned along with the reinstatement of the rule where a base on balls is scored as a free pass to first base.

A rare but historic player transaction episode dotted the spring of 1905. The Detroit Tigers, managed by William Armour, were training at Augusta, Georgia. Among the spring hopefuls was Detroit home-product Eddie Cicotte, the same pitcher who later became one of the game's top hurlers, only to be involved in the blemished 1919 Black Sox scandal. When the time came to reimburse the Augusta club for the use of its spring training facilities, Armour left Pitcher Cicotte behind. It's true. There was a bit more. A proviso in the settlement also called for Armour to have first pick of the Augusta players later in the season for a $500 payment.

A twist of fate in baseball history followed. Detroit suffered many outfield injuries, so Armour ordered a visitation trip to Augusta for Tigers' scout Heinie Youngman. He issued specific instructions for a good lookover of "an irrational rookie outfielder we viewed during spring sessions."

Upon Youngman's arrival, the rookie, Ty Cobb, was missing

from the lineup due to a thumb injury. Youngman had to settle for the ever-so-glowing reports issued by the Sally League on the young outfielder. Impressive words convinced Youngman, and he set in motion the deal for Cobb. The Tigers' scout tossed in an extra $250 bonus with owner Frank Navin's approval. The Detroit club also allowed Augusta to keep Cicotte. Thus, Cobb, the greatest ballplayer of all time, became a Detroit Tiger.

Cobb moved to Detroit and made his debut at Bennett Field on August 30, 1905. Two years later, Detroit captured its first AL pennant.

Cicotte, used as payment for spring training facilities, later developed into a star pitcher.

One other significant procurement was clutch-hitting Claude Rossman. Claude, a burly first baseman, was a long-ball hitter with the ability to come through in run-producing situations. The 1907 spring training season saw Cleveland's Nap Lajoie faced with a problem of deciding between Rossman and George Stovall for the Indians' first base job. Nap selected Stovall and soon Rossman became a Tiger.

As 20-year-old Cobb began his spectacular career on a .350 effort, Rossman competing in all 153 games showed a .277 average and 69 RBIs during the Tigers' pennant drive, substantiating Navin's acquisition moves. Claude batted .400 in the World Series via an 8-for-20 route against the Cubs' pitching.

The 1909 Detroit team zoomed to a great start, but a summer slump tightened the race as the young Philadelphia A's fought their way into contention. Manager Hughie Jennings asked Navin for additional infield help, and Frank proceeded accordingly by getting Second Baseman Jim Delehanty from Washington in a swap for Germany Schaefer. Several days later, Frank sent Rossman to the St. Louis Browns in return for first sacker Tom Jones. Once again the front office maneuvers bolstered the Tigers' infield. Jones's defensive prowess along with Delehanty's keystone ability seemingly provided the impetus the Tigers needed for their third pennant in a row.

Not all of Navin's deals came up in champagne flavor. Before the 1923 season, Ty Cobb, now manager, and Navin collaborated in one of Detroit's subpar transactions as they sent away Pitcher Howard Ehmke. Ty traded Ehmke, Pitcher Carl Hollings, and rookie First Baseman Floyd ("Babe") Herman to the Red Sox for Pitcher Warren ("Rip") Collins and Second Baseman Del Pratt.

Herman was the unpredictable Babe Herman of future Brooklyn notoriety. The two Tigers' acquisitions slumped to new career lows. Pratt, with hard-hitting credentials, slipped considerably and Ty benched him after 60 games. Collins, plagued by arm trouble and injuries, won only three in 10 decisions. To add to the chagrin, Ehmke relished the transfer to Boston by winning 20 and losing 17 for the cellar-dwelling Red Sox.

The 1928 season was another depressing one for Tiger owner Navin. An off-season trade moved First Baseman Lu Blue and Outfielder Heinie Manush to the St. Louis Browns for Outfielder Harry Rice, Pitcher Elam Vangilder, and Shortstop Clarence Galloway in an effort to beef up Manager George Moriarty's pitching staff. Vangilder won 11 in 21 decisions. The fleet-footed Rice batted .302, while Manush displayed a nifty .378 for the Browns, missing the batting crown by a single point as Goose Goslin led the league with .379.

To add salt to the 1928 season wounds, Beaumont, the Tigers' Texas League connection, sold Carl Hubbell to the Giants for $40,000. Hubbell had developed his famous screwball pitch, and the NLers bought Hubbell from under the Tigers' noses.

Bucky Harris took over as manager in 1929. The Detroit fans had little to cheer about a sixth-place finish. They certainly put up a loud complaint on October 14 when Navin announced the sale of four-time AL batting champion Harry Heilmann to the Cincinnati team in the "other" league. The fans never forgave Harris for approving the Heilmann waiver deal.

On Memorial Day of 1930, Navin and Harris came up with another deal, not too popular with New York, for a pair of former Yankee star players. The Tigers welcomed Pitcher Waite Hoyt and Shortstop Mark Koenig for Outfielder Harry Rice, Pitcher Owen Carroll, and Infielder George Wuestling. Harris soon learned that Hoyt had lost his fast ball while Koenig arrived wearing glasses, and the shortstop problem remained unsolved. Harris tried to make a pitcher out of Koenig, but that trial did not last too long.

Bucky resigned on September 27, 1933, and the Harris five-year plan ended with second division blues. Navin began a search for a new manager. He was unable to land Babe Ruth, who bypassed Navin's managerial bid because of travel commitments to Hawaii. The Tigers' executive knew that the nation's depression had also hit Connie Mack's finances, and he needed instant cash like many other owners. Navin contacted Walter O. Briggs, now one-half owner of the Tigers, and discussed the merits of four managerial candidates. "Get Cochrane from the A's," said Briggs.

Navin finalized the deal for fiery Gordon Stanley Cochrane at the December 1933 meetings by sending Mr. Mack $100,000 and a young catcher, Johnny Pasek. "Cochrane is the Tigers' playing manager," proclaimed Navin.

The trade sunshine continued. Within forty-eight hours, Navin came up with another over-the-rainbow deal, this time with Clark Griffith of Washington. The Tigers obtained Outfielder Leon ("Goose") Goslin for Outfielder Jonathan Stone. In August 1934, Navin acquired Alvin ("General") Crowder, veteran pitcher from the Senators. The daring moves paved the way for the Tigers' first pennant in a quarter of a century, followed by another pennant and a World Series championship in 1935.

Not as lucky was George Susce, a catcher recalled by the Tigers from their Beaumont team. One of the Tigers, Marvin Owen, was on a batting spree when Susce arrived. Susce and Owen were chatting on the dugout steps as Manager Cochrane passed by.

"Whatcha hitting, Marv?" Susce asked.

"I'm hitting .365," answered Owen proudly.

"You'll soon be down to .280 where you belong," Susce remarked. The next day, Susce was sold to Milwaukee in the American Association. His nine tactless words cost him $372 apiece in World Series money that never came his way.

The December 1937 minor league sessions in Milwaukee provided the setting for the Tigers' next startling trade. The explosive transaction saw the Tigers send away popular Outfielder Gerald ("Gee") Walker, Third Baseman Marv Owen, along with young Catcher Mike Tresh to the White Sox in exchange for Pitcher Vern Kennedy, Outfielder Fred ("Dixie") Walker, and Infielder Tony Piet. The surprise deal was the most scorned ever in Detroit baseball history. The reaction caused an uproar from the fans, petitions threatening boycott of the ball park; newspapers were flooded with letters of protest. One daily paper asked for "penny contribution" from the youngster fans toward a goodbye gift for the ever-beloved "Gee" Walker.

The demonstrations caused Tiger owner Briggs to issue a statement from his home in Miami Beach, Florida. "I have told Detroit fans that I hoped to give them a championship team. I repeat that promise and the Walker-Owen-Tresh deal was made with my approval."

The fans not only missed Gee's six consecutive .300 seasons but also his flair of showmanship, dazzling base running, and sometimes unorthodox play afield that certainly annoyed Cochrane but had the fans cheering. Success easily justifies any baseball deal with the fans. There seemed some vindication when Tigers' new Pitcher Kennedy won his first nine games, but suddenly his mound magic vanished. He won only three more, finishing with a 12–9 record. "Dixie" never replaced "Gee" in the hearts of the Walker fans. He was destined for greater love from Brooklyn fans. Owen's departure left a gaping hole at third base as a parade of successors met with fans' disfavor, missing Marv's stylish defensive tactics.

Soon, Cochrane was fired. Del Baker finished out a fourth-place spot. Newly appointed General Manager Jack Zeller plugged the 1938 third-base problem by acquiring Michael ("Pinky") Higgins, also southpaw Pitcher Archie McKain for Pitcher Elden Auker and Outfielder Chet Morgan from the Red Sox in a postseason deal.

Continuing a desire to obtain that winning pitcher, Zeller and Bill DeWitt of the St. Louis Browns huddled for many days and finally on May 13, 1939, announced a ten-player package deal. Zeller moved a quartet of pitchers—Vern Kennedy, Alfred ("Roxie") Lawson, Bob Harris, and George Gill—also Outfielder Chet Laabs and Infielder Mark Christman to the Browns. In return, the much-traveled and talkative Louis ("Bobo") Newsom, Pitcher Jim Walkup, Infielder Ralph Kress, and Outfielder Roy Bell joined the Tigers. Newsom won 17 and lost 10 for the Tigers to chalk up a 20–11 season mark while the luckless Kennedy totaled only nine wins for the year and suffered 20 defeats.

Baseball Commissioner Kenesaw Landis liberated 91 Detroit minor leaguers on January 14, 1940, in his famous "Free Agent Decree." The white-haired former federal judge charged Zeller was cheating with wholesale "cover-ups," "fake" transfers of contracts, and "gentleman's agreements" in deals with his minor league players. Among the long list of freed players were the promising Outfielder Roy Cullenbine and Infielder Benny McCoy. Only a month earlier, Zeller had traded McCoy and Pitcher George Coffman to the Athletics for Outfielder Wally Moses. The deal was voided by Landis with McCoy eventually selling his services to Connie Mack for $45,000 while Cullenbine joined the Dodgers for $25,000.

The Landis setback caused Zeller to search anew, and the Cubs responded with an interleague deal. The Tigers received

("Rowdy") Richard Bartell for Billy Rogell in an exchange of shortstops. Then, Zeller traded Outfielder Roy Bell to Cleveland for Bruce Campbell. Loquacious Newsom missed three weeks with a broken thumb but came through with an amazing 21–5 log, including 13 victories in a row.

The new combinations contributed their share and clicked for the 1940 pennant, and Detroit fans were busy talking baseball once again. Then the Tigers slipped into the second division and Zeller went hunting. Before the 1942 play began, he traded Shortstop Frank Croucher and Bruce Campbell to Washington for Outfielder Roger ("Doc") Cramer and Second Baseman Jimmy Bloodworth. Another good trade for the Tigers. During the winter of 1944, Zeller swapped Infielder Joe Orengo to the Red Sox for Jimmy ("Skeeter") Webb, Manager Steve O'Neill's son-in-law. The Tiger field boss denied any knowledge of trade discussions until "I read about it in the morning paper."

Then came the April 30, 1945, trade that saw Zeller send Outfielder-Third Baseman Don Ross and Second Baseman Lambert ("Dutch") Meyer to Cleveland for Roy Cullenbine, one of the Detroiters freed by Judge Landis in 1940. The judge had specified that none of the new free agents could play for the Tigers for three years. Once again the player moves paid off for Zeller. The Tigers enjoyed pennant success and also a World Series triumph over the Cubs.

When George Trautman became the Tigers' new general

WOMEN PITCH IN TO SAVE BASEBALL

Judge Kenesaw Mountain Landis, baseball's first commissioner, was the original member of the "Tell It Like It Is, and Not Like You Hope It Is" club. During a visit to jam-packed Wrigley Field, with another fiery pennant race in progress in 1929, the colorful and silver-shocked jurist-commissioner looked around the crowded stands and observed:

"Many factors contribute to the success of baseball, but two things saved the game after the scandal ten years ago: Babe Ruth's home-run bat and the breakthrough of women's new and increasing interest. Only a fool would attempt to rate one ahead of the other from a popularity standpoint."

Such a declaration forty-seven years later would have qualified The Judge as a jewel-crowned champion of equal rights.

manager, he surprised Detroit fans—some not too happily—by trading away Barney McCosky, a homegrown favorite. McCosky went to the Philadelphia Athletics for George Kell, a class gentleman-athlete. The A's were in Detroit at the time, May 20, 1946, and Kell learned about the trade while riding the same elevator in the Book-Cadillac Hotel with his manager, Connie Mack. During the not too speedy stop-go descent, Mack explained: "Only sixteen players can make the plane trip to St. Louis, and you will have to stay here."

"But, Mr. Mack," Kell answered, "I like to fly. Can't I go on the flight?"

"I mean, you are staying here for good," Mack told the man who was to finish his career with a .308 batting average.

"For good?" the puzzled native of Swifton, Arkansas replied.

"Yes, we traded you to Detroit for Barney McCosky," Mr. Mack concluded as the elevator reached the lobby floor. After concluding his career of playing with the Tigers, Red Sox, White Sox, and Orioles, Kell returned to Detroit for an even longer stay. Since 1958 George has been associated with the Tigers' TV and/or radio broadcasting teams. He is, they say, the first player-broadcaster ever involved in a $100,000 trade. The White Sox gave the Red Sox Grady Hatton and 100 grand for Kell in 1954.

Two years later the Tigers unloaded another homegrown favorite: youthful lefty, Billy Pierce. Billy was regarded as expendable when the Tigers had Hal Newhouser, Dizzy Trout, Virgil Trucks, and Fred Hutchinson taking their regular rotation. Needing a catcher, the Bengals sent Pierce and $10,000 to the White Sox for Catcher Aaron Robinson. Long after Robinson retired, Pierce was still pitching—and winning—first for the White Sox and later the Giants.

The Tigers possess evidence that TV-radio sportscasters frequently find advancement to the majors as odd as some players. Something happened in 1948 which moved Ernie Harwell along the road to becoming the Tigers' radio voice in 1960. Harwell was broadcasting the Atlanta Crackers' games in 1948 when Branch Rickey heard him for the first time and was immediately impressed. Mr. R. asked Earl Mann, the Atlanta owner, if he would release Ernie so he could broadcast the Dodgers' games.

Rickey was in a bind. Red Barber was ailing, and the Dodgers needed help in the radio booth. Mann approved the release of Harwell if—if Rickey would give him Catcher Cliff Dapper of the

Montreal Royals. Mann wanted Dapper to manage his Atlanta club. Rickey agreed. Dapper, an off-season avocado farmer in California, moved to Atlanta to manage the Crackers, and Harwell moved to Brooklyn to broadcast the Dodgers' games. After later stops to air the Giants' and Orioles' games, Ernie Harwell arrived in Detroit— two years after George Kell checked in a second time.

A new broom sweeps clean, an adage that certainly applied to the owner "Spike" Briggs and General Manager Charlie Gehringer in the 1952–1953 tactics. In 1952 only five players who went to the Tigers' camp in Lakeland, Florida, weathered the winter trade storm, namely Hal Newhouser, Ted Gray, Gerry Priddy, Pat Mullin, and Steve Souchock. "Meet Me in St. Louis," became a popular expression among the Tigers in 1952 as the club made six deals, four with the Browns, involving 40 players: 20 going, and 20 coming. During this gigantic swap spree, Hoot Evers was believed to be the first player ever traded with a 1.000 BA. Hoot had been injured, and batted just once—getting a single the night before his departure to the Red Sox. In his final game for Boston, Don Lenhardt hit a grand slam home run, and it almost chilled the transaction.

A maneuver in 1955 provided the Tigers with a trivia topper: they signed Pitcher Joe Coleman, Sr., after he had been cut loose by the Orioles. Fifteen years later they obtained Pitcher Joe Coleman, Jr., in the Denny McLain deal with the Senators. It provided Detroit with a father-son pitching combination: the club's first ever.

John McHale, elevated to the general managership in 1957, didn't make many deals, but when he moved, he moved big. McHale traded away seven players to the Kansas City A's and got six in return. One of them was Billy Martin. The king-size deal didn't do too much for either club. The Tigers finished fourth, the A's seventh.

One of the Tigers' cream-of-the-crop transactions came in early 1960 when Detroit obtained Outfielder-First Baseman Norman Cash from Cleveland for Third Baseman Steve Demeter. Steve never made it to the big time with the Indians. Cash, however, became a longtime favorite with Tiger fans, eventually tagged with the nickname of "Stormin' Norman." He won the AL batting title in 1961 with .361 and parlayed that championship into a 15-year career with the Tigers even though he never again reached .300.

Five days after the Cash-Demeter trade, the Tigers swapped

AL batting champion Harvey Kuenn for Rocky Colavito as Detroit and Cleveland ended spring training exhibition games April 17, 1960. This player shuffle triggered heated discussions among base- ball fans—merits of a hitter versus the value of a slugger.

"We need more power in our lineup," explained Tigers' President Bill DeWitt, while Indians' General Manager Frank Lane expounded "We need someone to get on base more often." It was a switch of 42 HRs for 135 singles; a home-run champ for a batting champion. Cleveland fans were enraged at the Easter Sunday announcement. Little girls wept, so did their mothers. Some threat- ened to dent Lane's nose. Nevertheless, Lane was happy, delighted to see his name emblazoned on front-page headlines as he re- marked repeatedly "What's all the excitement about? I just traded a hamburger for a steak."

Kuenn remained with the Indians one season, then Lane traded him to the Giants. This seemingly was admittance that the Tigers got the best of the deal.

Almost four months later, on August 2, 1960, in a move unparalleled in baseball history, the Tigers traded managers with the Indians. Joe Gordon came from Cleveland to replace Jimmie Dykes, who was fired by prexy DeWitt. It all began as DeWitt's idea of a joke. For Frank Lane it was a master move, the epitome of a David Harum career. For both baseball executives it was a resolu- tion of an urgent dilemma: what to do about a couple of teams that looked like pretenders rather than contenders for a pennant.

It was becoming more embarrassing day by day for the sixth-place Tigers and the fourth-place Indians, both suffering late season slumps. The Tigers had lost 12 of their last 15 games, nine by a single run, while Cleveland dropped 18 of its past 25. DeWitt and Lane both started the season with a headline gamble in the Kuenn-Colavito spectacular. Each player was supposed to fit the missing piece in their new team's pennant puzzle. Despite credit- able performances, neither man provided the key part for which he was obtained. Thus, the managerial switch—a historical trade of managers.

Dykes, who had been in baseball for more than 40 of his 63 years at the time said "Baseball is the craziest business I know, and this is the craziest thing they have ever done." The odd trade formula came about as each team gave its manager an uncondi- tional release with the understanding they'd be hired in the other fellow's job.

James A. Campbell, current general manager of the Tigers, has been charged with being a status-quo type, conservative in the player market. 'Tis not so; the soft-spoken but thorough general manager has been involved in over 90 transactions since he took over late in 1962.

The Denny McLain deal in 1970 was the most lengthy affair. "The talks with Washington spanned the summer months before the key pieces were placed together in October," recalls Campbell. Finally, Commissioner Bowie Kuhn interrupted the World Series on October 9, called all the media personnel together, and with Campbell on one side and Bob Short, Washington owner, on the other, he announced that McLain was traded to the Senators. It was the first time a commissioner had ever announced a trade. This was a special exception since McLain was under suspension.

The most recent entry in Campbell's trade diary involves Nate Colbert, who came to the Tigers from San Diego in November 1974. The Tigers gave up Ed Brinkman, Pitcher Bob Strampe, and Outfielder Dick Sharon. "I'm very disappointed in the way things turned out," said Campbell, "but if I had the same information available, I'd certainly do the same thing." After a third of the season, Campbell sent Colbert to Montreal in a last minute waiver deal June 15, 1975.

PHIL COLLIER
Sportswriter, *San Diego Union*

Phil Collier has covered baseball for the *San Diego Union* since 1953, and shifted to the major league beat in 1958. Phil began newspapering in Baytown, Texas, when he was thirteen years old. He was a combat infantryman in Europe during World War II and enrolled in Texas Christian University upon his return. After a five-year stint with the *Fort Worth Star-Telegram,* Phil moved to San Diego and joined the *Union.* In 1965 Phil scooped the Cubs by sixteen hours on the signing of Leo Durocher as their new manager. He had a national beat "announcing" the early retirement plans of Sandy Koufax, the Dodgers' Hall of Fame left-handed pitcher.

Padres were born with deathbed commitment

The first deal the Padres ever made was agreed on in a hospital and before they had any players. A few months later, their thirtieth and final selection in the expansion draft was to become the second player ever to represent them in the major league All Star game.

In examining the trades they made during the five years they were owned by San Diego financier C. Arnholt Smith, it is important to understand that many of the transactions brought in cash that enabled the Padres to meet their payrolls. They made one trade to beef up a club bank account that had dwindled to $1,400 and another that kept them afloat when the account was down to $900.

"I'm proud that we never missed a payday," says Padre President E. J. ("Buzzie") Bavasi, who had been general manager of the Dodgers for 17 seasons, in Brooklyn and Los Angeles, before joining forces with Smith to gain a franchise for San Diego. "We never missed one, but there were many times when it was touch and go."

To a great extent, the early future of the Padres was shaped in a Fullerton, California, hospital in the late summer of 1968. The NL had awarded expansion franchises to San Diego and Montreal. Buzzie Bavasi left his job with the Dodgers, moved to San Diego, started the organization of a front office, and began to prepare for the expansion draft that was to be held at Montreal in October.

With his departure from Los Angeles, the Dodgers came under the command of the late Fresco Thompson, vice-president in charge of minor league operations. Shortly after Buzzie's departure, Thompson became gravely ill while scouting the Dodgers' Albuquerque farm club. The general manager there was Peter Bavasi, Buzzie's son. In late summer, Buzzie drove to Fullerton to see Thompson, his close friend and baseball associate for thirty years.

"I got to the hospital and Peg (Thompson's wife) was crying," Buzzie recalls, "but I didn't know that Fresco's condition was as serious as it was.

"When I went in to see him, Fresco was concerned about the expansion draft. Knowing the Dodger personnel as well as I did, I thought we would be able to draft three good players from them. The people I had in mind were Shortstop Bill Russell, Catcher Jeff Torborg, Second Baseman Ted Sizemore, and Outfielder Von Joshua.

"Fresco asked me to do him a favor. He named three players he wanted me to take—Outfielders Al Ferrara and Jimmy Williams, and Shortstop Zoilo Versalles.

"As ill as he was, I couldn't say no, but I thought he would get better and that I could talk him out of the agreement before we got to the expansion draft."

Tragically, Thompson died a short time later before the draft, and Buzzie Bavasi says he felt obligated to honor his commitment to his friend.

"People said I took Ferrara, Williams, and Versalles as a favor to Walter O'Malley, the Dodger owner, for his support in helping us get a franchise in San Diego," Buzzie says, "but that wasn't the case."

In 1968, I was in my eighth season of living my summers in the Los Angeles area, covering the home games of the Dodgers and Angels for the *San Diego Union*. With my many connections, I anticipated my return to San Diego to cover the Padres in 1969 and spent many hours in 1968 talking to scouts, managers, and players about people who might be available to help the new franchise. I was renting the Costa Mesa home of Pirate Pitcher Tommie Sisk when the phone rang in August of 1968. It was Buzzie, calling from San Diego.

"You've been scouting for us for nothing," he said, "and I know there is no game tomorrow, so I would like for you to drive down here. Our staff is having its first expansion draft meeting, and we would like for you to sit in with us.

"We're going to go down the list of players we think will be available in the draft, and we want your opinions."

It was a flattering and unprecedented opportunity for a member of the Fourth Estate, and I also had the privilege of sitting

with Bavasi and his staff in a Montreal hotel suite the day the
Padres and Expos each drafted 30 players. Bavasi had known for
several months that his first choice would be San Francisco Outfielder Ollie Brown, who never was to live up to his vast potential.
The Giants had optioned Brown to Phoenix in 1968, and Ollie
refused to report until Bavasi talked him into it.

The Padres went into the expansion draft armed with scouting reports generously provided them by several teams, including
Houston and San Francisco. San Diego and Montreal each had six
rounds to draft five players and were limited to taking three players
from each of the ten established NL teams. The draft was in its
eighth hour when a weary Bavasi bowed out of the proceedings
with one round remaining. "I'll let you guys pick the last five
(players)," he said.

When the Padres got down to their thirtieth and final choice,
pitching Coach Roger Craig and announcer Duke Snider, who was
to serve as batting instructor, had a simultaneous flash. They
recommended an obscure Atlanta farmhand, Shreveport Outfielder Clarence ("Cito") Gaston, they had seen in the Texas League.
Two years later (1970), Gaston batted .318, hit 29 HRs with 93
RBIs. He was a logical choice to represent the Padres in the
mid-summer All-Star game.

With 30 players under their wing, the Padres embarked on
what, in retrospect, can be regarded as a reckless course. In
December of 1968, they traded right-hander Dave Giusti, their No.
2 draft choice, to St. Louis for Third Baseman Ed Spiezio, right-
hander Phil Knuckles, Outfielder Ron Davis, and Catcher Danny
Breeden. In mid-June of 1969, the Padres dealt Outfielder Tony
Gonzalez, their No. 19 draft choice, to Atlanta for Outfielder Andy
Finlay and two infielders, Walt Hriniak and Van Kelly.

"At that point, we needed young players for our farm system,
and we were looking for bodies," Bavasi says. "Giusti has had a
fine career as a relief pitcher for Pittsburgh, but he wasn't going to
win a pennant for us and neither was Gonzalez."

The Giants and Braves both sought Gonzalez, who turned out
to be the determining factor in the five-way fight for first place in
the NL West in 1969. "If the Giants had gotten him, they would
have won, instead of us," said Paul Richards, the Atlanta general
manager at the time.

According to Buzzie Bavasi, the Padres have always operated in the black, and that has taken some doing, considering that

their home attendance totals for the first five seasons (1969–73) were 613,327, 633,439, 549,085, 644,272, and 611,806.

"We ran a very frugal operation, and we received money in almost every trade we made."

In December of 1969, Bavasi traded right-hander Joe Niekro to Detroit for right-hander Pat Dobson, Infielder Dave Campbell, and $27,500. Twelve months later, the Padres traded Dobson and reliever Tom Dukes to the Orioles for Shortstop Enzo Hernandez, three pitchers, and $20,000.

In the spring of 1971, the Padres signed veteran reliever Bob Miller, who had been released by the Cubs. Miller pitched so well that in August the Padres were able to trade him to Pittsburgh for two players and $50,000. That same year, Bavasi traded right-hander Al Santorini to St. Louis for left-hander Fred Norman, Outfielder Leron Lee, and an undisclosed amount of cash. It was one of the most profitable deals in San Diego history.

Norman hurled six shutouts for the Padres in 1972. In June 1973, when they were nearing insolvency, the Padres dealt Norman to the Reds for Outfielder Gene Locklear, reliever Mike Johnson, and $50,000. Lee batted .300 for San Diego in 1972 and was sold to the Indians for $25,000 during spring training in 1974.

Of all the players Bavasi has dealt with, his favorite would have to be Bob Miller. Though he helped the Pirates win a World Championship in 1971 and compiled a 5–2 record in 1972, Miller was given his release the next spring. For the second time in three years, the Padres signed Miller as a free agent, got him in shape again, and sold him two months later to Detroit for $30,000. "I gave Bob part of his purchase price because he kept us in business," Bavasi recalls. After going from Detroit to the Mets and getting another release in the fall of 1974, Miller was invited to the San Diego spring camp in 1975, was signed again, and was sent to Hawaii to serve as a player and pitching coach.

The Padres received another windfall in October 1973. St. Louis had a roster problem and asked the Padres to take veteran Outfielder Matty Alou off their hands. Bavasi bought him for $100. The next spring, he sold the little left-hand hitter to Japan for $50,000. "After he played there for a year, Matty was so pleased that he came to San Diego to thank us for sending him to Japan," Bavasi says.

In a span of little more than a year, the Padres sold five players to Japanese teams for a total of approximately $163,000. The five were Alou, Infielder Gary Jestadt ($35,000), Infielder John

Sipin ($35,000), Outfielder Bernie Williams ($25,000), and Pitcher Terry Lei ($18,000).

"We've had a fine relationship with Japanese teams," says Padre General Manager Peter Bavasi. "We sell them breaking-ball hitters and fast-ball pitchers. Sipin couldn't play for us, but they tell me he is an $80,000-a-year player in Japan."

In the fall of 1973—the first time in their history—the Padres went out and traded for "name" players. At the time, the franchise was in limbo. Owner C. Arnholt Smith signed a letter of intent to sell the team to Washington, D.C. interests headed by Joseph Danzansky. Peter Bavasi was prepared to move with the team. However, San Diego city attorney John Witt filed damage suits totaling approximately $85 million against the NL and all the parties involved. Witt's efforts to protect the city's San Diego Stadium lease was to prove effective. The Danzansky group withdrew from negotiations for the team after failing to satisfy the NL that it could guarantee to indemnify the league against possible losses threatened by Witt's suits.

During this impasse, Mrs. Marjorie Everett, principal stockholder in Hollywood Park racetrack, made a pitch to buy the Padres with the intention of keeping the team in San Diego. Partly because of Mrs. Everett's interest in acquiring "name" players and mostly because he wanted to make the Padres more appealing to any prospective buyers, Bavasi made several important deals.

On October 15, 1973, he traded left-hander Mike Caldwell to San Francisco for veteran First Baseman Willie McCovey, who was to become the Padres' first $100,000-a-year performer. On November 9, the Padres traded Pitcher Clay Kirby to the Reds for Outfielder Bobby Tolan and left-hand reliever Dave Tomlin. Tolan had been an All-Star performer who had been on four World Series teams— twice with St. Louis and twice with the Reds. Three days later, the Padres dealt Outfielder Jerry Morales to the Cubs for another All-Star, veteran Second Baseman Glenn Beckert.

The acquisitions of McCovey, Tolan, Beckert, and Alou whetted the interest of San Diego fans and drew the attention of Chicago multimillionaire Ray Kroc, chairman of the board of the McDonald hamburger empire. Kroc, whose wealth is estimated at $500 million, bought the Padres in January 1974, and, in his first season as owner, the last-place San Diego team surprised the baseball world by increasing its home attendance to 1,075,399.

Things have changed dramatically under Kroc's auspices.

"During our first five years," says Peter Bavasi, "the first thing we asked when we were trying to trade for a player was 'how much is he making?' During those lean years, the Padres passed up opportunities to acquire players such as Joe Torre, Billy Williams, Willie Davis, and Maury Wills because they couldn't afford their high salaries.

"Our budget had to be the lowest in modern major league history," says Peter Bavasi. "Never during those first five years did another team ask us if we wanted to buy a player. They knew we didn't have the money, and they didn't want to embarrass us.

"Since Mr. Kroc took over, every team in the majors has offered to sell us players."

Looking back on San Diego's trade, Buzzie Bavasi believes the most important was the one for Hernandez. "We had to have a shortstop," he says, "and we've had a good one now for five years." Bavasi is also proud of the trade he made in December of 1971 when he sent left-hander Dave Roberts to Houston for right-hander Bill Greif, Second Baseman Derrel Thomas, and a minor league pitcher, Mark Schaeffer. "Greif has become an important member of our bullpen," Buzzie says, "and we were able to trade Thomas to the Giants for Tito Fuentes, who turns a double play better than any second baseman we've ever had."

Peter Bavasi believes the most strategic trade in Padre history was the one involving McCovey.

"He became the new Padre image," Peter says. "He gave us credibility. When he walked into our training camp in 1974, the reaction of the younger players was exciting to watch. Willie became Mr. San Diego Padre, our leader. He did away with our defeatist attitude."

Baseball people say their best trades are the ones they didn't make, and the Padres feel that way in regard to left-hander Randy Jones. Randy was a 22-game loser in 1974 and a 20-game winner in 1975. "We had a lot of interesting offers for him," says Peter Bavasi, "but I'm glad we didn't accept any of them."

As they entered their seventh season, the Padres had only one of their original 30 expansion draft choices, Catcher Fred Kendall.

"If I ever went through another expansion draft, I would go for a better blend of experience and youth," says Peter Bavasi. "When Mr. Smith paid $10 million for the franchise, he didn't realize that he needed additional funds for player development.

"Montreal didn't have a financial problem, so they drafted a lot of players with identity—Donn Clendenon, Mack Jones, Manny Mota, and Maury Wills, to name a few.

"We started out with young players, most of them without any reputations, so we tried to sell our fans on coming out to see the stars on the visiting teams. It didn't work."

After six years of bringing up the rear in the NL West, the Padres made a move in the fall of 1974 that caused dramatic improvement in what had been the weakest pitching staff in the majors. They gave up slugging First Baseman Nate Colbert to the Tigers in a three-way swap that netted them three Cardinals' pitchers—Rich Folkers, Alan Foster, and Sonny Siebert. The Padres were among the leaders in NL pitching as the club took over fourth place—their highest finish ever in 1975 under Manager John McNamara. Meanwhile, Colbert had failed miserably at Detroit and had been sold to Montreal, causing Tiger General Manager Jim Campbell to comment that the deal with the Padres was the worst he had ever consummated. Recently, Buzzie Bavasi was reflecting on the Padres' early years.

"The thing that worried me the most was what might happen to the people in our front office and the people who were scouting for us," he said. "The concern about that put me under a terrible strain.

"The city of San Diego bailed us out of a jam on January 1, 1974. We were due to come up with deferred bonus payments to players we had drafted the previous June, and we didn't have the money. They could have been declared free agents and the scary thing is that one of them was Dave Winfield (the outfielder who has become the Padres' most valuable property).

"The city advanced us some money that would be coming to us for promotional purposes and for concessions. We were able to make all of the bonus payments."

Over the years, the impoverished Padres struggled along with many players who were deficient in one area or another. One was Outfielder Al Ferrara, long one of Buzzie Bavasi's pets. The Padres were on the road the day in 1971 that Ferrara got the word that he had been traded to Cincinnati. "The Bull," as he was called, was given a champagne farewell by the writers and broadcasters who traveled with the team. After several glasses of the bubbly, Ferrara waxed nostalgic as he turned to a longtime writer friend.

"Phantom, do you realize that the next time I see you I'll be trying to beat the Padres?" Ferrara said.

"Christ, Bull, you've been doing that for years," the writer replied.

SHIRLEY POVICH
Sportswriter, *Washington Post*

Shirley Povich was on the scene for the *Washington Post* for fifty-one years as sportswriter, columnist, and war correspondent in the Pacific theater. A native of Bar Harbor, Maine, Shirley interrupted his studies at Georgetown University to become sports editor of *The Post* at the age of twenty-one. For most of those fifty years, Povich covered almost every pennant race, World Series, Kentucky Derby, and championship fight. His story on Don Larsen's perfect no-hit game in the 1956 World Series was judged Best Sports Story of the Year. A former national president of the Baseball Writers' Association of America, he authored scores of magazine articles and two books the latest of which is *All These Mornings,* a semibiographical work. Shirley is also the only male who, through an inadvertency, was included in *Who's Who of American Women.*

19/THE SENATORS/TWINS

Cronin to Griffith: make deal, take the money

As some forgotten philosopher once said of money, "It is such an obedient servant." Another guy, after giving much thought to the subject, probably stated it as well. "Money makes you less nervous," he said. Nothing serves to better sharpen the awareness of the many splendid virtues of money than the lack of it. That was the plight of Clark Griffith in his early years as owner of the Washington Senators, the near indigents of the AL.

Keeping the Senators solvent was the nagging problem for Griffith. Unlike the wealthy club owners, he was forbidden the luxury of buying ballplayers as the need arose. Meeting the payroll was a prior necessity. Mainly, he was reduced to barter when a desperate need arose to fill a position on the Senators. In 1915, he acquired his Hall of Fame outfielder, Sam Rice, by canceling a bad debt, $600 owed to him by the Portsmouth, Virginia, club of the Virginia League that was about to go defunct.

Griffith was the canny little right-handed pitcher, circa turn of the century, for both the Cubs and the White Sox. He compensated for his lack of a fast ball by the shrewdness that earned him the name of Old Fox. As a club owner he reinforced that reputation with his trading skills and suddenly put together back-to-back pennant winners in 1924–1925.

Griffith traded the Senators into the third pennant they won for him in 1933. That was after he had consulted his new, rookie Manager Joe Cronin on the team's needs. "I'd like to have these ballplayers," said Cronin, handing Griffith a slip with the names of three pitchers on it, "with them, I think, we could win the pennant." Griffith scanned Cronin's list. On it were the names of Earl Whitehill of the Tigers, Jack Russell of the Indians, and Walter Stewart of the Browns.

"Whoa," Griffith said, "You just don't go taking ballplayers off other clubs simply because you'd like to have 'em."

"Well," said Cronin coyly, "They always told me you were a pretty good baseball trader." He began talking fast. "We need some pitchers who can beat the Yankees. Whitehill and Stewart and their left-handed stuff will give them fits." But Griffith noted that Jack Russell had no reputation for beating the Yankees. "No, but he beats the hell out of us," Cronin said. "We could get him on our side and get rid of a jinx."

One by one, Griffith acquired every player on Cronin's list, plus Catcher Luke Sewell, and Outfielders Goose Goslin and Fred Schulte. He had to give up Outfielders Sammy West and Carl Reynolds and Pitcher Lloyd Brown to St. Louis, and Pitchers Fred Marberry and Carl Fischer to Detroit; and to gain Russell from Cleveland, he had to toss in Catcher Roy Spencer and some cash. But Griffith had his pennant-winning team, with Whitehill blossoming as a 22-game winner and teaming up with Stewart to beat the Yankees when necessary.

If Griffith was chary of spending money for players, he also could truthfully boast, as he frequently did, "I never sold any of my good ballplayers for cash." But after a December day in 1934, he could no longer make that claim. When the Senators' owner did surrender to the siren call, it was with the biggest cash deal ever exploded on the face of big league baseball. He sold his son-in-law, shortstop and manager, all in the same person, to Red Sox owner Tom Yawkey. That was the famous Joe Cronin deal. Fourteen years later, Griffith gained unique status as the first club owner ever to make deals for two sons-in-law. In 1948, he swung a deal to make Thelma Griffith Haynes happy, although it took a five-player trade to bring back her pitcher-husband, Joe Haynes, from Cleveland.

The deal for Cronin that brought him a quarter million dollars was not Griffith's idea. When it was first rumored, the Red Sox were seeking Cronin, who as their hard-hitting shortstop manager had led the Senators to the 1933 pennant, Griffith was angered. He announced publicly that he had told Red Sox General Manager Eddie Collins, "Stop talking about my ballplayers. Besides," commented Griffith, "I wouldn't dare sell Cronin. I couldn't face the Washington fans after a deal like that and, anyway, nobody would pay what Cronin is worth."

He underestimated rich man Yawkey, a nabob of the game and director of countless corporations. During the 1934 World

Series at Detroit, Yawkey contacted Griffith on the phone and said, "If you're going to be in your hotel, I'd like to talk." Yawkey went bluntly to the point, asking if Cronin was for sale. Griffith said, "No, and consarn it, I don't like these stories about your trying to buy my ballplayers."

Whereat, Yawkey purred, "Would $250,000 interest you?"

"You can't offer that much, no ballplayer is worth a quarter of a million," Griffith said. "You're wasting your time, anyway. I'm not selling Cronin."

Yawkey could see the old gentleman's anger rising and discreetly took his leave, perhaps to return to the subject another day. Ironically, he also apologized to Griffith for offering a quarter million for a player Griffith had bought for $7,500 as a minor leaguer after the Pirates gave him a tryout and lost interest. But on returning to Washington, Griffith was assailed by some doubts. Was he doing the right thing for Joe? At the end of the 1934 season, Cronin had married into the Griffith family, taking as his bride Mildred Robinson, adopted daughter of Griffith. Other facts crossed Griffith's mind. With the 1934 Senators hopelessly in seventh place near the end of the season, Cronin for the first time was hearing the boos from the grandstand wolves. And now there would be that troublesome family angle if the Senators under Cronin continued down in the team standings.

Two months later, Yawkey called Griffith again, and he agreed to listen. They met in Yawkey's deluxe offices in New York's Tower Building, and Yawkey broached the $250,000 offer again, with Eddie Collins present.

"Maybe I'll make the deal if you toss in your shortstop, Lyn Lary," Griffith fenced.

"That's murder!" Collins shouted. "We just paid the Yankees $35,000 for Lary."

When Griffith indicated there would be no deal, and rose to leave, Yawkey asked him to stay. To Collins, Yawkey said, "Whaddayasay we give 'em Lary and make a deal?" When Collins simply shrugged, Yawkey grabbed the handiest piece of paper on his desk and wrote out the terms.

"No deal yet, Tom," Griffith said.

"What do you mean? What else is there to do?"

"I've got to call Joe Cronin first," Griffith said. "No deal unless it's all right with him. You'll hear from me soon."

That night, Griffith telephoned Cronin who had just completed his honeymoon trip to San Francisco with his bride, via the Panama Canal route. "Tell 'em it's a deal and take the money," Cronin told Griffith. He learned later that his father-in-law had taken the precaution to arrange for him a five-year, no-cut contract as player-manager of the Red Sox at a salary far in excess of what he was paid in Washington. For the next eleven years, Cronin was playing manager for the Red Sox and the hardest hitting shortstop in the AL. Lary flopped with the Senators, playing only 35 games and batting only .194 before he was traded to the Browns.

Neither as spectacular nor as profitable was Griffith's deal involving his other son-in-law, Pitcher Joe Haynes. One year after the Senators traded rookie Pitcher Haynes to the White Sox, in 1941, Thelma Griffith became his bride. Eight years he toiled for the White Sox, and with some distinction, but Mrs. Haynes missed her family and friends in Washington. And she had the ear of "Unc," her name for Mr. Griffith.

The White Sox refused Griffith's frequent offers for Haynes, but after they traded him to Cleveland in November 1948 for Catcher Joe Tipton, Griffith began new calculations to please his daughter Thelma. A deal with the Indians could be possible. Griffith went high to get Haynes, who had a 9–10 year with Chicago before going to Cleveland. He constructed a five-player deal that also brought First Baseman Eddie Robinson and Pitcher Ed Klieman to the Senators in a swap for First Baseman Mickey Vernon and Pitcher Early Wynn.

The deal was difficult to justify. Vernon, who had won one AL batting title, went on to win another later; Wynn became a 20-game winner for Cleveland in four of his next seven seasons. Neither Robinson, Klieman, nor Haynes served the Senators with much distinction. Haynes was 10–21 for his remaining years with Wash-

---

THIS IS RIDICULOUS!

Bobo Newsom, who quit pitching at the ripe old age of 46, was traded five times, sold four times, and was released five times. During these moves, 24 players changed uniforms, and an estimated $150,000 changed hands among his nine different owners. If deuces were wild, his record would break any bank in town. He won 211, lost 222, and was 2–2 in two World Series.

ington. There always was the solid suspicion that Bill Veeck shrewdly stage-managed the whole deal, and that it was Veeck's express idea that his Cleveland team could peddle Haynes to Washington at a huge profit by exploiting Thelma's desire to have hubby back with the Senators. Haynes never pitched a ball for the Indians after Veeck wangled him from the White Sox in the Joe Tipton swap.

Griffith's clever deals far outnumber his occasional errors. But one of these, and an egregious one, stemmed from a strange and sudden yearning to have Zeke Bonura on his ball club. After his Senators finished sixth in 1937, Griffith reasoned that with more batting punch he could climb high into the first division. He had been noting the .330 and .345 batting averages of First Baseman Bonura for the White Sox in 1936–1937.

Bonura came to the Senators in an even swap for fancy-fielding First Baseman Joe Kuhel who had bothered Griffith by hitting only .283 in 1937. The Senators' owner instantly regretted it. Inured to the smooth fielding of First Baseman Joe Judge and Joe Kuhel for the Senators for more than twenty years, Griffith sickened at the bumbling play of big Bonura, who had little range. After one season, in which Bonura hit .287, Griffith conspired to be rid of him.

Bonura, a native of New Orleans, was a warm, friendly bear of a man, but hardly the thinking man's ballplayer. At the end of his first season with the Senators, after putting in several years with the White Sox, Zeke announced to a baseball writer that he was driving his new car to New Orleans.

"This new job can fly," Zeke said. "I'll be in Chicago in twenty-four hours."

"Chicago?" the writer inquired. "I thought you were going home to New Orleans."

"That's right," said Zeke, "but from Chicago I know every inch of the road."

Griffith made money with Bonura. At the end of 1938, he unloaded Zeke to the New York Giants for $25,000 and two minor league players. When the Giants, disenchanted, put Zeke on the waiver list at the end of the season, no NL club took the bait. Griffith rebought him for $7,500. In effect, he had rented Zeke to the Giants for $17,500. By July, Griffith resold Bonura to the Cubs for $10,000.

During World War II, Griffith dealt largely in 4-F's and

slightly aged minor leaguers. One outfielder he signed was Eddie Boland, at no outlay except for his modest salary. Boland came to the Senators straight from the outfield of New York City's Sanitation Department team.

One of Griffith's superdeals was his cadging of slugger Roy Sievers from the Veeck-owned Browns-Orioles in 1954. He wangled Sievers in a straight swap for Outfielder Gil Coan, fast and long on promise but short on some of the necessary skills. Six years later, following Griffith's death, his son and successor, Calvin Griffith, again outdealt Veeck in a deal involving Sievers. Veeck was now operating the White Sox in 1960, and in a winter meeting at Palm Beach he showed interest in acquiring Sievers from the Senators. Veeck saw a pennant for the Sox with the help of Sievers' hitting.

In return for home-run-hitter Sievers, who was to have only a short career with the White Sox, the Senators ended up with the man who was to be their regular catcher for the next decade in Washington and Minneapolis where they were to be known as the Twins. Veeck shipped them young Earl Battey of the peerless throwing arm and superb catching skills. And also Don Mincher, a regular first baseman for both the Senators and the Twins. And also, according to informed reports, $150,000 in hard and useful cash, in the best tradition of the Griffith Clan.

ALLEN LEWIS
Sportswriter, *Philadelphia Inquirer*

Allen Lewis was a man in motion before he was graduated from Haverford College in Pennsylvania. Besides his classroom chores, Lewis played football and baseball and was the sports editor of the college newspaper. This experience led to a brief stint on a weekly in Connecticut, and later the *Evening Ledger* in Philadelphia. After a five-year army hitch, when he entered as a private and exited as a captain, Allen joined the *Philadelphia Inquirer* in 1946 and has been there ever since. He has concentrated on baseball for the past twenty years on a marathon basis: sixteen years as a correspondent for *The Sporting News* and fifteen years as chairman of the scoring rules committee.

20/THE PHILLIES

For sale or swap, anybody at anytime

If any one sign was appropriate for posting on a major league baseball club's marquee, this is it. This has been especially true of the Phillies during a quarter of a century as the Philadelphia club helped to set the stage for the game's bicentennial celebration. There was a time when the Phillies were the other team in town. Now they are the only team, housed in a castle-type home named Veterans Stadium.

From the fall of 1917 until the end of the 1942 season, the Phillies led the league or earned a photo finish at least in receiving cash in every major deal. After their first pennant in 1915, the Phillies finished second the next two seasons. This new-found success was blurred when the club's combined cash-player packaging shifted into high gear with the trading of Grover Cleveland Alexander.

Trade Alexander? It was unthinkable! In helping to pace the Phillies' 1-2-2 parade, the wonderful wizard with a toeplate won 94 games during this span. In successive seasons Alex had pitched his way to these incredible statistics:

> 1915—31 victories, 10 losses with a 1.22 ERA;
> 1916—33 victories, 12 losses with a 1.55 ERA;
> 1917—30 victories, 13 losses with a 1.83 ERA.

During the Phillies' successful pennant race in 1915, 12 of Alexander's 31 victories were shutouts. Also he won his club's only game in the Series, beating the Red Sox and Ernie Shore 3-1 in the opener. Thereafter the Bostons won the next four games, and the Championship.

The baseball world still was talking about the White Sox's surprise upending of John McGraw's Giants in the 1917 World

Series when the shocking news was announced November 11. The Phillies traded Alexander and his personal catcher, Bill Killefer, to the Cubs for Pitcher Mike Prendergast, Catcher Bill ("Pickles") Dilhoefer, and $60,000. The unbelievable announcement triggered a furor heard 'round the sports world. When the say-it-isn't-so anger reached the heights, William F. Baker, the Phillies' owner and former New York City police commissioner, admitted he made the deal because "I needed the money."

The trading of Alexander broke the ice for Baker and Gerry Nugent, who ran the club from 1932 through 1942. It was the first of many similar transactions in which the Phillies received important money in trading away their top players. Surprisingly, many of the lesser-light players, which both Baker and Nugent received in the exchanges, progressed to the point where they were involved in later deals.

Five weeks after the Alexander trade, Baker proved he wasn't afraid of criticism when he swapped Outfielder George Paskert, a seven-year veteran with the Phillies, to the Cubs for Fred ("Cy") Williams, a lanky left-handed slugger. Cy was to become one of the greatest in the club's history. Taking aim on the short right-field fence in Baker Bowl—an early-day counterpart to the Green Monster in Boston's Fenway Park—Williams hit 222 homers during the next thirteen years. Williams, who was graduated from the University of Notre Dame with a bachelor of science degree in architecture, played until he was 42 years old and then became a player-manager for Richmond, Virginia, in the Eastern League in 1931. Paskert, meanwhile, never did enjoy the same success with the Cubs and bowed out four years later.

Casey Stengel was traded by the Pirates to the Phillies in August 1919 for Outfielder Possum Whitted, but refused to report after a salary dispute. Finally Stengel and Baker patched up their differences, and Ol' Case was a 129-game player with a .292 BA for the Phillies in 1920. In mid-season of 1921, Stengel was on the march again, going to the Giants for cash and players valued at $75,000.

Owner Baker finally qualified for the $100,000 sweepstakes. He traded Dave Bancroft, the NL's Number One shortstop, to the Giants for Shortstop Art Fletcher, who was 35 and nearing the end of the trail, Pitcher Bill Hubbell, and 100 grand in early June of 1920. Besides adding to Baker's bank account, the deal produced added benefits for both Bancroft and Fletcher. Bancroft played in three straight World Series with the Giants, and Fletcher was in the right spot at the right time to become the Phillies' new manager in 1923.

Baker continued to collect greenbacks in excessive amounts while aiding the Giants' gold rush in the 1921, 1922, and 1923 World Series. In surrendering Irish Meusel, Baker talked John McGraw out of Catcher Butch Henline (who later became an NL umpire), Pitcher Jesse Winters, Outfielder Curt Walker—and you guessed it: money. This time it was $35,000.

The mention of Frank ("Lefty") O'Doul's name means something more in Phillie history than the .398 he hit in 1929 to win the NL batting championship, or his .383 in 1930 before moving to Brooklyn. The Phillies obtained the colorful Irishman from the Giants with $25,000 for Fred Leach, another outfielder. Phillie fans were most unhappy when O'Doul and Fresco Thompson went to the Brooklyn Dodgers for Pitchers Jim ("Jumbo") Elliott and Clise Dudley, and Outfielder Hal Lee. Meanwhile Baker whistled all the way to the bank to deposit the $100,000 check which arrived along with the three players.

To provide the club with another big name, Baker sent Shortstop Tommy Thevenow to the Pirates for Dick Bartell, a full-of-fire competitor who had four good years for the Phillies before moving on to the Giants, Cubs, and Tigers, in that order, before doubling back to the Giants.

Baker died shortly after making this deal. Gerry Nugent, whose wife had been Baker's secretary and inherited a large block of stock, took over the running of the club. Nugent operated in the same manner Baker did: with dollar signs sparkling in his eyes. Gerry, however, warmed up slowly with a no-money three-club deal. The Phillies sent Outfielder George ("Kiddo") Davis to the Giants, getting Outfielder Chick Fullis in return. The Pirates sent First Baseman Gus Dugas to Philadelphia after receiving Freddie Lindstrom from the Giants. Nugent followed this transfer with a mini-money trade by Phillie standards. In exchange for Pitcher Ray Benge, Nugent received $15,000 and three players from the Dodgers: Infielders Mickey Finn and Jack Warner, and Pitcher Cy Moore.

Having lost his apprentice rating in the swap shop, Nugent next trained his eyes on Chicago and a bundle of Cubs' cash. The Phillies traded slugger Chuck Klein, the triple crown winner in 1933, to Chicago for Pitcher Ted Kleinhans, Infielder Mark Koenig, and Outfielder Harvey Hendricks—all members of the Over 30 Set—and $65,000.

At the same time the Phillies' Mr. Trader went to brand-new lengths finding a new manager. He sent Catcher Spud Davis and Infielder Eddie Delker to the Cardinals for Catcher Jimmy Wilson, who launched a four-and-a-half-year tenure as the Phillies' skipper immediately. The Wilson-Davis swap was a duplicate of the late-late TV movie: a rerun. In 1928 Boss Baker traded Wilson to the Cardinals for Outfielder Homer Peel and a catcher named—you guessed it—Spud Davis. There was just one difference in the two swaps. Baker received $50,000 in the first one; Nugent, nary a penny in completing the second.

Astute man that he was, Nugent stayed in close contact with the Cubs. Gerry apparently had all three dials of his Atwater Kent radio set tuned to Chicago when the Cubs decided to have a more experienced first baseman than Dolph Camilli. Reacting like some-body who had just walked in from the outside to get warm, Nugent "suggested" he had a seasoned first baseman and left-handed power hitter who might help the Cubs make a better run against the Cardinals in the 1934 showdown.

His name? Don Hurst. Was he available? Nugent reasoned he could be for a price. What was the price? He might be able to suffer along without Hurst if the Cubs would give him Camilli and $30,000. The Cubs agreed to Nugent's terms, and therein conclud-ed one of the worst deals in the history of the Cubs, the city of Chicago, and major league baseball. Hurst batted .199 for the Cubs and retired at the season's end. Camilli? Dolph went to spring training with the Phillies in 1938, but returned to the NL wars with the Dodgers. Nugent got $50,000 from Brooklyn and Outfielder Ed Morgan for Camilli. Now the Phillies' profit line on Camilli read $80,000, but what about Chuck Klein?

When Chuck didn't hit in Wrigley Field with the same authority that he did in Baker Bowl, the Cubs made him expend-able. Again Nugent had another "suggestion." He would take Klein, Pitcher Fabian Kowalik, and $50,000, and send Pitcher Curt Davis, a low-cost draftee in 1933, and Outfielder Ethan Allen to Chicago. In their desire to forget a bad trade as rapidly as possible, the Cubs accepted. Now the Phils' president didn't need an adding machine to learn his bank deposits represented entries of $115,000 for Klein, and $80,000 for Camilli—and he still had Klein.

The $50,000 deal tempo continued when Nugent sold Dick

Bartell to the Giants for that amount plus four undistinguished "fringers." Fifty thousand continued to be Nugent's magic number when the Reds paid him $50,000 and two players, Spud Davis (back for a second term), and Pitcher Al Hollingsworth for Bucky Walters. In 1939 another 50 grand swap developed when the Phillies sent Pitcher Claude Passeau to the Cubs for Outfielder Joe Marty, and two pitchers: Ray Harrell and Kirby Higbe.

After Higbe won 14 games for the Phillies in 1940, the Dodgers figured he might be a big help in their bid for the 1941 pennant—something Brooklyn hadn't seen in twenty-one years. Go-Getter President Larry MacPhail wouldn't trust the job of "getting Higbe" to anybody but himself. After a series of meetings with Nugent, MacPhail got his man. In return for Higbe, the Phillies received three players and a whopping $100,000.

Higbe won 22 games and lost only nine as the Dodgers edged out the Cardinals in another down-to-the-wire NL pennant race. Then the Yankees devoured them in the World Series, four games to one. About the $100,000 price tag on Higbe, who never had a better season, MacPhail claimed: "I would stand in line night and day to buy 22-game winners at $100,000 apiece."

In December 1942 and January 1943, the hep-dealing Nugent negotiated his last two cash-clad trades. Gerry got Pitcher Johnny Allen and $30,000 from the Dodgers for Pitcher Rube Melton, a Phillie pickup in the 1940 draft. After bowing in with a $15,000 deal, Nugent bowed out with one for $10,000. He swapped Nick Etten to the Yankees for another first baseman, Ed Levy, and Pitcher Allen Gettel. Compared to his big money dealing, Nugent probably tacked on the $10,000 as a service charge.

In the fall of 1943, it became a brand-new ball game for the Phillies. The cash-and-carry phase of the operation was over. Instead of collecting $485,000 as Gerry Nugent did in making ten deals, it would be a better bet the new owners would spend that much trying to build a winner. Some claimed a compass was needed to find the club which finished in the first division only once from 1918 to 1932, and once more from 1933 to 1949.

The Phillies became a family operation just like their rivals, Connie Mack's Athletics, when Robert R. M. Carpenter, married to a DuPont and a high official of that company, purchased the club in 1943 and installed his son, Robert, Jr., as president. The new president made Herb Pennock, an AL pitcher for twenty-two years and a veteran of five World Series, the club's new general manager.

For Pennock it was like playing checkers with the player personnel. The Phillies had lost more than a hundred games for five straight seasons, and six of the last seven. Bucky Harris, who was to become a 29-year manager with five clubs (three times with the Senators, and twice with the Tigers) was the Carpenters' first

---

THREE TEAMS IN FOUR HOURS

May First is a day reserved for parades and moving. So it was with Catcher Clyde Kluttz exactly thirty years ago. He paraded to three teams in three moves completed within an unmatchable four hours. It started at 9 AM and was all over by 1 PM.

Kluttz was in St. Louis with the New York Giants May 1, 1946. His breakfast was interrupted by a call from Manager Mel Ott to tell him he had just been traded to the Phillies for Vince DiMaggio. After wishing him well and thanking him for his contributions, Master Mel requested: "Stay close to the hotel because you will hear from the Phillies in an hour or two."

The Phillies' General Manager Herb Pennock called to welcome him to the club, and suggested that he report in Cincinnati the next day because "I doubt if you can get to Pittsburgh in time for our last game there tonight." Now it's 11 AM, and Kluttz had ample time to get to Cincinnati.

During a late lunch, Clyde was interrupted again. This time it was Eddie Dyer, the manager of the Cardinals, calling to tell big Clyde he had just traded Emil Verban to the Phillies for him. Checking his watch, Kluttz noted it was nearing 1 PM, and he was now with his third club in four hours.

"Come out a little early so we can visit, and I'll arrange to have your gear moved from the Giants' to our clubhouse," Dyer said. The third move proved a lucky break for Kluttz. The Cardinals beat the Dodgers in the NL's first-ever pennant playoff, and went on to win the World Series from the Red Sox, four games to three. For this Kluttz received a winning share in the amount of $3,742.34.

"Between the World Series and the extra two games we were paid for the playoff, I figured out I received around $1000 for each one of those four hours I sweated out back in May," Kluttz mused as he laughed his way to the nearest bank.

The Red Sox didn't do any laughing. Their losing shares ($2,140.89) were less than the four umpires were paid ($2,500.00 apiece) for officiating the classic. All this plus the fact it was the first time the Red Sox ever lost a World Series after winning five in a row. Bad day in Back Bay!

skipper. He lasted less than that first season, exiting after the Phillies won 40 and lost 53. Fred Fitzsimmons replaced Harris and remained until near mid-season in 1945.

Pennock made the deal which produced another new manager for the Phillies. He sent Catcher Johnny Peacock to the Dodgers for Ben Chapman, a former star outfielder who was in the midst of making a wartime comeback as a pitcher. It was Chapman who replaced Fitzsimmons. Herb made another major move, getting Harry ("The Hat") Walker and Pitcher Fred Schmidt from the Cardinals for Outfielder Ron Northey. Walker became the club's fourth player to win the NL batting championship with .363 in 1947.

Following Pennock's death in January 1948, Bob Carpenter doubled as both president and general manager until 1954. Following a slow and easy script, Carpenter got Shortstop Eddie Miller from the Cardinals for Outfielder Johnny Wyrostek and cash in 1948. Bob made another deal with the Cardinals, getting Dick Sisler in exchange for Infielder Ralph LaPointe and $20,000.

Carpenter then made two deals with the Cubs, and secured two players for the Whiz Kids' pennant-winning success in 1950. One was Pitcher Russ Meyer; the other Eddie Waitkus, a fancy fielding first baseman. The Phillies' second pennant in history was finalized on the last day of the season when Dick Sisler's three-run HR in the tenth inning gave the Phillies a 4–1 conquest of the Dodgers.

When the Whiz Kids didn't repeat in 1951, Carpenter researched Gerry Nugent's book titled: *Spend Big to Deal Big*. He gave the Pirates two players and $70,000 for Pitcher Murry Dickson. Fifty thousand plus a player went to the Cardinals for Infielder Bobby Morgan. The two deals added up to a $120,000 washout. Dickson ended up winning 22 while losing 34 for the Phillies before moving to the Cardinals. There he promptly posted 13 wins and 8 losses. Morgan, failing his second test with the Phillies, ended up with the Cubs.

In April of 1954 Carpenter turned the general managership over to Roy Hamey, who had earlier executive stints with the Yankees and Pirates. One of Hamey's first deals was most unusual: a five-pitcher trade, three to the Phillies and two to the Cardinals. Based on the theory "we can't stand still," Hamey dealt Del Ennis, the club's Number One power hitter, to the Cardinals. The deal was a dud, failing to help either team.

John Quinn, who built the Braves into a pennant-winner in Milwaukee, came aboard as Hamey's successor in January 1959. Quinn, a member of an old-line baseball family, hit an immediate jackpot when he completed a golden-fleece deal, trading veteran Gene Freese to the White Sox for Johnny Callison. The rapidly improving youthful Callison was the anchorman for a club which should have won a pennant in 1964, and didn't. The Phillies were out in front by six and a half games with 12 remaining. They ended up being lucky to tie for second place as the Cardinals clinched the flag on the last day of the season to stay a possible triple tie.

It was in 1966 that Quinn made another all-out effort to give the Phillies their third flag. The general manager made deals for such standouts as Bill White, Dick Groat, Bob Uecker, Larry Jackson, and Bob Buhl. When the 1966 club failed to win, Quinn was subjected to the second guess for including Fergie Jenkins, then one of the Phillies' farmhands, in the deal for Jackson and Buhl with the Cubs. Jenkins had six consecutive 20-game winning seasons for the Cubs, who followed the 1964 Phillies' script by blowing the pennant in 1969. In fact, this particular wake was held in Philadelphia when the Phillies, aiming for fifth place in the NL East, bowled over the Cubs in three straight sets.

Within a month after the close of the 1969 season, the Phillies once again broke up the Old Gang. Unhappy Dick Allen was traded to the Cardinals, and Johnny Callison went to the Cubs in a two for one swap. Curt Flood, one of the seven players in the Allen transfer, refused to report. After Quinn exhausted every possible way to get Flood to join the club, Curt retired from baseball to devote full-time to his various enterprises in Denmark. When Quinn asked for a replacement for the absentee Flood, the Cardinals surrendered title to Willie Montanez.

Operating much like the Hollywood director who saves the best for last, Quinn's last deal was a blockbuster. He traded Rick Wise to the Cardinals for Steve Carlton, who debuted with 27 victories in 1972—his first year with the Phillies. Besides being the first Phillies' pitcher to win the Cy Young Memorial Award, Steve is only the second NL southpaw to top three hundred (310) strikeouts. Sandy Koufax was the first.

Paul Owens moved in as the club's fourth general manager under the Carpenters' ownership in June of 1972. His entry was unusual inasmuch as Paul managed the club for 80 games after Frank Lucchesi left the organization.

Later the same year, November 22 to be exact, there was another change in the executive batting order. Bob's son, R. R. M. ("Ruly") Carpenter III, took over as president. His father became chairman of the board. Thirty-two at the time, Ruly still is the youngest president in the major leagues.

Even with the A's possessing a seven-up edge—nine pennants to two in representing Philadelphia—there is considerable similarity comparing the two clubs. After winning their sixth pennant in 1914, the A's staggered under a string of eight straight last-place finishes. The Phillies waited until 1938 to dip into the NL basement seven times in eight years.

Steve Carlton's sensational debut with the Phillies recalled shades of Lefty Grove, who was forced to play first base in semiprofessional competition because his team lacked a catcher who could handle his blazing fast ball. The Phillies secured Carlton in a trade while Connie Mack purchased Grove from the then Baltimore's minor league Orioles. The big pitcher cost Mack big money because he was called a $100,600 addition when he joined the A's in 1925. Why the $600 tacked on to the 100 grand? History has it that Jack Dunn, who owned the Orioles, wanted to make Grove the biggest sale in his club's history. Mack reportedly obliged and added this amount to the check he sent to his friend Jack Dunn. Also the figure helped Dunn forget that he sold Babe Ruth, Ernie Shore, and Catcher Ben Egan to the Red Sox for $8,500 in 1914.

Both clubs possessed potent Polish Power. During the A's last hurrah, Connie Mack's last powerhouse, Aloysius Harry Simmons, nee Szymanski, helped power it with more than a hundred RBIs for nine years, starting in 1924 and concluding in 1932. Twice the Milwaukee-born Simmons had such impressive RBI totals as 157 and 165. During this span the man they nicknamed "Bucketfoot Al" had back-to-back .381 and .390 hitting percentages. The Phillies' present Mr. Power is Greg Luzinski. The youthful slugger they affectionately call "The Bull" led the majors with 121 RBIs and trailed teammate Mike Schmidt, 38–34, in the HR department in 1975.

If Danny Ozark, the Phillies' sixth manager since 1968, can continue the club's present procession, there is an NL Eastern Division championship in the immediate future. The Phillies were third in 1974, second in 1975, and ? in 1976. Incidentally, the A's won three straight pennants after a second-place finish in 1928.

JIM ENRIGHT
Sportswriter, *Chicago Today*

Chicago's Comiskey Park has been the scene of many thrilling moments for Jim Enright, author of the White Sox chapter. As fan or writer, Jim viewed the first All-Star game there (1933); Bob Feller's opening-day no-hit, no-run game (1940); Lou Boudreau's only major league stint as a catcher (1943); Larry Doby's AL debut as a pinch runner (1947); Satchel Paige's bow in the bigs with a five-hit 5–0 zip of the White Sox before 51,013 fans (August 13, 1948), and two of the longest back-to-back games ever played. The Red Sox beat the White Sox 5–4 in the second game of a twi-night doubleheader (July 12, 1951) in 17 innings spanning 4 hours and 1 minute. The next night the White Sox won 5–4 in 19 innings. This marathon continued for 4 hours and 47 minutes before ending at 1:17 A.M.—and the two teams met in a day game the next afternoon.

21/THE WHITE SOX

Powerhouse in palace: Old Roman builds both

Whenever the White Sox take inventory of their player swapping or buying, there is a definite division between the commonplace and the extraordinary. In many cases only a banker would deal in dollars as Charles Albert Comiskey did in building two projects on Chicago's South Side, to establish himself as a master architect among baseball's family dynasty-builders. In doing what was then fashionable, keeping up with the Griffiths, the Macks, the Stonehams, and not too much later the Wrigleys and the Yawkeys, the Old Roman built a powerhouse baseball team. Once this chore was completed, he built a new home to house it. The new playpen was named Comiskey Park, and quickly labeled the baseball palace of the world.

In becoming one of the most colorful pioneers in the game's history, the Old Roman went for the cycle climbing to the top. In the 1880s he was both a first baseman and manager leading St. Louis to four straight pennants in the American Association. Returning to his native Chicago at the turn of the century, Comiskey was both the owner and president of the White Sox. Warming up for his wheeler-dealer player maneuvers, the Old Roman had no fewer than five different managers during the first eleven years of White Sox operations. During this span the club won two pennants, the first under Clark Griffith in 1901, and the second in 1906 when the "Hitless Wonder" White Sox, under the leadership of Fielder Jones, bowled over the favored Cubs in the World Series.

With seven nonwinners to show for the next seven seasons, 1907 through 1913, Comiskey's first deal was a blockbuster. He spent what was then a fortune, $50,000, to purchase Eddie Collins from the Philadelphia Athletics. The size of this outlay staggered the imagination of baseball buffs everywhere. This was at the time they were still replaying the success of the 1914 Braves as the new Miracle Team that sprung out of last place on the Fourth of July to win the pennant and then the unbelievable sweep of the Athletics in the World Series. With Collins, Comiskey reasoned he had the anchorman he desired to "build the best team ever."

Seeking a powerful bat for his team, the Old Roman trained his sights upon the Indians' Joe Jackson. Hardly anyone knew Jackson was available, but Comiskey did, and the overall price for "Shoeless Joe" was even bigger than Collins's purchase for 50 grand. To get Jackson, the White Sox shelled out $31,500 in cash and three players whose original costs added up to $34,000. That made it a total deal of $65,500—$15,500 more than Collins's cost.

With a $115,500 addition to the budget—some clubs' entire payroll—to get both Collins and Jackson, the White Sox climbed to third in 1915 and second in 1916, although they won four games less than they did in 1915. With Collins and Jackson came Pants Rowland as the team's new manager. There was even more bounce to Comiskey's new team as it won 100 games to win the AL pennant in 1917. What happened in that year's World Series between the White Sox and the Giants still remains an unmatched milestone in Chicago's baseball history. The White Sox won the Series four games to two to reign with distinction as the long suffering Land of Losers' last World Championship team.

The joys of this spectacular success didn't last long as the Old Roman proved a supersleuth in helping to break open the 1919 Black Sox scandal in the World Series against the Reds. The man who spent more than $115,000 for two players in building the team, heard himself stamped as a penny pincher by the fixers. Comiskey's army of friends—and they were legion—called this charge a hollow alibi in the shameless players' efforts to blame him for the scandal they engineered. Nevertheless, it was baseball's as well as Comiskey's most perilous and darkest hour.

After the 1922 season, the heartbroken but still aggressive Comiskey applied a brand-new shot of adrenaline to his fifth-place team with a 77–77 record. This move was an even bigger blockbuster than the one which put Eddie Collins and Joe Jackson in White Sox uniforms. The Old Roman paid the San Francisco Seals $100,000 for a minor league third baseman named Willie Kamm. That's right: a 22-year-old player who had spent four seasons playing for the Seals brought $100,000. The skeptics wouldn't believe that a minor league player would cost that kind of money, but Comiskey had the canceled check to prove it. Kamm, always an outstanding fielder, paid an immediate dividend with a rookie season batting average of .292. Fifty-four of Willie's 159 hits went for extra bases as he pounded 39 doubles into a collection of 87 RBIs. Kamm was good as advertised, but the White Sox weren't. The 1923 machine sputtered into a seventh place finish as the Old Roman asked himself, "What am I going to do next?"

The first answer to that question was discovered on the Baylor University campus in Waco, Texas, in the person of a 23-year-old right-handed pitcher, Ted Lyons. When word leaked out that Connie Mack was interested in Lyons, Comiskey dispatched Catcher Ray Schalk to check this particular prospect immediately. At the suggestion of Frank Bridges, the Baylor baseball coach, Schalk caught Lyons during a warm-up. Schalk was so impressed that he hurried to the first available telephone after the workout to call Comiskey in Chicago to recommend the signing of Lyons, "the sooner the better because some club is a cinch to grab him." Two or three Waco-to-Chicago phone calls later, after he weighed both Mack's and Comiskey's offers, Lyons accepted the White Sox bid.

In view of the vast amounts of money he spent to get Collins, Jackson, and Kamm, the Old Roman must have thought he was dealing in a basement bargain sale. Ted settled for a $1,000 bonus and a $550 monthly salary. The season would be half over by the time the talented newcomer would report following graduation, meaning the first-season cost of Lyons to the White Sox would be $2,650—or $97,350 less than the club originally paid for Kamm. During his twenty-one seasons with the White Sox, Lyons won 260 games and managed the club for more than two and a half years—this despite a three-year time-out spent with the marines. Altogether, Lyons missed by 10 reaching 500 major league decisions as he won 260 and lost 230—one of them a 21-inning 6–5 loss to the Tigers on May 24, 1929.

If it hadn't been for a massive postgame fight following a Baylor-Texas A & M game during Lyons' freshman year, his entire career might have turned in a different direction. After picking Baylor over Louisiana State, the Louisiana-born Lyons showed up at Waco with a trombone and a desire to study law. During the football melee somebody stepped on the trombone, breaking it beyond repair, and Ted lacked the money to buy a replacement. At Coach Bridges's urging, Lyons forgot his budding career in music to concentrate on pitching, when he wasn't playing first base or in the outfield. While multiyear-bonus contracts of six or seven figures are the rage of the day in current professional sports, it's interesting to learn how Lyons spent his $1,000 payment in exchange for his first pro autograph, "I spent almost half of it ($458.00) to buy a new Ford roadster," Ted explained, "and drove it about five years. Whenever it broke down, I'd wire the motor back together again and keep right on driving. I was both a driver and a mechanic."

Attempting to get lucky again with a costly addition from the Pacific Coast League, the Old Roman shelled out $75,000 in cash and the equivalent of $48,000 in players to purchase Shortstop "Bill" Cissell from Portland, Oregon, prior to the 1928 season. The newcomer with the first name of Chalmer had four good seasons with the White Sox before he followed the Kamm script: traded to the Indians. This same season the White Sox purchased a first baseman named Arthur ("The Great") Shires from Waco in the Texas League. Shires batted .341 for his first 33 games in the majors before attempting to prove he was a better boxer than player. Manager Lena Blackborn was his first unscheduled opponent before he took on the Chicago Bears' center, George Trafton, in a scheduled encounter that didn't do too much for boxing's progress. When Shires challenged the Cubs' Hack Wilson for an off-season match, Judge Landis stepped in and ordered an immediate stop to such shenanigans.

Following Comiskey's death in 1931, the leadership of the White Sox was continued first by his son, J. Louis Comiskey, and later by his daughter-in-law and two grandchildren. No matter how hard they tried, they still couldn't match the Old Roman's wild spending sprees for players like he owned and operated his personal and private mint. J. Louis Comiskey's first step in this direction came after the 1932 season when he was in on the ground floor of Connie Mack's bust-up of his all-powerful Athletics. The White Sox got Jimmie Dykes, Mule Haas, and Al Simmons for $150,000.

With three new regulars, baseball interest in Comiskey Park soared in 1933, especially when the first major league All-Star game was played there in connection with Chicago's Century of Progress. The AL, led by Connie Mack, beat the NL, managed by John McGraw, 4–2 before a crowd of 47,595. Sad, but true is the fact that this winning magic didn't rub off on the White Sox. Even with the three new standouts, the White Sox slumped to a sixth-place finish and dropped into the AL cellar in 1934.

During this time Lew Fonseca, obtained from Cleveland in a trade for Willie Kamm in mid-May of 1931, managed the team. During the 1934 skid into the cellar, Fonseca was replaced by Jimmie Dykes, the colorful and strong-armed third baseman who launched a managerial reign that carried into 1946. While the heights of Dykes's success were wrapped up in a total of six first-division finishes, the Li'l Round Man never lost his sense of humor. A master of the one-liner, Dykes often claimed, "I tell all my pitchers they'll win if they pitch a shutout. Our offense is a one-time shot, if we're lucky, comprised of a walk, a sacrifice bunt, a wild pitch, and a bad hop single. It isn't much but it's consistent."

Typical of the Comiskeys' lack of luck was a mid-season movement in 1936 designed to bolster the club's drawing power both at home and on the road with the addition of a good Jewish player. The scouts' search for just such a player came to an end with the purchase of Outfielder Larry Rosenthal from St. Paul, Minnesota, of the American Association. Rosenthal reported, and played well, batting .281 in 80 games. There was just one catch; Rosenthal wasn't Jewish. He was Polish. "I just took it for granted that Rosenthal was Jewish," J. Louis Comiskey mused, "until somebody in the office checked out his background. That is when it was discovered he was Polish. He played well for us, and I'm happy we were able to deal for him."

At the close of the 1936 season, Dykes made his debut as a master trader, and this maneuver produced one of the most humorous "scoops" in journalistic history. During the winter meetings in New York, Dykes traded Pitcher Jack Salveson to the Senators, who sent Pitcher Earl Whitehill to the Indians. In return for Whitehill, the Indians shipped Pitcher Thornton to the White Sox. The three-player–three-team deal was made and announced early in the afternoon.

Before the announcement, Jimmy Gallagher, the baseball writer for the *Chicago Evening American,* asked John P. Carmichael, his friend and competitor from the *Chicago Daily News,* "Please cover for me Old Buddy because I have tickets to a musical which I would like to see." Carmichael agreed, saying, "Have fun. If anything breaks, I'll protect you all the way." Something did break. The announcement of the White Sox-Senators-Indians deal. True to his promise, Carmichael rushed to the press room and wrote the story under Gallagher's by-line and filed it to the *Evening American.* The job well done, Carmichael repaired to the bar to fortify himself for the next stint. It wasn't too long before the page boy called out his name. "Here I am," Carmichael answered as he traded a tip for a telegram. It read:

"*American* has story Sox get Thornton Lee in three team deal. Do you know anything about it?" Signed Lloyd Lewis, Sports Editor, *Chicago Daily News.*

The embarrassed Carmichael hurriedly scribbled his answer to Lewis, "I know all about it. I wrote it but forgot to cover for myself."

The following year at another meeting, Carmichael didn't forget to cover for himself when Dykes arranged one of his biggest deals. The White Sox sent three regulars—Vernon Kennedy, Tony Piet, and Dixie Walker—to the Tigers for Gerald Walker, Marv Owen, and Mike Tresh, a catcher who was still waiting to play in his first major league game. Jimmie's wisdom was apparent in connection with Tresh. Mike became one of the game's outstanding catchers during the next eleven years with the White Sox.

Nobody but Dykes knows whether it's true or not, and he isn't talking, but rumors of romance reportedly resulted in the deal of Zeke Bonura to the Sentators for Joe Kuhel during spring training in 1938. J. Louis Comiskey didn't exactly relish Zeke's interest in his daughter, Dorothy. Zeke drove a new convertible, and he frequently drove Dorothy to and from work whenever the White Sox played at home. During his four seasons with the Chicago club, the big, easygoing Italian from New Orleans, Louisiana, had 79 HRs and 440 RBIs, with a .318 batting average for this productive stay. Nevertheless, Zeke was suddenly replaced by the fancy-fielding Kuhel in a surprising one-for-one exchange.

Some years later Miss Comiskey became Mrs. John Duncan Rigney, the wife of the pitcher and popular executive in the team's

---

DO AS I PREACH—MARSE JOE

Joe McCarthy, baseball's winningest manager, had good reason to follow a "don't do as I do, but do as I preach" philosophy. Playing 15 minor league seasons, Marse Joe hit a total of 32 HRs. Wouldn't you know he managed such all-time great sluggers as Hack Wilson, Babe Ruth, Lou Gehrig, and Ted Williams?

front office. It wasn't, however, Zeke's last hurrah in Chicago. He returned to play 49 games for the Cubs in 1940 to close out his seven-season career. And still the veteran buffs talk about the famous Bonura salute, his inability to reach a ball hit sharply into the hole between first and second. As a belated gesture, he would wave his mitt at the bouncing baseball and retreat to cover the base.

Mrs. Grace Comiskey reigned as the First Lady of baseball, with a rank of White Sox president from 1941 to 1956. It wasn't always a happy tenure for J. Louis Comiskey's widow, who worked with Attorney Roy Egan to retain ownership of the club, following her husband's death in 1939.

There was one thing to be said for Mrs. Comiskey; nobody ever accused her of sameness in the selection of two general managers. Leslie O'Connor was a sedate man who always remained in the background—the result of his long association with Judge Landis, the game's first commissioner. Frank Lane was the other. He came on like Gangbusters whether he was trading a superstar or berating an umpire. Lane never played the middle of the road, and seldom did he miss having the last word. He was the telephone company's best customer making 192 moves involving 298 players during his first six seasons as the White Sox general manager.

They talk about operating from A to Z—Frantic Frankie did: all the way from Luis Aparicio to Al Zarilla. His first deal, Aaron Robinson to the Tigers for Billy Pierce and $10,000 in cash, may have been his best one, but he never quit trying. How else did the White Sox get title to Chico Carrasquel, Nellie Fox, Eddie Robinson, Minnie Minoso, Jim Rivera, Sherman Lollar, Ferris Fain, Vern Stephens, Virgil Trucks, Walt Dropo, George Kell, and Sam Mele? In successive seasons, Lane also managed to pick up three Cubs, Carl Sawatski, Phil Cavarretta, and Bill Serena, all this at a time when the two Chicago clubs operated on a "you keep your players and we'll keep ours" basis. During a five-day period, May 26 to May 31, 1950, Frank fired a manager (Jack Onslow) hired a new one (Red Corriden) and traded away three players—Johnny Ostrowski, Cass Michaels (née Casimir Kwietnieski), and Bob Kuzava. In their farewell speeches neither manager nor player spared any words. Onslow called Frank a "second-guessing SOB." Ostrowski summed up his feeling, saying, "That SOB just doesn't like Polacks."

After the happy headline hunt of Lane and Manager Paul

Richards ended in 1954, Frank's last major move before going to St. Louis as the Cardinals' general manager was signing of Marty Marion as Richards' replacement on July 21, 1954.

Thereafter, the big White Sox year was 1959 under Bill Veeck's ownership and Al Lopez's managerial savvy. In winning the club's first pennant since 1919, the key deal developed when Outfielder Harry Simpson and Infielder Bob Sagers were traded to the Pirates for Ted Kluszewski. Big Klu's bat was most helpful in the stretch, and his .391 batting average in the World Series tied him at the top of the list with the Dodgers' Gil Hodges as Los Angeles won the classic four games to two.

Whereas Lane was strictly a volume dealer, the new leadership duo of General Manager Roland Hemond and Manager Chuck Tanner leaned mainly to the blue chip variety in the swap shop. Ken Henderson was obtained from the Giants along with Pitcher Steve Stone for Pitcher Tom Bradley. Bill Melton was purchased from Hawaii, Wilbur Wood moved up from the Pirate's farm in Columbus, Ohio, and lefty Jim Katt came in a cash deal with the Twins. At the 1971 winter meeting in Phoenix, Arizona, the club stole all the headlines by trading Pitcher Tommy John and handyman Steve Huntz to the Dodgers for Richie Allen. The slugger, who was joining his fourth club in as many years, was envisioned as being a down payment on the AL pennant. Allen compiled three batting averages of .308, .316, and .301 despite two stretches on the disabled list during his second season. Becoming disenchanted in 1974, Allen retired September 14. The following December he was sold to the Braves for a player to be named later, but he refused to report to Atlanta. The Braves finally dealt him to the Phillies after the 1975 season was well underway.

During the 1973 winter meetings in Houston, Texas, all hell broke loose and the White Sox were left totally defenseless as they were backed into a corner without an escape hatch. The Cubs, on another rebuilding binge, thought they had a deal arranged with the Angels: Ron Santo for two young but still untested prospects. When Santo was called for his approval—the right of every 10-year veteran player who had spent five or more seasons with the same club—Ron balked. He minced no words saying: "I'll play in Chicago, or not at all."

Because the Cubs claimed he didn't fit in their plans and wouldn't take him back under any consideration, Santo put the cap on the White Sox. They were the only other team in Chicago, and

Ron never missed a beat emphasizing "It's Chicago or nothing." Daily the controversy blossomed into new headlines. White Sox fans envisioned the longtime Wrigley Field hero returning happy days to Chicago's South Side. Finally the White Sox succumbed to the fan clamoring, trading three pitchers—one of them Steve Stone—and Catcher Steve Swisher, a highly regarded high draft choice, to the Cubs for Santo. This pleased both the fans and Ron.

Now the media members had another new picnic. They drummed up a "feud" between the old (Bill Melton) and the new (Ron Santo) White Sox third basemen. One, they reasoned, would have to go. Manager Chuck Tanner had a different idea. He'd play Melton at third, and use Santo at second—a new position for Ron—when he wasn't his designated hitter. It sounded good during the winter, but unfortunately it didn't work out that way during the summer. Melton batted .242 compared to Santo's .221. Bill hit 21 HRs to Ron's five. Coupling this lowly production with Richie Allen's early retirement, the White Sox finished a .500 club, nine games off the pace in the AL West.

Unhappy over his lowest percentage in 14½ major league seasons, Santo retired after 1974 to enter business, never knowing what he might have missed by not trading Chicago for Anaheim in sunny California.

After the White Sox were involved in a twin collapse—on the field as well as the box office—in 1975, the Old Guard became the New Guard in Comiskey Park. Bill Veeck, who followed the hit-and-run sign after the team's pennant success in 1959, returned as the new owner.

Once approved by AL club owners, Veeck began to wheel and deal as only he can, trying to pump new life into his latest venture. One of his first moves was hiring Paul Richards, 67 years old and away from active field leadership for 14 years, as his new manager. In rapid manner Chuck Tanner shifted to the helm of the Oakland A's, with three years remaining on his White Sox managerial contract. Veeck's activity on the trade market produced one very significant addition: the deal for Ralph ("Roadrunner") Garr with the Braves.

CHARLES FEENEY
Sportswriter, *Pittsburgh Post-Gazette*

Charles Feeney was brought up a die-hard Dodger fan, and his first assignment on the major league beat was covering the Yankees. Once he recovered from the shock of covering the "wrong" team, Feeney was quick to learn that being a fan doesn't insure a writer's success if he isn't informed and informative. In short time he moved from the *Long Island Star-Journal* to the *New York Journal-American* to the *Pittsburgh Post-Gazette.* In Pittsburgh Feeney hasn't lacked an opportunity to cover a winner, with the Pirates capturing five divisional championships during the last six seasons. Feeney's career as a basketball writer ended early and understandably when he wrote this lead on a tense game: "Scoring in every period, ..."

22/THE PIRATES

See what you can get for Roberto Clemente

Baseball legend in Pittsburgh says there were two players who would have broken down and cried if they had been traded. The legend also says that the franchise wouldn't have been in deep trouble if these Hall of Famers had left Pittsburgh.

Shortly after the turn of the century, Honus Wagner, baseball's greatest shortstop, asked Pirates' owner Barney Dreyfuss to give him a contract for the following year.

"You don't need a contract," Dreyfuss told Wagner. "I'm never going to trade you."

Wagner explained that officials of the Federal League were trying to get him to jump. "If I tell them I'm signed for next year, they'll let me alone," Wagner told Dreyfuss. Legend says that Wagner signed a blank contract, and legend also says Wagner didn't particularly care how much he was paid to play baseball. Legends almost always are made up of half-truths.

Years later, Pie Traynor, the greatest third baseman in baseball history who played for both Dreyfuss, who died in 1932, and his son-in-law Bill Benswanger, told of his feelings about the fans in Pittsburgh and the thrill of playing for the Pirates.

"I often wondered what would happen if I was traded," Traynor said. "I wondered if I ever could feel at home with another club. I loved the people in Pittsburgh, and I was proud of the Pirate uniform." In 1934, Traynor heard all sorts of trade rumors. "I was going to New York, Chicago, St. Louis," he said. "When I was called to Mr. Benswanger's office in 1934, he said: 'Pie, please sit down.'

"I began to think: 'Oh, is this how he is going to tell me that I'm traded.' He was going to tell me to sit down, to tell me he was throwing me out of Pittsburgh." Later, Traynor, reflecting on the meeting, said: "I should have known better. Mr. Benswanger was my friend and he wouldn't do anything to hurt old Pie."

That day in 1934, Benswanger appointed Traynor the playing-manager of the Pirates.

Years later, there were other Pittsburgh heroes. One was traded away an hour before game time to a team the Pirates were playing that day. The other was never traded, but he had a manager who suggested the Pirates try to trade him.

Ralph Kiner, the biggest gate attraction in Pittsburgh's sports history, was the main man in a nine-player swap with the Cubs. The trade was completed on June 4, 1953, and, according to Kiner, it was not unexpected simply because Branch Rickey was running the Pirates at the time.

In 1969, Larry Shepard, who was managing the Pirates, suggested to the club's general manager, Joe L. Brown, that he try to trade Roberto Clemente. "At least see what you can get for him," Shepard suggested to Brown. Shepard was talking to the wrong general manager. If Rickey had been operating the team, he would have been on Shepard's wavelength. Clemente was in his thirties and earning a big salary. Rickey made a habit of trading aging high-salaried stars. He often said: "It's better to trade a player one year too soon than one year too late."

Brown, who replaced Rickey as general manager in 1955, wouldn't think of tempting other clubs by offering them Clemente, who went on to help the Pirates win three consecutive Eastern Division titles, beginning in 1970, and a World Championship in 1971. Death in a plane crash on New Year's Eve 1972—stopped Clemente from playing baseball.

The Kiner trade to the Cubs in 1953 was not unexpected to the big home-run slugger. When Rickey was hired as Pirates' general manager in 1950, Kiner knew his time was limited. Rickey tried to trade Kiner in 1951 and 1952 to avoid contract hassles and obtain younger players whose contracts were much less than the $80,000 plus that Kiner received.

The morning of June 4, 1953, Kiner went to the Forbes Field and did the routine things. He arrived at the clubhouse and checked his mail which was abundant in those days because he was the most popular man in Pittsburgh. When it came time to take batting practice, Kiner and the rest of the Pirates, which included Joe Garagiola, George Metkovich, and Howie Pollet, were on the field. Pollet was shagging fly balls in the outfield. Garagiola, who often spent the pregame practices warming up high-school pitchers who were being scouted by Rickey, took his batting practice with the subs—the scrubinies. Metkovich and Kiner batted with the other six men. They were listed to start by Manager Fred Haney, who had replaced Billy Meyer after the 1952 season.

A couple of Chicago players stood near the batting cage. They were joking about a trade. Twenty-five Cubs for 25 Pirates. They were sure Rickey would go for it because the Cubs, minus Kiner, had a smaller payroll. There is little question that during Rickey's career, he took into consideration a player's salary when he dealt in the trade market. Like any man, Rickey made mistakes. Fewer than most baseball men, but he made mistakes.

Hours before the Cubs and Pirates were to play that June afternoon in 1953, Rickey had his mind on one Cub player. He felt he could land him in any deal and that it was worth giving up Kiner and let the Pirate fans scream. Rickey also figured the attendance had dipped to 688,673 at Forbes Field in 1952, and this was an indication that even Kiner's home-run magic couldn't keep the turnstiles moving at a profitable pace.

There were more than 20 names bantered about in the trade talks with the Cubs. Rickey had one name in mind—Preston Ward. Ward, a Rickey protégé when he was general manager in the Brooklyn organization, was a first baseman, who Rickey felt could play the outfield. Rickey also thought Ward had the potential to hit a lot of home runs. When the Cubs agreed to make Ward part of the deal, it was completed. It was shortly before one o'clock, and Kiner and the Pirates had nearly finished batting practice. When Kiner

---

WHAT PRICE MUSCLE!

Why was Branch Rickey considered the king of baseball trade makers?

Ask this question of Red Foley, of the *New York Daily News,* and he says:

"Nobody could match Rickey's ability to place price on a pound of muscle. He was fast and accurate, and very convincing—once he set the price. Not all times, but most times, the estimate would end up in his favor.

"Remarkable man, Mr. Rickey."

reached his locker, he noticed that his large baseball bag, with his extra spiked shoes, extra gloves, etc., had been packed.

"What's the joke?" Kiner asked the clubhouse man.

"You've been traded to the Cubs," the clubhouse man said.

When Kiner learned there was no joke involved, he picked up his bag, left the Pirates' home clubhouse, and walked about ten feet to the entrance of the visitors' clubhouse at Forbes Field. Accompanying Kiner were Metkovich, a first-baseman-outfielder, Garagiola, a catcher, and Pollet, a left-handed pitcher who had some outstanding seasons with the Cardinals earlier. Accompanying Ward to the Pirates' clubhouse were Catcher Toby Atwell, Outfielders Gene Hermanski and Bob Addis, Infielder George Freese, and Bob Schultz, a left-handed pitcher. Kiner didn't hit any home runs for the Cubs that afternoon, but there was much confusion in the Kiner apartment in Pittsburgh and among the fans listening to Rosey Rowswell and a youngster named Bob Prince, who broadcast the Pirates' games through 1975.

Kiner's wife, Nancy, had been out of the house shopping, and when she returned, she turned on the radio. After listening for a few minutes, she heard Rowswell say: "Kiner is on the on-deck circle for the Cubs." She thought it was a slip of the tongue by Rowswell. A moment later, Nancy Kiner heard Rowswell say: "Kiner is ready to bat." Then Rowswell mentioned how the Pirates were defensing for Kiner.

"No, it can't be," Nancy Kiner thought. She was not alone in her thoughts. The radio station broadcasting the game was flooded with telephone calls.

"Is Rowswell going nuts? . . . Is Prince going out of his tree? Is everybody hearing things?"

The word had not yet spread in Pittsburgh about the Kiner trade. The late editions of the two afternoon newspapers had not hit the streets. In time, the news was out. The Kiners were not unhappy because Kiner's relationship with Rickey was described in newspapers as "strained."

"I couldn't call the trade a shock or anything like that," Kiner now says. "I had heard of Rickey's style, and I was expecting the trade for some time. But being traded just after batting practice, to a team we were supposed to play . . . that was a surprise. Looking back now, it is almost funny."

Ward never lived up to Rickey's expectations, and Brown, in one of his first deals as Rickey's successor, traded Ward to Cleveland for Catcher Hank Foiles in 1956.

Ten years earlier, before Rickey or Brown had come to Pittsburgh, one of the new Pirate owners arranged a trade just to get Billy Herman to manage the Pirates. Herman, a great second baseman with the Cubs and the Dodgers, was playing out the string with the Braves in 1946.

Frank McKinney headed a group which included John Galbreath, Tom Johnson, and Bing Crosby. The group bought the club from Barney Dreyfuss's widow for a reported $2,250,000. Roy Hamey was named the general manager and, following McKinney's orders, traded Bob Elliott to the Braves for Herman, who didn't finish the 1947 season, as Pirate manager. Elliott went on to become the NL's most valuable player in 1948 when the Braves won the pennant.

There was much disenchantment in Pittsburgh when Brown replaced Rickey in 1955. Beginning in 1952, the Pirates had finished in last place for four straight seasons. Five years earlier, Galbreath and Johnson had bought out McKinney. In the early days of McKinney's time as club president, the Pirates completed a trade with the Braves. The Pirates gave Pitcher Al Lyons, Catcher Bill Salkeld and Outfielder Jimmy Russell in exchange for Johnny Hopp, an outfielder-first baseman and an infielder.

"I was strictly a throw-in," Danny Murtaugh says. "The Pirates wanted Hopp and decided a three-for-two trade would look better than a three-for-one. It was the best thing that ever happened to me."

Murtaugh had some good years at second base in Pittsburgh, and when he decided he wanted to manage, he was given a chance to manage the Pirates' farm club in New Orleans in 1952. The club president and general manager in New Orleans was one Joe L. Brown, a young minor league executive struggling for recognition. Before the 1955 season, Brown joined the Pirates for special scouting and administrative work. It was the forerunner to taking over as general manager. Brown appointed Bobby Bragan in 1956, and midway in the 1957 season Brown fired Bragan and named Murtaugh, by then a Pirate coach, as interim manager.

"I didn't think of Danny as a permanent manager," Brown said, "because I thought he had too much compassion to manage a big league club."

Murtaugh's Pirates played .500 ball the remainder of the 1957 season, earning him a new contract. The Brown-Murtaugh team helped the Pirates win World Championships in 1960 and again in 1971.

The trade that helped mold the Pirates into a championship club in 1960 was completed by Brown before the 1959 season. Frank Thomas, Pittsburgh's best home-run hitter since Kiner, was among four players sent to Cincinnati. The others were Outfielders Jim Pendleton and Johnny Powers, and Pitcher Whammy Douglas. In return, Brown received Don Hoak, a third baseman who was the aggressive leader of the 1960 World Champions, Smoky Burgess, a solid left-handed hitter who caught for the 1960 champs, and Harvey Haddix, who pitched 12 perfect innings against the Milwaukee Braves in 1959, only to lose, 1–0, in the 13th. In 1960, Haddix won 11 games for the Pirates and was the winning pitcher in the seventh World Series game against the Yankees.

Before Brown could put all the pieces together for a 1960 championship, he had to make one deal in June 1960. He obtained left-handed Pitcher Vinegar Bend Mizell from the Cardinals for Julian Javier, a minor league second baseman who later played in the big leagues for years. Mizell gave the 1960 Pirates the added pitching they needed to win.

"It wasn't difficult for me to make that deal," Brown said, "because we were dealing from strength. We had a young fellow named Bill Mazeroski playing second base for us."

Brown has made his share of clunker deals. In 1962, he traded Dick Groat and Diomenes Olivo, a pitcher, to the Cardinals for Pitcher Don Cardwell and handyman Julio Gotay. Groat, the NL's most valuable player in 1960, helped the Cardinals win a pennant and World Championship in 1964. Of course, Brown also traded Dick Stuart in 1962, and he didn't win a pennant for the Red Sox.

A plus trade for Brown which produced a batting champion in Pittsburgh was completed with the Giants before the 1966 season. The Pirates obtained Matty Alou for Pitcher Joe Gibbon and Infielder Ozzie Virgil. Alou, a .240 hitter at best in San Francisco, won the batting title in 1966 with a .342 BA.

One of Brown's earlier successful deals was almost forced upon him. Frank Lane, who was general manager of the Cardinals, and his manager, Fred Hutchinson, were high on a young Pirate outfielder.

"When I saw Bobby DelGreco hit two home runs in one game against us," Lane said, "I decided I had to have him." For DelGreco, Brown received Bill Virdon, an outstanding center fielder for years, who later was to be hired and fired by Brown as Pirate manager.

Pirate fans and Brown were hungry for a pennant after failing from 1960 on. In 1966, the Pirates lost out in a three-team race with the Dodgers and Giants. They stumbled to sixth place in 1967, and pitching was to blame because the Pirates were loaded with hitters. Brown traded for Jim Bunning, a winning right-hander with the Phillies. He gave up Pitchers Woodie Fryman, Bill Laxton, and Harold Clem, plus Don Money, a minor league infielder whom the Phillies insisted be included in the deal.

Brown took out an ad in the two Pittsburgh newspapers after the Bunning trade. In effect, the ad said to the fans: "You said we needed a class pitcher. We've gone out and got you one. Buy your tickets now." Injuries reduced Bunning's efficiency with the Pirates, and after one and one-half seasons with them, he was sold to the Dodgers.

Following the 1969 season, Brown completed what appeared to be just another trade with the Cardinals. It turned out to be one of Brown's best—perhaps his best ever. Brown sent utility man Carl Taylor and minor league Outfielder Frank Vanzin to St. Louis for Pitcher Dave Giusti and Catcher Dave Ricketts. Giusti emerged as one of the game's outstanding relief pitchers. His desire to win rubbed off on players who had been with the Pirates' losing teams. Giusti arrived to pitch in Pittsburgh in 1970, and it's no coincidence that they began winning division championships.

Prior to the 1971 season, Brown made two trades. One turned out good. The other had results where Brown least expected. Brown gave Shortstop Freddie Patek, Catcher Jerry May, and Pitcher Bruce Dal Canton to the Kansas City Royals for Pitcher Bob Johnson, Catcher Jimmy Campanis, and Jackie Hernandez, a shortstop who couldn't hit and whose fielding in the clutch had been questioned. Johnson, the key man for the Pirates, was of little help. Hernandez, filling in for Gene Alley, played excellent short-stop in August and September and continued his fine play in the playoffs against the Giants and in the seven-game World Series win over the Orioles.

The other pre-1971 trade was with the Cardinals. Brown sent Matty Alou and veteran left-hander George Brunet to the Cardinals for Nelson Briles and Vic Davalillo. Briles, as a spot starter, won eight games and won the fifth Series game in 1971. Davalillo batted over .300 as a pinch hitter in 1971.

Over the years, the Pirates have come up short with pitchers from their farm system. Brown has dug into the trade market and come up with a Giusti . . . a Briles . . . a Jim Rooker (for Gene

Garber to Kansas City) . . . a Ken Brett, and a Jerry Reuss. In landing Brett and Reuss, Brown was dealing, as he says, from strength. The Phillies are most happy with the trade for Brett because they received Dave Cash, an All-Star second baseman. The Astros are happy with the Reuss deal because they received Milt May, one of the fine young catchers in the big leagues.

"After I trade I never look back," Brown says. "I do a lot of thinking before I make a trade, but once it's made, I don't worry how it will turn out What's the use of worrying. The deal has been made. I try never to trade to get rid of a player. I try to get a player who I think will help our club."

Brown's track record is well above average. Of course, he receives some help from Danny Murtaugh, a man Brown once felt had too much compassion to manage a big league club.

JOSEPH DURSO
Sportswriter, *The New York Times*

Joseph Durso hasn't missed a World Series or an All-Star game during the last twelve years, and he has logged something close to a million miles in behalf of his various activities. Joe was a U.S. Air Force pilot for three years and filled another three-year stint in radio news and sports. Covering the Mets or Yankees in such faraway places as the Caribbean and Japan, Joe did the research and writing of nine books. A Phi Beta Kappa graduate of New York University, he earned his master's degree from Columbia, where he also taught in the graduate school for fifteen years as a professor of journalism. Durso became a Timesman in 1950, working as an editor on the national news staff, assistant city editor, broadcaster, and columnist.

Ruppert's magic words to Frazee: Babe Ruth

He was a strapping teen-ager in overalls at St. Mary's Industrial School in Baltimore, a catcher who threw left-handed, and who also swung the bat and pitched left-handed, and who did all three better than anybody else in town. His name was George Herman Ruth and, after he had been signed right out of school by Jack Dunn, he reported to the Baltimore Orioles' spring training camp in 1914 and immediately became Jack's boy, or Jack's baby—"the Babe."

It was the eve of World War I and, by the time Johnny came marching home again, Jack Dunn's "baby" had started marching through baseball history: He was sold to the Red Sox, where he pitched on some days and played the outfield on others; he won 18 games in 1915, then 23 a year later, and 24 the year after that; and in 1918, as the great war began to ebb, he won 13 times—and hit 11 home runs. By then, he was the best left-handed pitcher in the AL, the best power hitter anywhere, and the leading candidate for the talent trade that would revolutionize the old ball game.

Babe Ruth, in fact, was the leading candidate for a series of moves that resulted in the rise of the New York Yankees, a team that would take 29 pennants and 20 World Series during the following 45 years, and that would negotiate some of the most unusual swaps in the business.

But the die was cast up there in Boston where a general manager named Edward Grant Barrow decided that he would rather have Ruth's long ball every day instead of his fast ball every fourth day. Ruth responded by hitting .322 with 29 HRs, a record for baseball, and the crowds gathered. They included the two colonels from New York, Jacob Ruppert and Tillinghast l'Hommedieu Huston, the owners of the Yankees, and their quarry was Harry

Frazee, the owner of the Red Sox. It proved a marriage of true minds because Frazee, a onetime billposter from Peoria, had a weakness for the theater—a weakness that kept him in red ink as a relentless "angel" for stage flops.

So Frazee turned to New York for help, asking Ruppert to lend him half a million dollars. Ruppert's answer: Babe Ruth. When they finally cleared the transaction, Frazee had $100,000 in cash and a personal loan of $350,000; Ruppert had a mortgage on Fenway Park in Boston as collateral; and the Yankees had Babe Ruth, who joined them in 1920 by hitting .376 with 54 HRs while Yankee attendance doubled to 1,289,422. Never was so much owed by so many to so few.

As often happens in the strange business of exchanging professional talent, a chain reaction set in. Later that fall, Barrow followed Ruth to New York as business manager of the Yankees. Then he quickly swung an eight-man deal—though, to some people, it seemed more like a raid—that pried four players from his old club in Boston. They were Waite Hoyt and Harry Harper, both pitchers; Wally Schang, a catcher, and Mike McNally, a third baseman. The Red Sox gained Herbert Thormahlen, a pitcher; Muddy Ruel, a catcher; Derrill Pratt, a second baseman, and Sam Vick for their outfield. But the new Yankee magic prevailed: Hoyt, who had been 6–6 at Boston, won 19 games in each of the next two years and joined Babe Ruth in building the empire.

Less than three years later, Barrow raided the old till again. This time, he favored the Red Sox with Outfielder Camp Skinner, Infielder Norman McMillen, Pitcher George Murray, and all-purpose cash. In return, the Yankees acquired one left-handed pitcher: Herb Pennock, who had won 10 games and lost 17 for Boston, but who promptly won 19 and then 21 for New York *plus* two games in the World Series against John McGraw's Giants. It was the year Yankee Stadium opened its gates, and it was the year the Yankees and their new ballplayers overpowered the Giants in the celebrated Battle of Broadway.

If there was any doubt that the Yankees already were masters of playing their cards across the trading table, consider the festive scene when they opened their new stadium in the Bronx. It was April 18, 1923: a cool and somewhat cloudy day in New York, where topcoats were going for $27.50 to $54.75 at Macy's, and caps at $1.88, or Lansdowne hats at $4.89. All might be useful, the newspaper ads suggested, because "it is apt to be a bit chilly during the opening game of the baseball season, especially near the close of the game." Smokers could stock up on Tampa blunt cigars (the can of 50 went for $2.49), Italian briar pipes (at 39 cents each) or Three Castles Cigarettes (airtight tins of 50 each at $1.88).

Across the ten acres that once formed part of the estate of William Waldorf Astor, a throng of 74,200 was jammed into the gleaming ball park across the Harlem River from McGraw's Polo Grounds. The Seventh Regiment Band paraded, John Philip Sousa conducted, and Harry Frazee watched. He watched with mixed emotions, too, because his Red Sox were beaten that afternoon, 4–1, by the Yankees and their hired hands: Bob Shawkey, the pitcher, who had been sold by Philadelphia; Wally Schang, his catcher, sold by Boston; and Babe Ruth, who watched while Howard Ehmke "tried to fool him with one of those slow balls that the Giants used successfully in the last World Series." This time, it landed ten rows back for three runs.

Even when they weren't making trades, the Yankees sometimes developed the knack of making other people regret trades. Remember Mark Koenig, the infielder who was on third base with a triple in 1927 when Ruth whacked No. 60? He was later traded to the Tigers and Cubs, who got him from the Pacific Coast League during the 1932 season and shortchanged him on a World Series share. During the bench-riding of the Series, the Babe reminded the Cubs of their thrifty behavior with his old teammate, and then delivered the *coup de grace* by "calling the shot" just before unloading one over the center field fence off Charley Root.

One depression and another World War later, the Yankees got back to their old tricks in the open market as they turned into Phase II of their "era." They kicked off on October 16, 1946, during somebody else's World Series when they swung one with the Indians. They sent two infielders, the acrobatic Joe Gordon and Eddie Bockman, to Cleveland for the right-handed hardball pitcher from Oklahoma, Allie Reynolds (chiefly on the advice of Joe DiMaggio), and again they struck gold. Reynolds, 11–15 for the Indians that season, promptly pitched 19 victories for the Yankees in 1947 as they began to piece together the team that would win five straight world titles under Casey Stengel starting in 1949.

When they needed help, even during their heyday, they displayed an uncommon instinct for getting it in the nick of time—as they did during the summer of 1949 when their bid for the pennant was complicated by a siege of 73 injuries. In August, with things getting sticky, Dan Topping and George Weiss figured out the equation: Horace Stoneham and his Giants needed money, Casey and his Yankees needed muscle. Result: $50,000 in cash for Johnny Mize, the 36-year-old slugger who in eleven seasons with the Cardinals and Giants had led the NL in HRs four times.

Mize, in fact, had led the league two years running, in 1947 and 1948, and had been named to the All-Star team that very summer. But Leo Durocher, the Giants' new manager, had begun to phase out some of his older players, and so Johnny Mize and his bat switched sides. He did all right, too, despite age and injuries; he stayed five years with the Yankees; he led them in pinch hitting three times and finished his career with 359 HRs. "In 1950," he said later, pinpointing his remarkable value after the trade, "I only had 76 hits for the entire season and I drove in 72 runs."

But the blockbuster of all—maybe of all time in sheer numbers—came toward the end of 1954. The traders were George Weiss for the Yankees and Paul Richards for the Orioles, recently transplanted from St. Louis where they had alternately amused and amazed people as the Browns.

The wheeling and dealing began on November 18 with nine players involved, and it closed 15 days later on December 3 with eight more involved. By then, it counted 17 men, everything but the kitchen sink in a virtual exchange of armies. This is the way the travel orders read:

To the Yankees: Don Larsen, Bob Turley, and Mike Blyzka, three pitchers; Darrell Johnson, a catcher; Dick Kryhoski, first baseman; Billy Hunter, shortstop; Ted del Guercio and Tim Fridley, outfielders. Total: eight bodies.

To the Orioles: Harry Byrd, Jim McDonald, and Bill Miller, three pitchers; Hal Smith and Gus Triandos, catchers; Don Leppert, second baseman; Kal Segrist, third baseman; Willy Miranda, shortstop, and Gene Woodling, outfielder. Total: nine bodies.

Behind the quantity, enough quality accompanied the migration to help the Yankees prolong their rank in baseball for another decade while established stars like Mickey Mantle, Whitey Ford, and Roger Maris (the traders' delight) carried the main load. Specifically, they obtained two hard-throwing right-handers, Turley at 25 and Larsen at 26, plus Hunter at shortstop to support the 37-year-old Phil Rizzuto. For the Orioles that year, Turley had been 14–15; for the Yankees the next year, 17–13, and the year after that, 21–7. For the Orioles, meanwhile, Larsen had won three games and lost 21—that's right, 21. For the Yankees two years later, he pitched the first perfect game in World Series history.

"The only thing he fears," Jimmie Dykes observed, "is sleep."

But if the massive swap with the Orioles made mathematics history, the Yankees found an even more willing collaborator during the 1950s in Kansas City. Once their farm club in the American Association, some folks snickered, and later their "farm club" in the AL. For openers: Billy Martin in June 1957.

Billy was a knobby, impudent, fighting little guy whose chief talent seemed to be—well, being in the right place at the right time. He played for the Oakland Oaks for a month in the Pacific Coast League in 1947 and again in 1948, when they won the league title under the spindly old Casey Stengel. A year later, the spindly old Stengel went to the Yankees; a year after that, Martin followed him there. And for the next seven years, he was the Professor's pet.

Martin's best batting average during that span was .267 in 1952, but the Yankees had plenty of power to spare and didn't mind carrying a guy with other skills. Besides, in five World Series he hit .333 with five home runs. But along the way, he was Peck's Bad Boy—or so he seemed to the Victorian ringmaster of the club, George Weiss, who tended to blame Billy for being a bad influence on choice property like Mantle. The payoff came in May 1957 when Mantle, Ford, and a flock of Yankees and their wives made headlines after celebrating Martin's twenty-ninth birthday at the Copacabana Club in Manhattan, a celebration that reached a climax when one of the non-Yankee patrons was decked by person or persons unknown.

One month later—on June 15, the deadline for making trades in the big leagues, to be exact—Martin was sitting in the bullpen. In the middle of the game, "the Old Man called me and said, 'We want to talk to you.'" A few moments later in the clubhouse: "We traded you to Kansas City." This is the way it went: Billy Martin, Ralph Terry, Woodie Held, and Bob Martyn to Kansas City for Ryne Duren, Jim Pisoni, and Harry Simpson. An infielder, pitcher, and two outfielders for a pitcher and two outfielders. And later, Martin traveled from Kansas City to Detroit to Cleveland to Cincinnati to Milwaukee to Minnesota, all within 4½ years.

"My birthday was May 16," he lamented later, "and June 15 I was gone. How can you be a bad influence on six pennant winners?"

Two and a half years later, while Billy Martin was still shipping around the landscape, the Yankees reached into Kansas City for another big one. And if Kansas City now had replaced Boston as the "other" city in empire-building, then Roger Maris was about to replace Babe Ruth as the prize cargo. Maris had signed with the Cleveland system in 1953 when he was 19 years old, and he cast a shadow of sorts by hitting 32 HRs at Keokuk, Iowa, in his second season as a pro. He made it all the way to Cleveland in 1957 and hit 14 HRs, then raised a few eyebrows by hitting 28. Then he broke two ribs while sliding, was platooned, and finally was traded by Frank Lane to Kansas City. Ah, Frank Lane.

On December 11, 1959, came the blockbuster. The Yankees sent Don Larsen (who had been pitching some imperfect games, too) along with Marv Throneberry, Hank Bauer, and Norm Siebern. The Yankees got Kent Hadley, a first baseman; Joe DeMaestri, a shortstop, and Roger Maris. The following season, Maris cleared the fence 39 times with a memorably smooth left-handed swing of the bat. The year after that, 1961, he cleared the fence 61 times and broke the record set 34 years earlier by that other New York acquisition, Babe Ruth.

But a trade is usually a two-way street, and Roger Maris traveled the "other" side of the street when the Yankee era disintegrated during the 1960s. He hit "only" 33 HRs in 1962, the year after he had stirred the great commotion; then 23 the year after that in 90 games; then 26 in 1964; then, injured and serving on part-time duty, only eight in 1965 as the Yankees fell from the peak. Finally, in December of 1966, as the most successful team in history spiraled deeper, he was traded to the Cardinals for the journeyman infielder, Charlie Smith.

By then, the Yankees were left with their memories—of the time when they could deal from strength. The time, for instance, when they could bring a Luis Arroyo to the surface to help extend their success. Arroyo, the chubby little cigar-smoking Puerto Rican who pitched in the minors from 1948 (Greensville and Greensboro) to 1955 (Cardinals), and then pitched back in Omaha. He made Pittsburgh in 1956 and then briefly in 1957, and he had pitched for eight teams in the minors (including Havana) when the Yankees bought him during a summertime collapse in 1960.

He already had worked that year in Havana and Jersey City, but the old magic again worked miracles: In 29 appearances for New York that summer, he won 5 games, lost one and finished with an ERA of 2.81 as a bullpen stopper. A year later, he won 15 times and lost 5. A year after that, his record dwindled to 1 and 3, and then he retired. But he had helped the Yankees with their final 15 games of 1960 and the pennant, he had pitched in two World Series, and he had written another footnote to the Yankees' bizarre record in the market.

Or, for memories, they could recall Enos Slaughter, who was 38 years old when the Yankees snatched him on April 11, 1954, from good old Kansas City. The price was Emil Tellinger; a rookie outfielder named Bill Virdon, who returned twenty years later as manager, and a pitcher named Mel Wright, who returned as one of Virdon's coaches. Old Country Slaughter, meanwhile, stuck around long enough to play in three World Series for the Yankees after he already had played in two for the Cardinals.

Or, again for memories, there was Pedro Ramos, who was annexed from Cleveland in September 1964 when things looked gloomy for Yogi Berra. He arrived with cowboy hat, boots, Cuban cigars, a frequently wet "palm ball," and a superior style that led Ralph Houk to say: "The way he throws, I don't see how they ever hit him." They didn't hit him much, and the Yankees regained first place that time on September 17 with Pete Ramos adding another chapter to their intriguing history of dealing in the open market.

The memories fade, though . . . Maris to St. Louis in 1966 . . . Clete Boyer to Atlanta in 1967 . . . Jim Bouton to Seattle in 1968 . . . Joe Pepitone to Houston in 1970. The trading slows, the era fades. Then the seventies . . . Catfish Hunter "trades himself" to the team for $3.75-million . . . Elliott Maddox from Texas . . . Bobby Bonds from San Francisco . . . Mickey Rivers from California. . . . The trading quickens, another era dawns, half a century after Jacob Ruppert looked at Harry Frazee and replied: Babe Ruth.

And the surprise of 1976: Billy Martin back as manager, and Yogi Berra back as a coach in another new era's dawning.

RITTER COLLETT
Sports Editor, *Dayton Journal Herald*

Ritter Collett is the only sports editor the *Dayton* (Ohio) *Journal Herald,* formed in a 1949 merger, has ever had. He was only twenty-eight years old at the time, and is still going strong in the 1970s. His father, a native of Ironton, Ohio, owned a newspaper, and Ritter grew up in the business. Ritter is a graduate of Ohio University, and he spent three and a half years in World War II. He joined the *Dayton Herald* in January of 1946. His coverage spans from his first World Series in 1946 to the Olympics in Munich. Ritter is chairman of the Phi Delta Theta fraternity's Lou Gehrig Memorial Award committee, and national secretary-treasurer of the Hutch Fund.

24/THE REDS

Rickey's pocket picking in dear old Zinzinnati

Frank C. Lane, who became one of the legendary traders of the game, never had an opportunity to engineer a deal for the Cincinnati Reds when he broke into baseball. "But I got a good idea of what it was all about from observing Branch Rickey pick Sid Weil's pocket several times," Lane recalled, chuckling at the reference to the late, great Rickey.

Sid Weil was the owner of the Cincinnati franchise when it was going broke during the Great Depression. When civic interests persuaded industrialist Powel Crosley Jr., who had absolutely no personal interest in the game, to take over the club in 1933 by assuming Weil's debts, the industrialist was to hire Larry MacPhail to run the Reds. Lane was the farm director in this operation.

"The only thing was, we didn't have a farm system when we started out in 1933," Lane said. Frank C. did sign a number of players who made it to the majors. He parlayed a bus ticket that brought a young man from New York City to Beckley, West Virginia, into a Most Valuable Player winner long after Lane had left the club. The young man who came by Greyhound to West Virginia was Frank McCormick, the graceful and hard-hitting first baseman.

Lane's reference to Rickey picking Weil's pocket seems well attuned to the uneven history of Cincinnati trades. Over the years, the Reds' general managers Warren Giles, Gabe Paul, Bill DeWitt, and the incumbent front office boss, Bob Howsam, have made some incredible "steals" at one time or another. The first three were also badly burned on occasion, a fate that Howsam has managed to avoid up to this point in time.

Giles would like to forget the 1948 maneuver, carried out under the ticking away of the clock against the June 15 trade deadline, in which he sent Hank Sauer and Frank Baumholtz to the Cubs. In exchange he took Harry ("the Hat") Walker and Peanuts Lowrey, both of whom, in parlance of the racetrack, had dropped from the handicap to the claimer class.

As for Gabe, after a string of highly successful deals, he stumbled in 1959 going for slugger Frank Thomas. That deal paid off in a pennant—for the Pirates—who got excellent mileage out of Don Hoak, Smokey Burgess, and Harvey Haddix.

DeWitt hastily changes the subject when the name of Frank Robinson is brought up. The man, whom DeWitt labeled an "old 30" when he traded him to the Orioles, went strong for a decade afterwards and acquired the stature to become baseball's first black major league manager. The trio that came to Cincinnati in exchange for Robinson has long since passed into the discard, two of them on short notice. The third one became the central figure in a simmering dispute linked, of all things, to the tragic assassination of Senator Bobby Kennedy. Milt Pappas, who became the Reds' player representative, wanted baseball to cancel its schedule during the period Kennedy lay in state before burial. Somehow that seemingly admirable sentiment stirred up all sorts of animosity in the ranks.

Tracing the history of Cincinnati trades should start with Edd J. Roush, perhaps the greatest player ever to wear a Cincinnati uniform—a contention that may someday soon be disputed by partisans of Johnny Bench and Pete Rose. Roush came to the Reds in a trade, departed in one, and then bounced back to the Rhineland again in a maneuver that perhaps involved more future Hall of Famers than any other swap.

In 1916, John J. McGraw, the legendary "Little Napoleon" of the New York Giants, traded not one, but three, future Hall of Famers to the Reds. Accompanying Roush to Cincinnati, was the great Christy Mathewson and a third baseman named Bill McKechnie. The Giants took Buck Herzog and Wade Killefer in exchange. Mathewson was then going on 36 and had next to nothing in his arm. Perhaps even then he was suffering from the tubercular condition that led to his early death in 1925.

McGraw, however, made a mistake on Roush, who had spent two seasons in the Federal League. Roush's batting averages for the next 10 seasons in Cincinnati uniform are incredible and noteworthy. The hard-bitten Hoosier hit .341, .333, .321, .339, .352, .352, .351, .348, .339 and .328 before the Reds traded him back to the New York Giants. This time McGraw gave up another future Hall of Famer in a more even deal. First Baseman George "High-pockets" Kelly came to dear old Zinzinnati. After Roush became the only player in history to sit out a full season as a holdout in 1930 against the Giants, he came back to Cincinnati for one more year.

McKechnie's fame in baseball was not as a player, but later as a manager. Coincidence providing a fascinating strand in life, the Reds have had only four managers who directed them to pennants. Two of them, McKechnie and Fred Hutchinson died in the same hospital in Bradenton, Florida, less than a year apart. McKechnie, known as Deacon Bill, led the Reds to the NL pennant in 1939 and 1940, and won the World Series in 1940 at the expense of Bobo Newsom and the Tigers.

Most of McKechnie's key players were acquired in trades, and most of those were engineered by Warren Giles who came on the scene as general manager in 1936. Pitching standouts Paul Derringer, William ("Bucky") Walters, Milkman Jim Turner, and relief ace Joe Beggs all came from other clubs. So did Ernie Lombardi, the huge and moody catcher who was positively the slowest runner ever to win a major league batting title. Third Baseman Bill Werber and Second Baseman Lonnie Frey, as well as the parade of left fielders the Reds had in that span were acquired in either cash purchases, deals, or maneuvers involving both.

Whatever advantage Mr. Rickey may have taken of the Reds, he did give them Paul Derringer, and in that context—taking advantage of the other man in a trade is what it is supposed to be all about. Derringer came to Cincinnati in a multiplayer deal in 1933, which saw the Reds give up Shortstop Leo Durocher. Durocher became a key man in the pennant surge of the Cardinals' Gashouse Gang a year later. Derringer's dividend in Cincinnati was far into the future, but it was a big one when it came.

The Reds had become solvent with a bit of cash in the bank, thanks to pioneering night baseball in the big leagues. Thus Giles could purchase Werber from Connie Mack's Philadelphia A's and buy Bucky Walters from that club's equally insolvent NL counter-part, the Phillies. Giles was not averse to spending, because cash was the main ingredient in bringing Jim Turner over from Boston as insurance for the 1940 drive.

Ernie Lombardi had come to Cincinnati in a deal with the Brooklyn Dodgers way back in the Sid Weil era in 1931. He was accompanied by the hard-hitting but ever so eccentric Babe Herman. Herman was beginning to bounce around like the baseballs he frequently shadowboxed off the high right field wall in old Ebbetts Field. But Lombardi became a fixture in Cincinnati for the next decade and an excellent catcher and dangerous hitter.

"If Ernie Lombardi could have run with anything approaching average speed, he would have been one of baseball's all-time great hitters," Giles said of his burly catcher. "They played a six-man outfield against him and he still hit over .300 most of the time."

The advent of World War II cast a pall of darkness over the world that all but engulfed baseball. The Reds suffered as much as any team in the aftermath, because West Germany was on its feet long before the Cincinnati team, despite the Reds' good fortune in coming up with the dazzling Ewell Blackwell.

It was an arm injury to Blackwell in 1948 that created the situation which saw Giles make his ill-fated deal with the Cubs. Sauer hit a lot of home runs, won an MVP and became a longtime favorite of Chicago fans. Baumholtz nearly won a batting title whereas Lowrey and Walker were unable to help the Reds.

When Warren C. Giles was offered the presidency of the NL in 1951, the Reds had a ready-made executive to step into his shoes. Gabe Paul had filled many a role in an undermanned Cincinnati front office without benefit of title, and he was a first-rate baseball man from the outset.

Gabe made his first deal within days, and as it turned out, it was better than he thought. He sent Outfielder Bob Usher and Catcher John Pramesa to the Cubs for Outfielder Bob Borkowski and Smokey Burgess—then an unknown catcher who had to overcome the reputation of his roly-poly build. Burgess was sent right on to Philadelphia in a seven-player deal that brought Andy Seminick to Cincinnati. Rock-hard, egg-bald Seminick was a workmanlike catcher in the Queen City, but when Burgess was reacquired from Philadelphia, Seminick was part of the price.

Gabe's first masterpiece was getting Gus Bell from Pittsburgh and the aging Branch Rickey, prior to the 1953 season, in exchange for three guys named Cal, Joe, and Gail, and letting that trade be remembered in precisely that manner. Bell was to become a mainstay in the rebuilding of the Reds to respectability, and much later he got the first hit for an expansion franchise known as the New York Mets.

Gabe made a practice of obtaining highly serviceable players in deals that stirred few headlines when he made them. But the likes of John Klippstein, Brooks ("The Bull") Lawrence, and Bob

Purkey attest to his good judgment. The price for Lawrence was southpaw Jackie Collum, and "The Bull" became a 19-game winner in his first season in Cincy under Manager Birdie Tebbetts. The Collum deal was made with St. Louis when Lane was in charge of the Cardinals.

On an occasion in the winter of 1957–1958, both Gabe and Lane appeared at a speaking engagement in Dayton, Ohio. They talked trade on the drive back to Cincinnati, but could arrive at nothing.

"Okay, so it isn't a wasted evening, I'll trade you the 25th man on my roster for the 25th man on your roster," suggested Lane.

Tebbetts vetoed the deal, advising his boss, Gabe, "I know how bad our guy is. I might be tempted to use the one they send us when I should know better."

Perhaps it was poetic justice that the Pirates stung Gabe in the Frank Thomas deal. The Cincinnati boss had picked their pockets again in getting Bob Purkey for southpaw Don Gross. Earlier, Gabe had picked up Jim Brosnan and Bill Henry in

---

HOW THE BIG RED MACHINE WAS ASSEMBLED

Altogether the Cincinnati Reds, 1975 World Series winner, went to the trade market eight times to get thirteen players in building the team which won 108 games to clinch the NL Western division title, swept the Pirates in three straight in the NL championship series, and inched past the Red Sox in the World Series, four games to three.

The 1975 Big Red Machine was assembled by General Manager Bob Howsom in this order:

Joe Morgan, Jack Billingham, Cesar Geronimo, Pat Darcy, Ed Armbrister from Astros;
Fred Norman, Clay Kirby from Padres;
Merve Rettenmund from Orioles;
Pedro Borbon from Angels;
Clay Carroll from Braves;
George Foster from Giants;
Bill Plummer from Cubs;
Terry Crowley from Rangers.

Also there was a touch of luck attached to the Reds' success. Ken Griffey, acquired in the free-agent draft of June 1969, was the club's Number Twenty-Nine choice. Three players, Dave Concepcion, Dan Driessen, and Doug Flynn, were picked up as undrafted free agents—in other words, walk-ons.

relatively minor deals, and the two of them became standout relief pitchers. Gabe has always had a fascination for power, and he was completely mesmerized by big Frank's 35 HRs and the 109 runs he had driven in for the Pirates in 1958.

As it turned out, Thomas had a bad hand and his .227 average (12 homers, 47 RBIs) ruined Mayo Smith's brief managerial whirl in Cincinnati and was a source of much chagrin among Cincy fans. Among the players who accompanied Thomas to Cincinnati was "Whammy" Douglas, a pitcher who had only one good eye. Already on hand in Cincinnati was Bobby Mabe, who had lost an eye in a boyhood B-B gun incident. In years after his firing, Mayo would regale audiences at baseball gatherings by talking about his problems. "I was the only manager in baseball with two one-eyed pitchers and a one-handed slugger," he would say. But it wasn't so funny when it cost him his job.

Gabe would make one more worthy deal for the Reds before resigning at the end of the 1960 season. He sent the fiery but fading Second Baseman Johnny Temple to the Indians for Cal McLish, Billy Martin, and the then unknown Gordy Coleman. The latter turned into a solid hitting first baseman. McLish was used in a deal that brought Gene Freese to the club in time for the 1961 pennant surge. Freese, who was to fracture an ankle in spring training a year later that would prematurely end his career, drove in 83 runs from his third base position in his one big season.

When DeWitt arrived as general manager in the fall of 1960, he was ready to wheel and deal. He made the move for Freese and then sent veteran Shortstop Roy McMillan to Milwaukee for Joey Jay, who was to win 21 games in successive years for the Reds. Early in the 1961 season, with Manager Fred Hutchinson insisting he needed a second baseman, DeWitt sent Catcher Ed Bailey to San Francisco for Don Blasingame, even though the Reds had no established catcher in reserve. Darrell Johnson, the current manager of the Red Sox and young John Edwards came through nicely.

After the 1961 pennant, the Reds were relatively inactive in the trading market until the Robinson fiasco. Most unbiased observers feel that DeWitt was guilty of two serious lapses. First, he let his personal feelings about Robinson influence the deal, and secondly, he did not investigate the background of the players he acquired. None could argue that the Reds needed pitching, but at his absolute best, Pappas had never been a pitcher of the stature that Robinson enjoyed as a hitter. As it turned out, it was the best break of Robinson's career. And just as the Frank Thomas deal put

Mayo Smith on the skids as a manager, the Robinson deal did in Don Heffner, whom DeWitt fired in mid-season of 1966 amidst the shambles of an aimlessly drifting club.

Robert L. Howsam, the incumbent head honcho of the Reds with the title of executive-president, has proven himself a very astute manipulator of talent. Not all of his deals have been "steals," but no one has picked his pocket either.

His first major maneuver paid a whopping dividend. As June trading deadline approached in 1968, with Pappas and Manager Dave Bristol not on speaking terms, the general manager solved that by sending Pappas, Ted Davidson, and Infielder Bob Johnson to Atlanta for Clay Carroll, Woody Woodward, and Tony Cloninger. The Reds got excellent mileage from all three—and Carroll, known as "The Hawk," is still one of the game's better relief pitching specialists.

Howsam still needed pitching as he went into the 1969 season. He sent the veteran Vada Pinson to St. Louis and got Wayne Granger and Bobby Tolan in exchange. Tolan had two excellent seasons before suffering a torn Achilles tendon. Granger was a standout relief pitcher in 1969. Howsam gave up Shortstop Leo Cardenas to the Twins to get Jim Merritt, who was to become the club's first 20-game winner in 1970 as the Reds won the West and the NL championships. Going into that season, the Reds needed more pitching, and Howsam got it from the Angels, bringing Pedro Borbon, Jim McGlothlin, and Vern Geishert in exchange for the moody Alex Johnson. McGlothlin helped for three seasons, and Borbon found a home in the bullpen.

Howsam's masterpiece was the blockbuster with the Astros in December of 1972, that restored speed and defensive balance after the club had stumbled badly in its first full season in its new home in Riverfront Stadium. Joe Morgan, "Mr. Excitement" himself, was the headman among the impressive imports that also included Jack Billingham, Cesar Geronimo, Denis Menke, and Ed Armbrister. Although the Reds surely got the better of the deal, Howsam did give up a trio of solid performers in First Baseman Lee May, Second Baseman Tommy Helms, and Jimmy Stewart. The latter, a hustling utility man, earned the nickname of "Super Sub" in Cincinnati.

Howsam has never rested on his laurels as the addition of Fred Norman in 1973 and Clay Kirby a year later attests. At the same time, the Cincinnati farm system has been whipped up into a very productive training ground to develop future stars.

Hall of Fame
trade box score

The foremost word in getting to the Baseball Hall of Fame in Cooperstown, New York, is *ability*. It isn't the only word, however. Residents in Cooperstown know that trades have added special emphasis to players' careers in qualifying them for the shrine in upstate New York.

Burleigh Grimes, class of 1964, was involved in eight different deals as he won 270 games for seven clubs, thirteen in a row for the Giants in 1927. Ol' Stubblebeard pitched his way into four World Series spanning the period from 1920 through 1932. Players changing clubs in swaps for Grimes ranged all the way from Vic Aldridge to fabled Hack Wilson—who still hasn't found the right road to Cooperstown. Nobody had a better book on the declining values on the trade mart than Al Simmons. In successive deals his price tag fell from $150,000 to $75,000, and finally to $15,000 before the Milwaukee-born slugger was the party of the first part in two lesser sales, going first to the Boston Braves and then the Reds.

Think it was possible for Paul ("Big Poison") Waner to know every word and every comma in the unconditional-release clause in his contract? Altogether this supersouthpaw swinger balanced the scales by getting a career total of 3,152 hits and drawing his unconditional release five times—twice from the Dodgers. Honus Wagner, Mr. Shortstop of his era, was one of fourteen players to join the Pirates in a mass move after Louisville dropped out of the NL. Colorful Casey Stengel learned early in his playing career to keep his suitcase packed at all times. Stengel went through four different deals before finding managerial security in New York. Ol' Case was the Yankee skipper for twelve years before laughing his way through Fun City during four seasons with the hapless Mets.

Ralph Kiner figured as one of ten players in a deal between the Pirates and the Cubs, which the Chicago club sweetened by tossing $100,000 into the swap. Joe Garagiola could devote a full chapter to this deal about the Baseball World of Joe Garagiola. He was one of the players to move to Chicago from Pittsburgh.

Formula! If you want to get to the Hall of Fame, a trade or two might help. It won't make it official, but it certainly won't hurt as this Box Score proves—all the way from Alexander to Young.

Jim Enright

Name of Player	Type of Deal	Other Players Included	Selling or Releasing Team
Grover Cleveland Alexander	1. Traded	Bill Killefer	Phillies
	2. Released		Cubs
	Signed		
	3. Traded	Harry McCurdy	Cardinals
Earl Averill	1. Sold		San Francisco Seals (PCL)
	2. Traded		Indians
Franklin ("Home Run") Baker	1. Sold		Philadelphia A's
Dave Bancroft	1. Traded		Phillies
	2. Traded	Casey Stengel Bill Cunningham	New York Giants
Roger Bresnahan	1. Jumped	John McGraw Frank Bowerman Joe McGinnity John Cronin	Baltimore
	2. Traded		New York Giants
Dan Brouthers	1. Sold	Hardie Richardson Jim White Charles Rowe	Buffalo
Mordecai Brown	1. Traded	Jack O'Neill	Cardinals
	2. Released Signed		Cubs
	3. Traded		Louisville
Max Carey	1. Released		Pirates
	Signed		
John Clarkson	1. Sold		Cubs
Ty Cobb	1. Released Signed		Tigers
Mickey Cochrane	1. Traded		Philadelphia A's
Eddie Collins	1. Traded		Philadelphia A's

| Buying or Receiving Team | Dealt For | | Date |
	Player	Cash in Dollars	
Cubs	Mike Prendergast Pickles Dilhoefer	60,000	11-11-1917
		waiver price	6-22-1926
Cardinals			6-22-1926
Phillies	Homer Peel Bob McGraw		12-11-1929
Indians		50,000	April 1928 season
Tigers	Harry Eisenstat	cash	6-14-1930
Yankees		35,000	2-17-1916
New York Giants	Art Fletcher Wilbur Hubbell	100,000	6-8-1921
Boston Braves	Joe Oeschger Billy Southworth		11-15-1923
New York Giants			7-16-1902
Cardinals	Bugs Raymond John Murray George Schlie		12-10-1908
Tigers		cash	For 1886 season
Cubs	Jack Taylor		After 1903 season
			Oct. 1912
Louisville			Oct. 1912
Reds	Grover Lowdermilk		1-10-1913
		waiver price	7-15-1926
Brooklyn Dodgers			7-15-1926
Boston Braves		10,000	Between 1887–1888 season
			11-2-1926
Philadelphia A's			Feb. 1927
Tigers	John Pasek	100,000	12-15-1933
White Sox		50,000	12-8-1914

Name of Player	Type of Deal	* Other Players Included	Selling or Releasing Team
Stanley Coveleskie	1. Traded		Indians
	2. Released Signed		Washington Senators
Joe Cronin	1. Traded		Washington Senators
Kiki Cuyler	1. Traded		Pirates
Dizzy Dean	1. Traded		Cardinals
Buck Ewing	1. Traded		Giants
Jimmie Foxx	1. Traded	John Marcum	Philadelphia A's
	2. Released Signed		Red Sox
	3. Released as player Signed as coach		Cubs
	4. Signed		
Frankie Frisch	1. Traded	Jimmy Ring	Giants
Lefty Gomez	1. Sold		San Francisco Seals (PCL)
	2. Sold		Yankees
	3. Released Signed		Boston Braves
Goose Goslin	1. Traded		Washington Senators
	2. Traded	Walter Stewart Fred Schulte	St. Louis Browns
	3. Traded		Washington Senators
	4. Released Signed		Tigers

Buying or Receiving Team	Dealt For		Date
	Player	Cash in Dollars	
Washington Senators	Byron Speece Carr Smith		12-12-1924
			6-12-1927
Yankees			Dec. 1927
Red Sox	Lyn Lary	250,000	Oct. 1934
Cubs	Sparky Adams Floyd Scott		11-28-1927
Cubs	Curt Davis Clyde Shoun Tuck Stainback	185,000	4-16-1938
Indians	George Davis		Mar. 1893
Red Sox	Gordon Rhodes George Savino	150,000	12-10-1935
		waiver price	6-1-1942
Cubs			6-1-1942
			7-6-1944
Cubs			7-6-1944
Phillies			2-10-1945
Cardinals	Rogers Hornsby		12-20-1926
Yankees		35,000	After 1929 season
Boston Braves		cash	1-25-1943
			5-19-1943
Washington Senators			5-24-1943
St. Louis Browns	Alvin ("General") Crowder Heinie Manush	20,000	6-14-1930
Washington Senators	Lloyd Brown Carl Reynolds Sam West	20,000	12-14-1932
Tigers	Jonathan Stone		12-14-1933
			May 1938
Washington Senators			May 1938

Name of Player	Type of Deal	Other Players Included	Selling or Releasing Team
Hank Greenberg	1. Sold		Tigers
Burleigh Grimes	1. Traded	Charles Ward Al Mamaux	Pirates
	2. Traded (3-way deal)		Brooklyn Dodgers
		Fresco Thompson Jack Scott	New York Giants
		George Harper	Phillies
		Butch Henline	Phillies
	3. Traded		New York Giants
	4. Traded		Pirates
	5. Traded		Boston Braves
	6. Traded		Cardinals
	7. Released		Cubs
	Signed		
	8. Released		Cardinals
	Signed		
	9. Released		Yankees
	Signed		
Lefty Grove	1. Traded	Max Bishop Rube Walberg	Philadelphia A's
Chick Hafey	1. Traded		Cardinals
Gabby Hartnett	1. Released Signed as player-coach		Cubs
Harry Heilmann	1. Released		Tigers
	Signed		
Billy Herman	1. Traded		Cubs
	2. Traded		Brooklyn Dodgers
	3. Traded	Whitey Wietelmann Elmer Singleton Stan Wentzel	Boston Braves

| Buying or Receiving Team | Dealt For | | Date |
	Player	Cash in Dollars	
Pirates		cash	1-18-1947
Brooklyn Dodgers	George Cutshaw Casey Stengel	20,000	1-8-1918
New York Giants			1-9-1927
Phillies			
New York Giants			
Brooklyn Dodgers			
Pirates	Vic Aldridge		2-11-1928
Boston Braves	Percy Lee Jones	cash	4-9-1930
Cardinals	Willie Sherdel Fred Frankhouse		6-16-1930
Cubs	Arthur Teachout Hack Wilson		Dec. 1931
		waiver price	8-4-1933
Cardinals			8-4-1933
		waiver price	May 1934
Yankees			May 1934
			Aug. 1934
Pirates			Aug. 1934
Red Sox	Harold Warstler Bob Kline	125,000	12-12-1933
Reds	Harvey Henrick Benny Frey	cash	4-11-1932
			11-13-1940
New York Giants			12-2-1940
		waiver price	10-29-1929
Reds			10-29-1929
Brooklyn Dodgers	Johnny Hudson Charley Gilbert	50,000	5-6-1941
Boston Braves	Stewart Hofferth		6-15-1946
Pirates	Bob Elliott Hank Camelli		9-30-1946

NAME OF PLAYER	TYPE OF DEAL	OTHER PLAYERS INCLUDED	SELLING OR RELEASING TEAM
Rogers Hornsby	1. Traded		Cardinals
	2. Traded		New York Giants
	3. Traded		Boston Braves
	4. Released Signed		Cubs
Waite Hoyt	1. Traded	Harry Harper Wally Schang Mike McNally	Red Sox
	2. Traded	Mark Koenig	Yankees
	3. Released Signed		Tigers
	4. Released Signed		Philadelphia A's
	5. Released Signed		Brooklyn Dodgers
	6. Released Signed		New York Giants
	7. Released Signed		Pirates
Wee Willie Keeler	1. Traded	Dan Brouthers	Brooklyn Dodgers
King Kelly	1. Sold		Cubs
Ralph Kiner	1. Traded	Howie Pollet Joe Garagiola George Metkovich	Pirates
	2. Traded		Cubs

Buying or Receiving Team	Dealt For		Date
	Player	Cash in Dollars	
New York Giants	Frank Frisch Jimmy Ring		12-20-1926
Boston Braves	Jimmy Welsh Shanty Hogan	cash	1-10-1928
Cubs	Bruce Cunningham Percy Lee Jones Doc Leggett Fred Maguire Harry Seibold	250,000	11-20-1928
			10-24-1932
Cardinals			10-24-1932
Yankees	Herbert Thormahlen Muddy Ruel Derrill Pratt Sam Vick		12-15-1920
Tigers	Owen Carroll George Weustling Harry Rice		5-30-1930
		waiver price	June 1931
Philadelphia A's			June 1931 Jan. 1932
Brooklyn Dodgers			
			June 1932
New York Giants			June 1932 Nov. 1932
Pirates			Nov. 1932
			June 1937
Brooklyn Dodgers			June 1937
Baltimore (NL)	Billy Shindle George Treadway		Jan. 1894
Boston Braves		10,000	Oct. 1886
Cubs	Bob Schultz Toby Atwell Preston Ward George Freese Bob Addis Gene Harmanski	100,000	6-4-1953
Indians	Sam Jones Gale Wade	65,000	11-16-1954

Name of Player	Type of Deal	Other Players Included	Selling or Releasing Team
Napoleon Lajoie	1. Joined		
Henry Manush	1. Traded	Lu Blue	Tigers
	2. Traded	Alvin Crowder	St. Louis Browns
	3. Traded		Washington Senators
	4. Released Signed		Red Sox
	5. Released Signed		Brooklyn Dodgers
Rabbit Maranville	1. Traded		Boston Braves
	2. Traded	Wilbur Cooper Charlie Grimm	Pirates
	3. Released Signed		Cubs
	4. Sold	George Harper	Brooklyn Dodgers
Rube Marquard	1. Sold		Indianapolis
	2. Released Signed		New York Giants
	3. Traded		Brooklyn Dodgers
	4. Traded		Reds
Christy Mathewson	1. Drafted		Reds
	2. Traded		Reds
	3. Traded	Edd Roush Bill McKechnie	New York Giants
Iron Man McGinnity	1. Transferred		Baltimore
	2. Jumped	John McGraw	Brooklyn (NL)
	3. Jumped	John McGraw	Baltimore (AL)

Buying or Receiving Team	Dealt For		Date
	Player	Cash in Dollars	
(Philadelphia A's) Cleveland (AL)[1]			June 1902
St. Louis Browns	Elmer VanGilder Chick Galloway Harry Rice		12-2-1927
Washington Senators	Goose Goslin		6-13-1930
Red Sox	Roy Johnson Carl Reynolds		12-17-1935
			9-28-1936
Brooklyn Dodgers			12-9-1936
		waiver price	May 1938
Pirates			May 1938
Pirates	Billy Southworth Fred Nicholson Walter Barbare	15,000	Feb. 1921
Cubs	Vic Aldridge Al Niehaus George Grantham		10-27-1934
		waiver price	Nov. 1925
Brooklyn Dodgers			Nov. 1925
Boston Braves		cash	12-8-1928
New York Giants		11,000	Jan. 1908
		waiver price	Sept. 1915
Brooklyn Dodgers			Sept. 1915
Reds	Walter Ruether		12-15-1920
Boston Braves	John Scott William Kopf		2-20-1922
			Sept. 1900
New York Giants	Amos Rusie		Nov. 1900
Reds	Charles Herzog Wade Killefer		7-20-1916
Brooklyn (NL)			1900
Baltimore (AL)			1901
New York Giants			July 1902

1. Lajoie joined Cleveland after the Philadelphia Phillies obtained an injunction against his playing with the A's.

NAME OF PLAYER	TYPE OF DEAL	OTHER PLAYERS INCLUDED	SELLING OR RELEASING TEAM
John McGraw	1. Sold	Wilbert Robinson Billy Keister	Baltimore
Joe Medwick	1. Traded	Curt Davis	Cardinals
	2. Sold		Brooklyn Dodgers
	3. Traded	Ewald Pyle	New York Giants
	4. Released		Boston Braves
	Signed		
	5. Released		St. Louis Browns
	Signed		
	6. Released		Brooklyn Dodgers
	Signed		
	7. Released		Yankees
	Signed		
	8. Released		Cardinals
	Re-signed		
Herb Pennock	1. Sold		Philadelphia A's
	2. Traded		Red Sox
	3. Released		Yankees
	Signed		
Edd Roush	1. Traded	Christy Mathewson Bill McKechnie	New York Giants
	2. Traded		Reds
Red Ruffing	1. Traded		Red Sox
	2. Inducted into U.S. Army Air Forces		
	Return		
	3. Released		Yankees
	Signed		
Babe Ruth	1. Sold		Red Sox
	2. Released		Yankees

| Buying or Receiving Team | Dealt For | | Date |
	Player	Cash in Dollars	
Cardinals		150,000	End of 1899 season
Brooklyn Dodgers	Carl Doyle Sam Nahem Ernie Koy Berthold Haas	125,000	6-12-1940
New York Giants		50,000	7-6-1943
Boston Braves	Clyde Kluttz		6-14-1945
			2-8-1946
St. Louis Browns			3-3-1946
			4-5-1946
Brooklyn Dodgers			6-28-1946
			10-9-1946
Yankees			Jan. 1947
			4-29-1947
Cardinals			4-29-1947
			10-10-1947
Cardinals			1-23-1948
Red Sox		waiver price	June 1915
Yankees	Camp Skinner Norman McMillan George Murray	cash	1-30-1923
			Jan. 1934
Red Sox			Jan. 1934
Reds	Charles Herzog Wade Killefer		7-20-1916
New York Giants	George Kelly		Jan. 1927
Yankees	Cedric Durst	50,000	5-6-1930
			12-29-1942
Yankees			7-16-1945
			9-20-1946
White Sox			12-6-1946
Yankees		125,000	1-3-1920
Boston Braves			2-26-1935

Name of Player	Type of Deal	Other Players Included	Selling or Releasing Team
Al Simmons	1. Sold	Jimmie Dykes Mule Haas	Philadelphia A's
	2. Sold		White Sox
	3. Sold		Tigers
	4. Sold		Washington Senators
	5. Sold		Boston Braves
	6. Released		Reds
	Signed		
	7. Released		Philadelphia A's
	Signed		
	8. Released		Red Sox
	Signed as player-coach		
George Sisler	1. Sold		St. Louis Browns
	2. Sold		Washington Senators
Tris Speaker	1. Traded		Red Sox
	2. Resigned as manager		Indians
	Signed		
	3. Released		Washington Senators
	Signed		
Casey Stengel	1. Traded	George Cutshaw	Brooklyn Dodgers
	2. Traded (Refused to report)		Pirates
	3. Traded		Phillies
	4. Traded	Dave Bancroft Bill Cunningham	New York Giants

Buying or Receiving Team	Dealt For		Date
	Player	Cash in Dollars	
White Sox		150,000	9-28-1932
Tigers		75,000	12-10-1935
Washington Senators		15,000	4-4-1937
Boston Braves		20,000	12-20-1938
Reds		15,000	8-31-1939
			End of 1929 season
Philadelphia A's			12-11-1939
			After 1942 season
Red Sox			2-2-1943
			10-15-1943
Philadelphia A's			Dec. 1943
Washington Senators		25,000	12-14-1927
Boston Braves		7,500	5-27-1928
Indians	Sam Jones Fred Thomas	50,000	4-12-1916
			12-2-1926
Washington Senators			12-2-1926
			2-5-1928
Philadelphia A's			2-5-1928
Pirates	Chuck Ward Burleigh Grimes Al Mamaux		1-9-1918
Phillies	George Whitted		8-19-1920
New York Giants	players valued at	75,000	July 1921
Boston Braves	Billy Southworth Joe Oeschger		Nov. 1923

Name of Player	Type of Deal	Other Players Included	Selling or Releasing Team
Joe Tinker	1. Traded	Grover Lowdermilk Harry Chapman	Cubs
	2. Sold (Refused to report. Jumped to Federal League.)		Reds
	3. Sold in peace agreement		
Honus Wagner	1. Transferred with 14 other players when Louisville left NL		Louisville
Lloyd ("Little Poison") Waner	1. Traded		Pirates
	2. Traded		Boston Braves
	3. Released Signed		Reds
	4. Traded	Al Glossop	Phillies
	5. Released Signed		Brooklyn Dodgers
Paul ("Big Poison") Waner	1. Released Signed		Pirates
	2. Released Signed		Brooklyn Dodgers
	3. Released Signed		Boston Braves
	4. Released Signed		Brooklyn Dodgers
	5. Released		Yankees

Buying or Receiving Team	Dealt For		Date
	Player	Cash in Dollars	
Reds	Bert Humphries Pete Knisely Red Corriden Art Phelan Mike Mitchell		12-15-1912
Brooklyn Dodgers			Dec. 1913
Cubs			Jan. 1916
Pirates			After 1899 season
Boston Braves	Nick Strincevich		5-7-1941
Reds	John Hutchings		6-12-1941
Phillies Dodgers	Babe Dahlgren		10-8-1941 12-4-1941 3-8-1943 6-14-1944
Pirates			6-15-1944
			12-10-1940
Brooklyn Dodgers			1-31-1941 5-11-1941
Boston Braves			5-24-1941 1-19-1943
Brooklyn Dodgers			1-21-1943 Sept. 1944
Yankees			Sept. 1944 5-3-1945

Name of Player	Type of Deal	Other Players Included	Selling or Releasing Team
Early Wynn	1. Traded	Mickey Vernon	Washington Senators
	2. Traded	Al Smith	Indians
	3. Released Signed		White Sox
Cy Young	1. Transferred	pick of team	Cleveland Spiders (NL)
	2. Jumped		St. Louis (NL)
	Signed		
	3. Sold		Red Sox
	4. Released		Cleveland Naps (AL)
	Signed		

| Buying or Receiving Team | Dealt For | | Date |
	Player	Cash in Dollars	
Indians	Joe Haynes Ed Klieman Eddie Robinson		12-14-1948
White Sox	Fred Hatfield Minnie Minoso		12-4-1957
			11-20-1962
Indians			6-21-1963
St. Louis (NL)			After 1898 season
			After 1900 season
Red Sox			
Cleveland Naps (AL)		12,500	Before 1909
			Aug. 1911
Boston Braves			Aug. 1911

Tops in trades

The following are considered the most important trades
in baseball history:

NAME OF PLAYER	TYPE OF DEAL	OTHER PLAYERS INCLUDED	SELLING OR RELEASING TEAM
Grover Cleveland Alexander	1. Traded	Bill Killefer	Phillies
	2. Released		Cubs
	Signed 3. Traded	Harry McCurdy	Cardinals
Earl Averill	1. Sold		San Francisco Seals (PCL)
	2. Traded		Indians
Franklin ("Home-run") Baker	1. Sold		Philadelphia A's
Dave Bancroft	1. Traded		Phillies
	2. Traded	Casey Stengel Bill Cunningham	New York Giants
Mickey Cochrane	1. Traded		Philadelphia A's
Walker Cooper	1. Sold		Cardinals
	2. Traded		New York Giants

Buying or Receiving Team	Dealt For		Date
	Player	Cash in Dollars	
Cubs	Mike Prendergast Pickles Dilhoefer	60,000	11-11-1917
		waiver price	6-22-1926
Cardinals			6-22-1926
Phillies	Homer Peel Bob McGraw		12-11-1929
Indians		50,000	After 1928 season
Tigers	Harry Eisenstat	cash	6-14-1930
Yankees		35,000	2-17-1916
New York Giants	Art Fletcher Wilbur Hubbell	100,000	6-8-1921
Boston Braves	Joe Oeschger Billy Southworth		11-15-1923
Tigers	John Pasek	100,000	12-15-1933
New York Giants		175,000	1-5-1946
Reds	Ray Mueller		6-13-1949

NAME OF PLAYER	TYPE OF DEAL	OTHER PLAYERS INCLUDED	SELLING OR RELEASING TEAM
Lawrence ("Spud") Davis	1. Traded	Homer Peel	Cardinals
	2. Traded[1]	Eddie Delker	Phillies
	3. Sold		Cardinals
	4. Traded	Al Hollingsworth	Reds
	5. Sold		Phillies
	6. Released as active player		Pirates
	Returned to active list		
Dizzy Dean	1. Traded		Cardinals
Bob Dillinger	1. Traded	Paul Lehner	St. Louis Browns
Jimmie Dykes	1. Sold	Mule Haas Al Simmons	Philadelphia A's
Jimmy Foxx	1. Traded	John Marcum	Philadelphia A's
	2. Released		Red Sox
	Signed		
	3. Released as player Signed as coach		Cubs
	4. Signed		
Larry French	1. Traded	Freddie Lindstrom	Pirates
	2. Released		Cubs
	Signed		
Lefty Gomez	1. Sold		San Francisco Seals (PCL)
	2. Sold		Yankees
	3. Released		Boston Braves
	Signed		

1. Phillies made this deal to get a new manager as Wilson took over the club from Burt Shotton at the start of the 1934 season.

| Buying or Receiving Team | Dealt For | | Date |
	Player	Cash in Dollars	
Phillies	Jimmy Wilson		5-11-1928
Cardinals	Jimmy Wilson		11-15-1933
Reds		15,000	12-2-1936
Phillies	Bucky Walters	55,000	6-13-1938
Pirates		15,000	10-27-1939
			10-2-1941
Pirates			Apr. 1944
Cubs	Curt Davis Clyde Shoun Tuck Stainback	185,000	4-16-1938
Philadelphia A's	Frank Gustine Billy DeMars Ray Coleman Rocco Ippolitto	100,000	12-13-1949
White Sox		150,000	9-28-1932
Red Sox	Gordon Rhodes George Savino	150,000	12-10-1935
		waiver price	6-1-1942
Cubs			6-1-1942
			7-6-1944
Cubs			7-6-1944
Phillies			2-10-1945
Cubs	Guy Bush Babe Herman Jim Weaver		11-22-1934
		waiver price	8-20-1941
Brooklyn Dodgers			8-20-1941
Yankees		35,000	After 1929 season
Boston Braves		cash	1-25-1943
			5-19-1943
Washington Senators			5-24-1943

Name of Player	Type of Deal	Other Players Included	Selling or Releasing Team
Joe Gordon	1. Traded[2]	Eddie Bockman	Yankees
Goose Goslin	1. Traded		Washington Senators
	2. Traded	Fred Schulte Walter Stewart	St. Louis Browns
	3. Traded		Washington Senators
	4. Released Signed		Tigers
Burleigh Grimes	1. Traded	Charles Ward Al Mamaux	Pirates
	2. Traded (3-way deal)		Brooklyn Dodgers
		Fresco Thompson Jack Scott	New York Giants
		George Harper	Phillies
		Butch Henline	Phillies
	3. Traded		New York Giants
	4. Traded		Pirates
	5. Traded		Boston Braves
	6. Traded		Cardinals
	7. Released Signed		Cubs
	8. Released Signed		Cardinals
	9. Released Signed		Yankees
Charlie Grimm	1. Traded	Rabbit Maranville Wilbur Cooper	Pirates
Lefty Grove	1. Traded	Max Bishop Rube Walberg	Philadelphia A's

2. Gordon was involved in the only outright trade of managers in major league history. After 95 games of the 1960 season as manager of the Indians, Gordon was traded to the Tigers for Jimmie Dykes. At the time of trade Gordon's record with the Indians was 49–46; Dykes's 44–52 with the Tigers. Gordon finished 26–31 with Tigers, Dykes 26–32 with Indians.

Buying or Receiving Team	Dealt For		Date
	Player	Cash in Dollars	
Indians	Allie Reynolds		10-19-1946
St. Louis Browns	Alvin ("General") Crowder Heinie Manush		6-14-1930
Washington Senators	Lloyd Brown Carl Reynolds Sam West	20,000	12-14-1932
Tigers	Jonathan Stone		12-14-1933
			May 1938
Washington Senators			May 1938
Brooklyn Dodgers	George Cutshaw Casey Stengel	20,000	1-8-1918
New York Giants			1-9-1927
Phillies			
New York Giants			
Brooklyn Dodgers			
Pirates	Vic Aldridge		2-11-1928
Boston Braves	Percy Lee Jones	cash	4-9-1930
Cardinals	Fred Frankhouse Bill Sherdel		6-16-1930
Cubs	Arthur Teachout Hack Wilson		Dec. 1931
		waiver price	8-4-1933
Cardinals			8-4-1933
			May 1934
Yankees			May 1934
			Aug. 1934
Pirates			Aug. 1934
Cubs	Vic Aldridge George Grantham Al Neihaus		10-15-1924
Red Sox	Harold Warstler Bob Kline	125,000	12-12-1933

Name of Player	Type of Deal	Other Players Included	Selling or Releasing Team
Babe Herman	1. Traded	Ernie Lombardi Walter Gilbert	Brooklyn Dodgers
	2. Traded		Reds
	3. Traded	Guy Bush Jim Weaver	Cubs
	4. Sold		Pirates
	5. Released		Reds
	Signed		
Billy Herman	1. Traded		Cubs
	2. Traded		Brooklyn Dodgers
	3. Traded[3]	Elmer Singleton Stan Wentzel Whitey Wietelmann	Boston Braves
Kirby Higbe	1. Traded	Joe Marty Ray Harrell	Cubs
	2. Traded		Phillies
	3. Traded	Hank Behrman Dixie Howell Gene Mauch Cal McLish	Brooklyn Dodgers
	4. Traded		Pirates
Rogers Hornsby	1. Traded		Cardinals
	2. Traded		New York Giants
	3. Traded		Boston Braves
	4. Released Signed		Cubs
Waite Hoyt	1. Traded	Harry Harper Wally Schang Mike McNally	Red Sox

continued p. 316

3. Pirates made this deal to secure Herman as their new manager in 1947 to replace Frankie Frisch, who resigned.

| Buying or Receiving Team | Dealt For | | Date |
	Player	Cash in Dollars	
Reds	Joe Stripp Tony Cuccinello Clyde Sukeforth		3-14-1932
Cubs	Bob Smith Rollie Hemsley Johnny Moore Lance Richbourg	45,000	11-30-1932
Pirates	Larry French Freddie Lindstrom		11-22-1934
Reds		15,000	6-21-1935
		waiver price	4-1-1937
Tigers			4-1-1937
Brooklyn Dodgers	Charley Gilbert Johnny Hudson	50,000	5-6-1941
Boston Braves	Stewart Hofferth		6-15-1946
Pirates	Bob Elliott Hank Camelli		9-30-1946
Phillies	Claude Passeau		5-29-1939
Brooklyn Dodgers	Vito Tamulis Bill Crouch Mickey Livingston	100,000	11-11-1940
Pirates	Al Gionfriddo	150,000	5-3-1947
New York Giants	Ray Poat Bobby Rhawn		6-6-1949
New York Giants	Frankie Frisch Jimmy Ring		12-20-1926
Boston Braves	Shanty Hogan Jimmy Welsh	cash	1-10-1928
Cubs	Bruce Cunningham Percy Lee Jones Doc Leggett Fred Maguire Harry Seibold	200,000	11-20-1928
			10-24-1932
Cardinals			10-24-1932
Yankees	Herbert Thormahlen Muddy Ruel Derrill Pratt Sam Vick		12-15-1920

NAME OF PLAYER	TYPE OF DEAL	OTHER PLAYERS INCLUDED	SELLING OR RELEASING TEAM
Waite Hoyt *continued*	2. Traded	Mark Koenig	Yankees
	3. Released		Tigers
	Signed		
	4. Released		Philadelphia A's
	Signed		
	5. Released		Brooklyn Dodgers
	Signed		
	6. Released		New York Giants
	Signed		
	7. Released		Pirates
	Signed		
George Kell	1. Traded		Philadelphia A's
	2. Traded	Hoot Evers Johnny Lipon Dizzy Trout	Tigers
	3. Traded		Red Sox
	4. Traded	Mike Fornieles Connie Johnson Bob Nieman	White Sox
Ralph Kiner	1. Traded	Howie Pollet Joe Garagiola George Metkovich	Pirates
	2. Traded		Cubs
Chuck Klein	1. Traded		Phillies
	2. Traded	Fabian Kowalik	Cubs
	3. Released Signed		Phillies
	4. Released Signed		Pirates

Buying or Receiving Team	Dealt For		Date
	Player	Cash in Dollars	
Tigers	Owen Carroll George Weustling Harry Rice		5-30-1930
		waiver price	June 1931
Philadelphia A's			June 1931
			Jan. 1932
Brooklyn Dodgers			Jan. 1932
			June 1932
New York Giants			June 1932
			Nov. 1932
Pirates			Nov. 1932
			June 1937
Brooklyn Dodgers			June 1937
Tigers	Barney McCosky		5-18-1946
Red Sox	Walt Dropo Fred Hatfield Don Lenhardt Johnny Pesky Bill Wight		6-3-1952
White Sox	Grady Hatton	100,000	5-24-1954
Orioles	Jim Wilson Dave Philley		5-21-1956
Cubs	Bob Schultz Toby Atwell Preston Ward George Freese Bob Addis Gene Hermanski	100,000	6-4-1953
Indians	Sam Jones Gale Wade	65,000	11-16-1954
Cubs	Ted Kleinhans Mark Koenig Harvey Hendrick	65,000	11-21-1933
Phillies	Curt Davis Ethan Allen	50,000	5-21-1936
			6-7-1939
Pirates			6-7-1939
			3-26-1940
Phillies			3-26-1940

NAME OF PLAYER	TYPE OF DEAL	OTHER PLAYERS INCLUDED	SELLING OR RELEASING TEAM
Harvey Kuenn	1. Traded		Tigers
	2. Traded		Indians
	3. Traded	Ed Bailey Bob Hendley	San Francisco Giants
	4. Sold		Cubs
Dick Littlefield	1. Traded	Joe Dobson Al Zarilla	Red Sox
	2. Traded	Joe DeMaestri Gordon Goldsberry Gus Niarhos Jim Rivera	White Sox
	3. Traded	Matt Batts Cliff Mapes Ben Taylor	St. Louis Browns
	4. Traded	Don Lenhardt Marlin Stuart Vic Wertz	Tigers
	5. Traded		St. Louis Browns
	6. Traded	Bobby DelGreco	Pirates
	7. Traded	Bill Sarni Red Schoendienst Jackie Brandt	Cardinals
	8. Traded[4]		New York Giants
	9. Traded	Bob Lennon	New York Giants
Joe Medwick	1. Traded	Curt Davis	Cardinals
	2. Sold		Brooklyn Dodgers
	3. Traded	Ewald Pyle	New York Giants
	4. Released		Boston Braves
	Signed		
	5. Released		St. Louis Browns
	Signed		
	6. Released		Brooklyn Dodgers
continued p. 320	Signed		

4. Deal was canceled when Robinson retired from baseball.

Buying or Receiving Team	Dealt For		Date
	Player	Cash in Dollars	
Indians	Rocky Colavito		4-17-1960
San Francisco Giants	Johnny Antonelli Willie Kirkland		12-3-1960
Cubs	Dick Bertell Len Gabrielson		5-29-1965
Phillies		25,000	4-23-1966
White Sox	Ray Scarborough Bill Wight		12-10-1950
St. Louis Browns	Sherman Lollar Tommy Upton Al Widmar		11-26-1951
Tigers	Cene Bearden Bob Cain Dick Kryhoski		2-14-1952
St. Louis Browns	Bud Black Jim Delsing Ned Garver Dave Madison		8-14-1952
Pirates	Cal Abrams	10,000	5-25-1954
Cardinals	Bill Virdon		5-17-1956
New York Giants	Ray Katt Don Liddle Alvln Dark Whitey Lockman		6-14-1956
Brooklyn Dodgers	Jackie Robinson	35,000	1-5-1957
Cubs	Ray Katt Ray Jablonski		4-16-1957
Brooklyn Dodgers	Carl Doyle Sam Nahem Ernie Koy Berthold Haas	125,000	6-12-1940
New York Giants		50,000	7-6-1943
Boston Braves	Clyde Kluttz		6-14-1945
			2-8-1946
St. Louis Browns			3-3-1946
			4-5-1946
Brooklyn Dodgers			6-28-1946
			10-9-1946
Yankees			Jan. 1947

Name of Player	Type of Deal	Other Players Included	Selling or Releasing Team
Joe Medwick *continued*	7. Released Signed		Yankees
	8. Released Re-signed		Cardinals
Johnny Mize	1. Traded		Cardinals
	2. Sold		New York Giants
Buck Newsom	1. Sold		St. Louis Browns
	2. Traded	Ben Chapman	Washington Senators
	3. Traded	Ralph Kress Colonel Buster Mills	Red Sox
	4. Traded	Jim Walkup Ralph Kress Roy Bell	St. Louis Browns
	5. Sold		Tigers
	6. Sold		Washington Senators
	7. Traded		Brooklyn Dodgers
	8. Sold		St. Louis Browns
	9. Traded		Washington Senators
	10. Released Signed		Philadelphia A's
	11. Released Signed		Washington Senators
	12. Released Signed		Yankees
	13. Released Signed		New York Giants
	14. Released Signed		Washington Senators

Buying or Receiving Team	Dealt For		Date
	Player	Cash in Dollars	
			4-29-1947
Cardinals			4-29-1947
			10-10-1947
Cardinals			4-23-1948
New York Giants	Ken O'Dea Bill Lohrman Johnny McCarthy	50,000	12-11-1941
Yankees		40,000	8-22-1949
Washington Senators		40,000	5-21-1935
Red Sox	Wes and Rick Ferrell Mel Almada		6-10-1937
St. Louis Browns	Joe Vosmik		12-2-1937
Tigers	George Gill Bob Harris Vernon Kennedy Roxie Lawson Mark Christman Chet Laabs		5-13-1939
Washington Senators		cash	3-31-1942
Brooklyn Dodgers		cash	8-31-1942
St. Louis Browns	Archie McKain Fritz Ostermueller		7-15-1943
Washington Senators		cash	8-31-1943
Philadelphia A's	Roger Wolff		12-13-1943
			6-3-1946
Washington Senators			6-5-1946
		waiver price	7-11-1947
Yankees			7-11-1947
			2-16-1948
New York Giants			4-10-1948
			4-8-1952
Washington Senators			4-8-1952
			6-16-1952
Philadelphia A's			6-16-1952

Name of Player	Type of Deal	Other Players Included	Selling or Releasing Team
Frank ("Lefty") O'Doul	1. Sold		Yankees
	2. Went to spring training on look-see basis, but never signed. Later signed.		
	3. Sold		San Francisco Seals (PCL)
	4. Traded		New York Giants
	5. Traded	Fresco Thompson	Phillies
	6. Traded	William Clark	Brooklyn Dodgers
Jimmy Ring	1. Traded	Earle Neale	Reds
	2. Traded		Phillies
	3. Traded	Frankie Frisch	New York Giants
	4. Traded	John Schulte	Cardinals
Robin Roberts	1. Sold		Phillies
	2. Released Signed		Yankees
	3. Released Signed		Orioles
	4. Released Signed		Houston Astros
Red Ruffing	1. Traded		Red Sox
	2. Inducted into U.S. Army Air Forces Returned to baseball		
	3. Released Signed		Yankees

| Buying or Receiving Team | Dealt For | | Date |
	Player	Cash in Dollars	
Red Sox		waiver price	10-12-1922
Cubs			Spring 1926
Hollywood (PCL)			1926
New York Giants			Before 1928 season
Phillies	Fred Leach	25,000	10-29-1928
Brooklyn Dodgers	Hal Lee Clise Dudley James Elliott	25,000	10-14-1930
New York Giants	Sam Leslie		6-16-1933
Phillies	Eppa Rixey		11-22-1920
New York Giants	Jack Bentley Wayland Dean		12-30-1925
Cardinals	Rogers Hornsby		12-20-1926
Phillies	Clarence Jonnard John Mokan Jimmy Cooney		Dec. 1927
Yankees		25,000	10-16-1961 4-30-1962
Orioles			5-21-1962 7-31-1965
Houston Astros			8-6-1965 7-13-1966
Cubs			For rest of season
Yankees	Cedric Durst	50,000	5-6-1930 12-29-1942
Yankees			7-16-1945
			9-20-1946
White Sox			12-6-1946

Name of Player	Type of Deal	Other Players Included	Selling or Releasing Team
Babe Ruth	1. Sold		Red Sox
	2. Released		Yankees
	Signed		
Everett Scott	1. Traded	Joe Bush Sam Jones	Red Sox
	2. Released		Yankees
	Signed		
	3. Released		Washington Senators
	Signed		
	4. Released		White Sox
	Signed		
Al Simmons	1. Sold	Jimmie Dykes Mule Haas	Philadelphia A's
	2. Sold		White Sox
	3. Sold		Tigers
	4. Sold		Washington Senators
	5. Sold		Boston Braves
	6. Released		Reds
	Signed		
	7. Released		Philadelphia A's
	Signed		
	8. Released		Red Sox
	Signed as player-coach		
George Sisler	1. Sold		St. Louis Browns
	2. Sold		Washington Senators
Billy Southworth	1. Traded	Fred Nicholson Walter Barbare	Pirates
	2. Traded	Joe Oeschger	Boston Braves
	3. Traded		New York Giants

Buying or Receiving Team	Dealt For		Date
	Player	Cash in Dollars	
Yankees		125,000	1-3-1920
			2-26-1935
Boston Braves			Feb. 1935
Yankees	Roger Peckinpaugh Bill Piercy Jack Quinn		Dec. 1921
		waiver price	Aug. 1925
Washington Senators			Aug. 1925
		waiver price	Mar. 1926
White Sox			Mar. 1926
		waiver price	July 1926
Reds			July 1926
White Sox		150,000	9-28-1932
Tigers		75,000	12-10-1935
Washington Senators		15,000	4-4-1937
Boston Braves		20,000	12-20-1938
Reds		15,000	8-31-1939
			End of 1939 season
Philadelphia A's			12-11-1939
			After 1942 season
Red Sox			2-2-1943
			10-15-1943
Philadelphia A's			Dec. 1943
Washington Senators		25,000	12-14-1927
Boston Braves		7,500	5-27-1928
Boston Braves	Rabbit Maranville	15,000	Mar. 1921
New York Giants	Casey Stengel Dave Bancroft Bill Cunningham		Nov. 1923
Cardinals	Clarence Mueller		6-14-1926

Name of Player	Type of Deal	Other Players Included	Selling or Releasing Team
Tris Speaker	1. Traded		Red Sox
	2. Resigned as manager Signed		Indians
	3. Released		Washington Senators
	Signed		
Eddie Stanky	1. Traded		Cubs
	2. Traded		Brooklyn Dodgers
	3. Traded	Alvin Dark	Boston Braves
George Uhle	1. Traded		Indians
	2. Sold		Tigers
	3. Released		New York Giants
	Signed		
Dazzy Vance	1. Traded	Gordon Slade	Brooklyn Dodgers
	2. Sold		Cardinals
	3. Released		Reds
	Signed		
	4. Released Signed		Cardinals
Honus Wagner	One of 14 players transferred when Louisville left NL		Louisville
Dixie Walker	1. Sold		Yankees
	2. Traded	Vernon Kennedy Tony Piet	White Sox
	3. Released		Tigers
	Signed		
	4. Traded	Hal Gregg Vic Lombardi	Brooklyn Dodgers

Buying or Receiving Team	Dealt For		Date
	Player	Cash in Dollars	
Indians	Sam Jones Fred Thomas	50,000	4-12-1916
			12-2-1926
Washington Senators			12-2-1926
			2-5-1928
Philadelphia A's			2-5-1928
Brooklyn Dodgers	Bob Chipman		6-7-1944
Boston Braves	Carvel Rowell	100,000	3-6-1948
New York Giants	Sid Gordon Willard Marshall Buddy Kerr Sam Webb		12-14-1949
Tigers	Jack Tavener Ken Holloway		12-11-1928
New York Giants		25,000	4-24-1933
			7-8-1933
Yankees			7-24-1933
Cardinals	Jake Flowers Owen Carroll		2-9-1933
Reds		15,000	2-6-1934
		waiver price	6-25-1934
Cardinals			6-25-1934
			Apr. 1935
Brooklyn Dodgers			Apr. 1935
Pirates			After 1899 season
White Sox		35,000	May 1936
Tigers	Marvin Owen Mike Tresh Gerald Walker		12-2-1937
		waiver price	7-24-1939
Brooklyn Dodgers			7-24-1939
Pirates	Billy Cox Gene Mauch Preacher Roe		12-8-1947

Name of Player	Type of Deal	Other Players Included	Selling or Releasing Team
Harry ("The Hat") Walker	1. Traded	Fred Schmidt	Cardinals
	2. Traded		Phillies
	3. Traded	Peanuts Lowrey	Cubs
	4. Traded		Reds
Lloyd ("Little Poison") Waner	1. Traded		Pirates
	2. Traded		Boston Braves
	3. Released Signed		Reds
	4. Traded	Al Glossop	Phillies
	5. Released Signed		Brooklyn Dodgers
Paul ("Big Poison") Waner	1. Released Signed		Pirates
	2. Released Signed		Brooklyn Dodgers
	3. Released Signed		Boston Braves
	4. Released Signed		Brooklyn Dodgers
	5. Released		Yankees
Lewis ("Hack") Wilson	1. Drafted		Toledo (New York Giants)
	2. Traded	Arthur Teachout	Cubs
	3. Traded		Cardinals
	4. Released Signed		Brooklyn Dodgers

| Buying or Receiving Team | Dealt For | | Date |
	Player	Cash in Dollars	
Phillies	Ron Northey	50,000	5-3-1947
Cubs	Bill Nicholson		10-4-1948
Reds	Hank Sauer Frankie Baumholtz		6-15-1949
Cardinals	Ron Northey Lou Klein		12-14-1949
Boston Braves	Nick Strincevich		5-7-1941
Reds	John Hutchings		6-12-1941
			10-8-1941
Phillies			12-4-1941
Brooklyn Dodgers	Babe Dahlgren		3-8-1943
			6-14-1944
Pirates			6-15-1944
			12-10-1940
Brooklyn Dodgers			1-31-1941
			5-11-1941
Boston Braves			5-24-1941
			1-19-1943
Brooklyn Dodgers			1-21-1943
			Sept. 1944
Yankees			Sept. 1944
			5-3-1945
Cubs		5,000	Oct. 1925
Cardinals	Burleigh Grimes		Dec. 1931
Brooklyn Dodgers	Robert Parham	45,000	1-23-1932
			Aug. 1934
Phillies			

INDEX